Compara

CU00819874

Comparative Management
A TRANSCULTURAL ODYSSEY

Stephen Gatley
European Management Laboratory, UK

Ronnie Lessem
City University Business School, UK

Yochanan Altman
Lyon Graduate School of Business, France

McGRAW-HILL BOOK COMPANY

London • New York • St Louis • San Francisco • Auckland
Bogotá • Caracas • Lisbon • Madrid • Mexico
Milan • Montreal • New Delhi • Panama • Paris • San Juan
São Paulo • Singapore • Sydney • Tokyo • Toronto

Published by
McGRAW-HILL Book Company Europe
Shoppenhangers Road, Maidenhead, Berkshire, SL6 2QL, England
Telephone 01628 23432
Facsimile 01628 770224

British Library Cataloguing in Publication Data

Gatley, Stephen
Comparative management
1. Management – Cross-cultural studies   2. Commerce
I. Title   II. Lessem, Ronnie   III. Altman, Yochanan
658
ISBN 0077091841

Library of Congress Cataloging-in-publication Data

Gatley, Stephen,
Comparative management: a transcultural odyssey / Stephen Gatley, Ronnie Lessem, Yochanan Altman
    p. cm.
Includes bibliographical references.
ISBN 0-07-709184-1 (pbk.)
1. Comparative management.   2. Management–Cross-cultural studies.
I. Lessem, Ronnie.   II. Altman, Yochanan.   III. Title.
HD30.55.G38   1996   95-49801
658–dc20   CIP

McGraw-Hill
A Division of The McGraw-Hill Companies

12345 CUP 99876

Typeset and printed and bound in Britain at the University Press, Cambridge
Printed on permanent paper in compliance with ISO Standard 9706.

To:

Marjorie Gatley
Edith Lessem
Sarah Altman

CONTENTS

PREFACE

This book emerged from the friendship of three people whose journey through life has led them to the conclusion that the world is best perceived from multiple points of view. As they write, the authors are aware that the world is full of conflicts, many caused by cultural differences between adjacent nations. They see that these conflicts obscure the potential synergies which exist between cultural opposites; the pendulum seems eternally stuck in only one of two possible directions.

Since long before Adam Smith wrote his *The Wealth of Nations*, business and society have existed as a seamless whole, and, as business executives, we therefore have a part to play in the evolution of our multicultural world.

Altruism apart, we have an interest in a peaceful, constructive place to live. Recognizing this, major companies have, for example, played an important role in the beginnings of a new South Africa. But we still have a long way to go — and that way must begin with an understanding of ourselves and our values in a broader context than simply that of the nation in which we are born.

The emergence of the Eastern economic world has proved, above all, that there is more to business than the 'scientific' systems of Western management — and we have yet to see what Africa can teach us. This book is therefore about the investigation of the nature and potential of our multicultural world — about its assets and its liabilities.

The reader is invited on a journey in which he or she will be transported through cultural time and space — an odyssey of new perspectives. Along the way we will meet some of the legends of transcultural travel, its economists, analysts and philosophers, and will see the world through their eyes. We will use them as guides in a journey of discovery, one which will take us to the west, the world of the pioneer, to the north, the world of cool rationality, to the south, the family world and finally to the east, the world of integration and *wa*.

Their journeys may be long or short, or they may be taken one step at a time. Our hope is simply that they will awaken in our readers a wish to travel further — on, from the clouds of conflict, through the mists of synergy, and from there to new horizons... .

Stephen Gatley
Cambridge, UK

ACKNOWLEDGEMENTS

Many thanks are due to all those who have contributed their imagination and enthusiasm to the writing of this book.

In particular, the authors would like to recognize the contribution from Sid Lowe and Cliff Oswick, whose work in the UK and Hong Kong provides illumination of the important differences which exist across the East–West divide. We would also like to express our thanks and debt to our French colleague Didier Cazal who has provided a cross-culturally encompassing overview of socio-economic theory, demonstrating so clearly strengths of the Cartesian culture into which he was born.

Thanks are also due to those companies who have contributed to the management innovation program which underpins this work, notably Anglian Water, the Rover Group, Minorco Minerals, Psion, and Integral. Each of these companies has recognized the importance of culture in the management of international operations and together they have allowed us to harden our theories in the fire of day-to-day business life. Thanks to all those who have taken part, in particular: at Anglian Water — Alan Smith, Debbie Dyson, David Latham and Terry Cook; at Rover — John Parkinson and his team, with special thanks to Peter Bailey and also to Laura Haines and her team; at Minorco, thanks are due to Ian Pughsley and to David Moore; at Psion we would like to thank David Potter, Charles Davies, Collie Myers and Colin Heaven; and lastly, at Integral our thanks go to Peter Hiscocks. Thanks also are due to the European Management Laboratory where the CPAS audit structure (see Chapter 8) was developed.

To the City University Management MBA team — Patti Davis, Cathy McSweeney and Catherine Butler — we are grateful for your help and support. Thanks are also due to the Open Business School and in particular its Centre for Cross-Cultural Management for supporting this endeavour.

The authors would like to acknowledge the work of Geert Hofstede, Mary Douglas, Salvador DeMadariaga, Charles Hampden-Turner and Fons Trompenaars, whose publications are discussed in this book.

Lastly, many thanks are due to our families, whose contribution we so often take for granted.

INTRODUCTION

'We all do a lot of feeling — and mistake it for thinking'
(Mark Twain).

With these words this well-known American not only commented on the ways in which our attitudes and decisions are influenced by unconsciously held values and beliefs but also aptly summed up how culture plays a role in fashioning the ways in which people live and work together.

Attitudes to the influence of culture in business vary widely, ranging from the 'business people are the same the world over' approach to the 'I treat everyone as an individual — everybody's different' position held by others. In between these polar views lies a somewhat larger body of opinion that acknowledges that people from different cultural backgrounds may have alternative views on business-related issues ranging from the degree of personal freedom considered to be normal to the role of the state in commercial affairs. This main body of opinion differs only in the extent to which the individual concerned feels that this affects the process of carrying out his or her business.

Leaving aside the thorny question of the degree to which our cultural heritage predisposes us to one or other of the above views, it is perhaps worth considering what we mean when we talk about our 'culture'. Many definitions have been proposed, but these mostly agree that culture is a set of values held by a group of people and which are passed on to new generations of individuals who grow up within it. Experience and education are certainly an important part of the cultural 'environment' in which we grow and develop as individuals, as are the people with whom we interact — our families, our friends, our mentors and our colleagues. This multiple input allows us to formulate a mental 'model' of the world around us and to test it against our observation of reality. This helps us to be confident that our view of the way things work is a satisfactory means of assessing new and unfamiliar situations as they arise. To do this we compare the new situation with our internal model and, if it fits, we use the rules which applied to the old situation rather than having to work out a new set of rules from scratch.

The more we find our model to be trustworthy, the more we put our trust in it and, in this way, we develop a 'paradigm' view of the world, or, in other words, we get stuck into a certain way of seeing things. The trouble with paradigms is that they do not just help us to understand the world, they can also make us blind to things which do not 'fit' our view of the way the world should be.

At best, this means we miss potentially useful information, at worst, it can lead us to make dangerous assumptions about the way things are when, in fact, they are really quite different from the way we see them. Take the Englishman driving along a deserted road and who, rounding the next corner, is faced by a car coming straight at him on the same side of the road. Angrily he swerves, narrowly avoiding collision with the other car, sure in his mind that the other driver is an idiot. Seconds later his paradigm shatters as he remembers that in France it is he who should be driving on the other side of the road.

Many businesses have actually failed by getting stuck in their paradigm view of the world. Take the American company whose paradigm told them they were in the railway business. With the introduction of the motor car, people's travel needs changed but not so the railway company — they were not able to make a 'paradigm shift' and respond to the changing needs of their customers and to develop a new view of themselves — that they were actually in the transportation business.

This book takes the reader on a reflective journey during which we will examine the extent to which our cultural backgrounds create for us a paradigm view of the world of business. In Part One we step back from our subject and use this distance as a means for comparing and contrasting the 'global' differences between nations. We look at the differences between Japan and the USA and gain an insight into what makes up the eastern and western paradigm views of the world. We also look at Europe and Africa to add an understanding of the northern and southern cultural paradigms and we go on to examine the extent to which these four 'paradigm worlds' represent potential synergies for transcultural business. In Part Two we take a more analytical/reductive approach to the subject of culture, looking more closely at the ways in which different cultural standpoints are in turn associated with economic and socio-psychological paradigms. Here we will investigate the ways in which theories of capitalism — how organizations and markets interact — differ according to the cultural setting in which they are developed. We will also investigate some of the culturally related psychological factors which are relevant to the workplace and will provide a broad overview of the models that have been proposed to aid the understanding of cultural diversity, from both a sociological and an anthropological viewpoint.

Finally, we review some of the practical ways in which cultural analysis may be used by businesses in the management of their intercultural assets and liabilities.

BACKGROUND

ONE

A WORD OF WELCOME TO THE TRANSCULTURAL TRAVELLER

As we awake into a new dawn of global enterprise, the Western world is sensing the emergence of a new and as yet unfamiliar form of capitalism. Following on the heels of Japan's success, the new 'Tigers' of the business world (Taiwan, Malaysia, etc.), are drawing on a deep vein of collective entrepreneurism which has roots in both the Western and Eastern worlds. After over half a century of Western domination of modern capitalism, the business world is now emerging with a new balance, with both Eastern and Western values and practices finding their place in the natural order of things.

The domination of the Western pole has had its price as well as its profits. We are beginning to recognize the importance of environmental issues; too late unfortunately for some habitats. It has also had its price in terms of profits, with the Eastern way now eating substantially into the Western domination of major markets such as those of the motor industry.

As we navigate our way through this new world, we should not forget that we have only just begun the process of evolution into a truly pluralist business world. Despite early stirrings in the Greek writings of the first century AD, it was not until 1492 that Martin Behaim designed the world's first globe, thus taking us from a 'flat world' view and catapulting us into a new era of 'round world' awareness. Dominated as we had been by the strong psychological influence of our main navigational aid, the east–west rhythm of the sun, we had, until this time, been largely blind to the existence of yet another dimension to our world; the north–south axis.

In a similar way, the predominance of the east–west poles of social and economic influence have led us to a myopic view of culture, in both a sociological and a business context. This has been further compounded by the nature and evolution of the post-nineteenth century world, this being dominated by the (mainly Anglo-Saxon) influences of the Industrial Revolution. Add to this the success of the mass-produced, mass-market product such as Mr Ford's famous black motor car and one sees the situation aggravated to the point where the world looks not only flat but also takes on a distinctly lopsided appearance. To quote Sir Peter Parker, the UK business-man and a leading exponent of the need for internationalism in business, 'add Pax Americana to Pax Britannica and suddenly the sun never sets on your smugness' (Figure 1.1).

From this perspective it may perhaps be judged fortuitous that, from the early 1970s onwards, we have seen first a trickle and now a tide of enterprise from the East, bringing with it not only fresh new products but also fresh new perspectives on the way business may be man-aged. The West has had, and still does have, a profoundly ambivalent response to this develop-

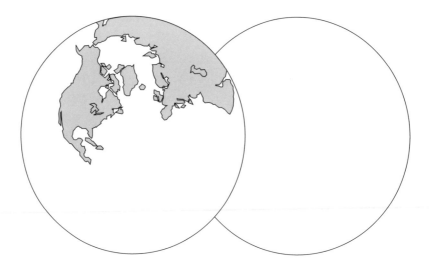

Figure 1.1 A Westerner's view of the world.

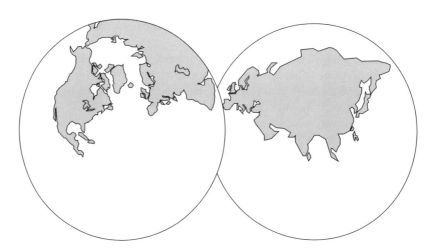

Figure 1.2 An east–west view of the world.

ment. On the one hand, it has sought to learn from its new Asian colleagues. Just-in-time manufacturing and worker participation are only two of a number of practices which have been successfully 'imported' to Western business. On the other, it has sought to isolate itself from the new 'threat' posed by the very same practices.

This ambivalence is far from resolved and, even as we write this book, America is locked into heated debate with Japan over what it sees as unfair trading relations, a discussion brought on not only by Japan's allegedly protected local markets, but resulting, perhaps more importantly, from the massive success of Japan in the US motor car and electronics markets.

Much has been written about the cultural differences which underpin these two poles of our business world but, valuable though such studies may be, they provide only points of light to illuminate what is still a black and incomplete art. We are still left with a rather less than complete view of things — it is as though our southern oceans were empty of land; it is as if our world was made up only of the eastern and western continental masses (Figure 1.2).

In this book we shall attempt, in order to go one step further, to take a step back from the subject, and begin the process of combining the various points of light into a wider beam with which to shine new light on our transcultural world. Our starting point is that, important though it may be to have a firm grip of the diversity of the east–west polarity, it should not be forgotten that we have, to a large extent, fallen into the trap of our forefathers in looking at the cultural world and thinking of it, too, as flat. It being the case that three-dimensional vision requires at least two points of view, then the true three-dimensional splendour of the world of culture may only become apparent when we look at it with at least two eyes. We must therefore build ways in which we can balance our understanding of the east–west polarity with that of the two other poles of our world — those of the north and south.

With the world locked into so many cross-cultural conflicts, it is perhaps worth remembering that we start our journey together in this book against a background of good progress. It took us over two and a half million years to evolve a 'round' world view — our understanding of culture is moving much faster than that! But to keep up the pace of progress we need not only new information, gathered from the four poles of the cultural world. We need also new models which help us to move on, first to look positively at the delights of east–west diversity — it has been said that the one without the other is as pointless as one hand clapping. Once we have achieved this, our models of the world then need to carry us forward to build a multidimensional view which takes into account the full beauty of our elegant and complex transcultural habitat.

THE EMERGENT BUSINESSPHERE

Universality turns into polarity

In the course of the 1990s, and in fact for the first time, 'the way we run the business' has been generally acknowledged to differ fundamentally depending on whether you and I are from one culture or another. As we have seen, most attention has been paid to the differences between the Anglo-Saxon and Japanese cultures.

In the 1980s McKinsey's Richard Pascale and Anthony Athos[1] compared and contrasted American and Japanese approaches to management and organization, but, finally concluded that the best-run companies in both countries adhered to common principles, duly enshrined in the 'seven S's'. These were alternately soft (shared vision, style, staff, skills) and hard (strategy, structure, systems). Pascale and Athos had begun the process of broadening their view on the world, but, in the end, were reluctant to surrender their culturally entrenched, pro-universalist (Western) perspective.

Conversely, and in the 1990s, both Michel Albert[2] in France and Lester Thurow in America have identified fundamental differences in the 'east–west' polarity. Whereas Albert is the head of France's largest insurance company, Thurow is the Dean of America's Sloan School of Management.

Both Albert and Thurow have compared, on the one hand, the British and the Americans, with, on the other, the Japanese and the Germans and they perceive these to be two discretely contrasting economic and managerial blocks. Moreover, as Thurow's assessment has gained wide-ranging appeal we shall focus on it here, also recognizing that Americans are somewhat more combative in orientation than their French counterparts. Lester Thurow, to begin with, positions his cross-cultural debate within the broader context of an emerging 'knowledge-based' economy that is crossing the world. As such, he is in tune with his renowned American colleagues, management guru Peter Drucker[3] and President Clinton's Secretary of State for Labour, Robert Reich.[4]

To the extent that such knowledge overtakes physical and financial capital as the primary factor of production, so culture enters the business foreground. In fact, in his book *Business as a Learning Community*[5] one of our authors has claimed that comparative philosophies, which in fact underpin our respective knowledge bases, may become the ultimate factors of production. For example, philosophical systems which favour development and renewal, be they based on German historicism or on Japanese Shintoism, may be better suited to present economic times than those favouring more pragmatically based business strategies.

Thurow[6] considers seven 'key industries' — microelectronics, biotechnology, the new materials industries, civilian aviation, telecommunications, robots plus machine tools and computers plus software. All he considers to be 'brainpower industries' each of which might be located anywhere in the world. Where they will be located depends on who can organize the brainpower to capture them. For Thurow, comparative advantage in the future will be man-made, and 'since technology lies behind man-made comparative advantage, research and development becomes critical...in the twenty-first century sustainable competitive advan-tage will come much more out of new process technologies and much less out of new product ones'.

For Thurow, the economic competition between Communism and capitalism is over, but another competition between two different forms of capitalism is already under way. This new competition, in his view, is between the individualistic Anglo-Saxon British American form of capitalism and the communitarian German and Japanese variants. America and Britain, in effect, champion the lone ranger — the heroic entrepreneur, the Nobel prize winner, the responsible individual. Underlying this individualistic approach is large-scale earnings differentiation, together with profit-maximizing policies as well as mergers and take-overs that serve the interests of the individual shareholder.

In contrast, the group-oriented Germans and Japanese believe in business clusters, teamwork, social responsibility for skills, company loyalty and industrial strategy. Whereas, Thurlow argues, the Anglo-Saxons believe in consumer economics, the Japanese believe in producer economics. Each national culture, as we shall see, notwithstanding certain company and industry variations, has a characteristically different business philosophy, culture, strategy and structure.

First World — Third World

The new 'east–west' divide then, no longer differentiating Communist from capitalist, now distinguishes the Anglo-Saxon from the Japanese–German ways of doing business. However, although this particular polarity underlies the primary field of economic tension today, we cannot afford to restrict our vision to this horizontal plane. After all, both in Europe in particular and in the world in general, there is also a great 'north–south' divide. Each contains both its positive and its negative manifestations, depending on the state of balance, or imbalance, within its national and corporate psyche[7] (Figure 1.3).

While, for the moment, there is no southern economic force to match the power of America — west, Europe — north, or Japan — east, we cannot merely write off two of the world's great continents, Asia and Africa. In fact, a remarkable African entrepreneur and visionary, Albert

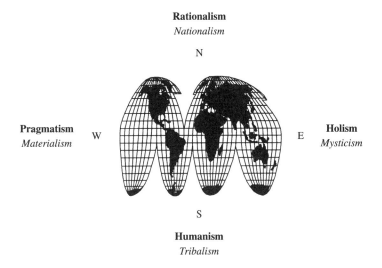

Figure 1.3   The global businessphere.

Koopman, has devoted his life to turning the north–south force field into one of creative tension as opposed to endemic conflict. During the course of the 1980s he created Africa's first viable worker democracy, and in the process developed a management ethos that in many ways straddled the 'north–south' divide. His company, Cashbuild, with its thousand-strong workforce supplying building materials across South Africa, has not only survived the country's prolonged depression better than most but has even prospered both economically and socially. Interestingly enough, since Koopman left Cashbuild in the late 1980s it has been further developed and consolidated by a more rationally based Frenchman.

Together with his colleagues at ITISA[8] (Interdependence and Transformation in Southern Africa), Koopman[9] is now attempting to spread his so-called 'pragmatic humanism' across indigenous enterprises. Their underlying approach involves sharing value to add value. Koopman combines two respectively 'northern' and 'southern' perspectives. There is first what he calls the 'having mode' of the north, encompassing individual wealth and control, wealth and status, goals and deadlines. Second, he characterizes the 'being mode' of the south, which he associates with team cooperation, dignity and respect, vision and faith.

Koopman has therefore helped us to make a start on our journey around the cross-cultural world. But for us to be able to find our way, and our way back, we will need some form of map and a guide to help us.

THE READER'S JOURNEY

Think therefore of this book as an illuminated atlas of culture, designed for the transcultural business voyager. The design of our atlas has been helped by a variety of experienced travellers. Some have spent their time on east–west voyages; others, like Koopman, have taken the north–south route. Our maps are built from two perspectives on the world — the so-called 'inside-out' perspective, that of the individual looking at culture from his or her own point of view and building these individual views into a broader view of the whole, and the other perspective, 'outside-in', where researchers have attempted to study societies as a whole and to deduce from these studies what principal differences exist between the different worlds in which they live (see Chapter 7).

We have chosen to present our atlas in three parts.

Part One

In Part One our travellers tell their stories. Chapter 1, in which the reader now stands, is the starting point for our journey. Here we will take a look at the map and set the sails. Here our guide tells us that, while the journey need not take us through all the points of the atlas, we should take care not to visit only those places where we feel most comfortable. An understanding of other cultures requires immersion in their point of view. For some voyagers this may cause some problems. For the north-westerner, the east and south may appear rather too fond of their humanist and visionary philosophy; for those from the south-east, the north-west may seem a place where science and a need for action obscure the true balance between people and the economic world in which they exist. We encourage our travellers to put aside, for a moment, their natural reticence and to dwell for a time in those places which are strange to them.

In Chapter 2 we begin our journey in the east and west. Here we will take a new look at the east–west tension. On this part of the journey we will meet two experienced travellers, Charles Hampden-Turner and Fons Trompenaars, and view the east–west polarity from their perspective. These authors, building on the seminal work of Geerte Hofstede (see Chapter 6), have drawn on an extensive international study of managers' responses to questions related to cultural preferences. In so doing, they are, true to their own cultural heritage, taking an individualist 'inside-out' perspective on their subject.

In Chapter 3 we begin to tease out Europe's complexity through the eyes of Salvador de Madariaga. This remarkable poet/diplomat has described in an extraordinarily insightful way the profound differences underpinning European culture. This intuitive/deductive approach seeks to examine the differences between different groups of Europeans and therefore falls into the 'outside-in' category of investigation. Through de Madariaga we begin the process of sensing the existence of the north–south poles of culture, using as our temporary harbour the southern cultures of Spain and Italy. De Madariaga's view, though eloquent, is inevitably conditioned by the culture in which it is set and is only able to take us part of the way towards a worldview of Europe.

Chapter 4 provides us with a broader, more complete view of European culture, where the traveller sees the world through the eyes of one of the authors, a South African now living and working in Europe. Chapter 4 is therefore in every respect an 'outside-in' perspective. Here our atlas introduces the reader to a fully three-dimensional view of culture, using Europe as a place of learning. Here we build on de Madariaga to arrive at a 'four-world' model of culture, a concept which the reader will see becomes the guiding principle of our journey. This chapter seeks to explore the metaphor of a four-polar world, drawing on Europe's rich diversity as a framework of reference to explore the east, west, north and south polarities in terms of the fundamental value systems on which they draw. Here the traveller is introduced to the pioneering, action-orientated cultures of the west, to the cool rational cultures of the north. We then travel south to the traditional family-oriented cultures and then move on towards the reflective, idealist cultures of the east.

This chapter begins the process of healing the rift between cultures, extolling the virtues of diversity and introducing the concept of a multicultural 'businessphere' in which the truly transcultural manager moves easily from one culture to the other, building on its strengths and girding its weakness with the strengths of others. Companies and their cultural environments thus become a seamless whole, with assets and liabilities being measured in terms not only of finance but also of their rich and fertile transcultural resources.

By now the reader will have sensed that, though we have started our journey in the east–west worlds, we have spent much of our time so far in the south and east, and have experienced the strongly humanist and idealist values of its cultures. Here the world is humanist rather than rational and idealist rather than pragmatic. We will not therefore dally further in this part of the world and will now turn again to the north-west, to the cooler world of rationalism and the action-oriented world of pragmatism.

Part Two

Part Two will take the reader through the world of cultural modelling. Here we will visit the northern analytical worlds of economics, psychology and, in an attempt to re-establish a healthy balance within this world also, will bring into play the perspective of the cultural anthropologist, looking at the roots and origins of culture and the ways in which these combine to produce the branches or 'above-ground' attributes of culture.

For our trip into the northern world we are helped by René Decartes, whose rational ideals are to be found exemplified in Chapter 5. Here our French colleague, Didier Cazal, provides the reader with an overview of the economic and social theory which underpins the world of cultural analysis. As we travel, using our rational 'northern' eyes, we begin the process of unravelling the theories which underpin cultural analysis, looking first at the evolution of the 'dualist' view of economics, introducing the concept that the operation of a market economy is not driven by price alone but by other, more human factors which come about through the existence of companies. This dualist approach caused a sea-change in economics theory, one which is particularly relevant to our journey since it made the business a relevant part of the chain of economic management and brought about an awareness of the importance of people in economic dynamics (see Figure 1.4).

Building on the dualists' approach we will take the reader again briefly to the east and look at the teachings of a group of Japanese economists who, it may already not surprise our travellers to find, have been responsible for the acceptance of the true importance of relationships in

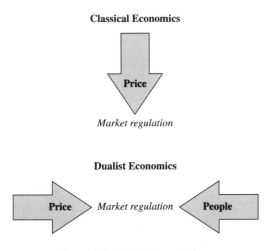

Figure 1.4 Market mechanisms.

market dynamics. The traveller will meet with the Japanese economics researchers Ouchi and Aoki, whose works serve to illustrate this part of our atlas and who bring to the fore the importance of people and their values in the understanding and management of commercial and economic entities. Lastly in this chapter we return to France where we complete our journey through economic theory and arrive at a comprehensive view of economics in a transcultural context.

In Chapter 6 we meet with a party of bridge builders, working between the north-west and the south-east. Sid Lowe and Cliff Oswick, based on their research in Hong Kong, will provide a perspective on the degree to which our analytical, individualist methodologies are themselves culturally transposable. They will introduce the traveller to Geerte Hofstede, a legendary cross-cultural traveller who has done more than most to light the way for wary voyagers. The traveller will see the world through his eyes and will begin to gain an understanding of the ways in which cultures can be compared and contrasted on the basis of a surprisingly small number of common issues. These guides will take the traveller back and forth between the east and the west, to gain a view not only of the complexity of culture but also of its essential simplicity, with certain 'higher-order' variables determining the structure of others in a predictable and elegant pattern — a continuum of predictable evolution.

In Chapter 7, and in the company of one of the authors, the traveller will take a trip back in time. In this part of the journey the traveller will meet the veteran cultural analyst, Mary Douglas and, through her eyes, will discover the ways in which group allegiance shapes and is shaped by the culture of the surrounding world. This anthropological excursion will also take the traveller deep into the world of the family and its evolution and will gain an insight into the ways in which the family affects the commercial world in which it exists.

In Chapter 8 we will turn fully west and explore the ways in which cultural analysis can be used to gain a competitive advantage in day-to-day management practice. One of the authors will act as a guide, introducing the traveller to the systems by which it is possible to begin the process of understanding of the degree to which we as individuals have been shaped by the cultural environment in which we grew up. We will look at how the same process of analysis can also be used to assess the value systems of the people in our working environment and the traveller will gain an insight into the ways in which this information can be used as the basis for a new approach to transcultural management; harnessing cultural assets and liabilities.

Part Three

As is appropriate to any journey, the last leg will be in reflective mode. Here the reader will be invited to take a short journey back to the south-east — a final process of reflection where traveller will take a moment to consider the implications of his or her journey of transcultural discovery. As is fitting for a journey's end, some questions will have been answered and some will not, some will have indeed emerged as a result of the journey itself. But before we can end, we must begin... .

REFERENCES

1. Pascale, R. and Athos, A., *The Art of Japanese Management*, Penguin, Harmondsworth, 1982.
2. Albert, M., *Capitalisme contre Capitalisme*, Edition du Seuil, Paris, 1991.
3. Drucker, P., *Post-Capitalist Society*, Butterworth-Heinemann, Oxford, 1993.
4. Reich, R., *The New Work of Nations,* Simon and Schuster, New York, 1992.

5. Lessem, R., *Business as a Learning Community*, McGraw-Hill, Maidenhead, 1993.
6. Thurow, L., *Head to Head*, p. 44, Nicholas Brealey, London, 1992.
7. Lessem, R. and Neubauer, F., *European Management Systems*, McGraw-Hill, Maidenhead, 1993.
8. ITISA, *Value Sharing*, internal publication, 1992.
9. Koopman, A., *Transcultural Management*, p. 147, Blackwell, Oxford, 1991.

TWO

INTO THE JAWS OF THE EAST–WEST DIVIDE: AMERICA VERSUS JAPAN

INTRODUCTION

The evolution of capitalism

In today's international economy, as France's Michel Albert has pointed out, a global perspective must be underpinned by an appreciation of the differences between the Anglo-Saxon and Japanese–German 'capitalisme contre capitalisme'. This is the primary field of force, or global economic template, within which the rest of the world would do well, at least initially, to position itself. Moreover, because globally less is known of the Japanese and indeed of the Germans than of the British and Americans, we shall devote relatively more attention to the former — particularly to the Japanese — than to the latter.

Charles Hampden-Turner, in fact one of the most globally oriented of Britain's management thinkers, has recently joined forces with the Dutchman Fons Trompenaars, to compare and contrast what they term *The Seven Cultures of Capitalism*.[1] These include Britain and the USA, France and Sweden, Germany, the Netherlands and Japan. As we shall see in Chapter 6, Trompenaars has devoted most of his working life to analysing the ways in which such different cultures manage their business affairs. Hampden-Turner, more recently, has added psychological depth to Trompenaars' anthropological breadth. In both their views, moreover, the Anglo-Saxon culture that helped capitalism to take off, and encouraged entrepreneurs to defy the orthodoxies of their day, may not encounter the complexities of the information revolution on good terms. *If capitalism is constantly evolving, so must be the values which engage it to best advantage.* The cultures that exemplified early capitalism may, in their view, have over-reached their once-winning combinations. What it took to create wealth in the pin factory described by the Anglo-Saxon hero Adam Smith, in 1776, may not be what it takes to dominate markets in consumer electronics, as the Japanese do today!

In this chapter, therefore, our journey will take us through a comparative analysis of America and Japan, beginning where Lester Thurow, whom we met in Chapter 1, left off.

Cultural dimensions

In Hampden-Turner's and Fons Trompenaars' view, *cultures are created from the effort of groups to deal with the basic dilemmas of human existence*. In that respect, and from the outset of their

Table 2.1   The east–west divide

	Japan (Eastern)	USA (Western)
Corporate philosophy	Integrated	Segmented
Corporate culture	Group	Individual
Corporate strategy	Long term	Short term
Corporate structure	Organic	Mechanistic

respective histories, a small set of islands like Japan and the North American landmass will have faced very different physical, economic and psychological dilemmas. It is in the face of these that cultures place one horn of the dilemma in the foreground, another in the background. This is dramatically illustrated in a modern-day comparison, in business, of the USA and Japan. In fact, for ease of assimilation, we have grouped the seven sets of dilemmas to which Hampden-Turner and Trompenaars refer into four categories: corporate philosophy, corporate 'culture', corporate strategy and corporate structure (Table 2.1).

We shall start our journey with a look at business philosophy in the West, that is, with 'Capitalism USA', and then turn eastwards, towards 'Capitalism Japan'. In each case, moreover, the one will be highlighted by way of comparison with the other. Finally, it goes without saying that particular industry, company and professional cultures will inevitably make their mark on management.

CAPITALISM USA

Corporate philosophy

American business philosophy is characterized, first, by universal codes of behaviour, rather than being oriented towards particular people and things. Second, the Anglo-Saxons tend to be 'atomistic' in their business approach, focusing on the part rather than the whole. In sum, they tend to individually segment their business, organization, work and relationships rather than integrate them altogether.

Preferring segmentation to integration
Universal codes supplant particular people and things   The dilemma in question here is whether to start with universals — that is, numbers, accounts, laws — or with particulars — with uniquely identifiable people and things. The new nation of the USA, when it was originally established, developed and promoted its universal codes as an invitation to immigrants to join it. Indeed, it is hard to see how a nation could play host to people from so many lands without substituting a universal code for many particular customs. As a result, you can be un-American but not un-Dutch. The US 'melting pot' became a powerful metaphor for the immigration process. American citizenship was less a uniform result than a ground rule for a fair contest. What the rules guaranteed was a field of play clearly marked, open to all and fairly refereed, and subject to clearly measurable performance.

America's leadership in the so-called 'Machine Age' therefore, according to Hampden-Turner and Trompenaars, was 'measurably' helped by the fast development of the hard sciences of accountancy, finance and economics. These professional disciplines lend themselves to universal codification.

The early success of Wall Street and the City of London is a testimony to such univer–salism. Similarly, American business schools were established in the belief that anything, from the running of a pig farm to the production of high-definition television sets, can be covered by a coherent set of universally valid laws. The preference for making money by remote control from the headquarters of conglomerates, Hampden-Turner and Trompenaars argue, all testify to the American faith in general formulae, whereby you can then avoid encountering particular persons and things. Coca-Cola and Pepsi, for example, are formulae prepared as condensed essences, and then distributed to bottlers who dilute them. McDonald's and fast foods generally appeal to stan-dardized tastes. Hotel and motel chains are often replicas of each other.

The problem is not the presence of universalism. It is axiomatic that businesses cannot develop without ever more elaborate codes to guide them. The problem is trying to substitute a prepared formula for the particularities of human encounters. There are large areas of life which it is not only very difficult to encode beforehand, Hampden-Turner stresses, but where this very attempt prevents you from being surprised by customers' particular desires. Moreover, there is another hazard. The insistence that knowledge only counts if it can be successfully systematized means that the most easily codifiable aspects of knowledge will dominate over the least easily codifiable. Finance, law and economics will be far more influential than human resources and quality, which remain subordinated to the more universal disciplines. In the USA and Britain, therefore, finance and accountancy rule over technology, design, marketing and human resources.

The problem with universals is that they can lose touch with the real clay of industrial experience. You mistake the shadows for the substance, the profit figures for the genuine satis-factions. When you distil all the mess of the factory into clean figures on crisp white paper that a manager can manipulate, Hampden-Turner cogently argues, much may be lost in the cleansing.

The teaching of such universals, finally, is an invitation to 'management by remote control', a board game of numbers and abstractions. Examples of 'hard' universalism include scientific management, operations research, market segmentation and SWOT analyses. All tend to ignore the particularities of product or technology. In soft universalism the style is different, but not the substance. 'Sticking to your knitting' and 'managing by wandering about', for Hampden-Turner, remain overgeneralized prescriptions for excellence. Behaviourism, a product of American cul-ture, has long aspired to develop a universal code of principles which allow E, the Experimenter, to condition the responses of S, the Subject, by preparing a schedule of responses to reward and punish. Similarly, empiricism, strongly grounded in Anglo-Saxon philosophy, as we shall see in Chapter 10, favours segmented parts over integrated wholes.

Atomism supplants holism   The dilemma in question here is whether to begin managing with 'atoms' — jobs, tasks, roles, targets, budgets, profits — or to start with wholes — to connect, contextualize, configure. These two orientations have been attributed to the relative dominance of the two brain hemispheres, the analysing reductive left brain, which seems to dominate the Western world and the synthesizing visuo-spatial right brain which seems to dominate in the East. Whatever the source of this bifurcation, according to Hampden-Turner and Trompenaars, the distinction is culturally strong.

By treating an organization as an assembly of multiple objects, Western managers feel that they can behave objectively. What an object is will then be considered to be independent of their desires, hopes and fears. Western enlightenment consisted of just such an advance against supersti-tion. We have inexorably progressed by scepticism, by reduction and by what we can verify. For Anglo-Saxon empiricists the atomistic-specific approach is dignified by science.

Yet the idea that reality is 'objective', Hampden-Turner and Trompenaars argue, is more a cultural preference than it is less a proven proposition, and is a preference which is particularly strong in Britain and the USA. Facts are interpreted by the contexts in which we see them. To regard these 'facts' as more basic than their contexts is not obvious in large parts of the world, especially Asia. However, Americans like to 'get to the point'.

Western business cultures tend therefore to focus on specifics, they tend to know the price of things rather than their value. Valuing something requires an understanding of its context and is therefore an integrative process. Such cultures find it sometimes difficult to encourage workers to see beyond the confines of their roles and 'day jobs', to capture the imaginations of employees and to build these into a greater vision. They tend to get stuck with specifically designed objectives, more money, more customers. This happens because specifics, being separate objects, tend to be seen as large or small, many or few. Westerners can therefore quickly eliminate subtle possibilities in favour of the gross extremities — excellent, extraordinary, world class — massive production for massive markets!

The traditional organization of the American factory followed Adam Smith's dictum that the wealth of nations is created by divisions of labour. Thus the USA became the world's leader in the mass manufacture of relatively simple products. The new (eastern) manufacturing is more integrative and diffuse. But perhaps the most limiting aspect of (western) atomistic-specific thinking is the reduction of multiple values with which an organization must deal to a single figure, or configuration, that of profitability.

Similarly, it would seem that the one universalist and atomistic phenomenon which dominates the consciousness of an organization is that of a mechanism. A machine is the sum of its parts and operates by universal laws. An individual, viewed in similar terms, stands apart from the whole.

Corporate culture

American corporate culture, first, focuses on personality, the employee's and the leader's personality, rather than upon the business and organization's communality. In essence, Anglo-Saxon culture favours the individual over the group. Second, the Western view is characteristically 'inner directed', or assertive. In contrast with Eastern 'outer directedness' or responsiveness, whereby direction comes from without, the Western culture therefore looks for energy and inspiration from within.

Favouring the individual over the group
Personality supplants communality   It was the great entrepreneurs who were responsible for first the British Industrial Revolution, then the American one. They defied the values of landed gentility and inherited privilege, struck out on their own, and transformed the world. James Watt, Richard Arkwright, Andrew Carnegie, Henry Ford and John D. Rockefeller — the roll call of capitalism's great individuals — are now part of Anglo-Saxon folklore.

Three cultural biases, for Hampden-Turner, underlie the belief that economic self-interest must have primacy over social concern. First, and as we have already seen, Anglo-Saxons have an analytic-specific bias, whereby they separate self-interest from benevolence because these are logically opposed categories. Second, they exhibit an individualistic orientation whereby the individual is considered prior to the group. Third, they exhibit a sequential bias, in that, as we shall see, one of two conflicting tendencies must come first. These respective biases, moreover, lead to their 'inner-directed' approach to life in general, and to management in particular.

Inner directed supplants outer directed   According to Hampden-Turner and Trompenaars, almost no issue distinguishes the American mind-set from Asian and Latin cultures as much as the idea that persons can and should exercise control over their environment from within themselves. The belief in 'being your own man', that 'the buck stops here', that 'when the going gets tough the tough get going' is intrinsic to the American 'inner-directed' way. Yet managers of other nations see themselves steered by external as opposed to internal forces, which are often perceived to be out of their control. The ideal for the Japanese, for example, is not that of Superman but 'The Way of the Monkey', a figure in their pop culture who uses agility and wits to redirect the force and momentum of its opponents.

America's preponderant inner-direction, in effect, is responsible for its spectacular record in starting up new companies and creating new jobs. However, it leaves such companies very vulnerable as they approach their organizational phase, the point at which they must serve a maturing market. For at maturity, markets typically subdivide into hundreds or even thousands of niches, and the quality and variety of such products, rather than their very existence, is what makes them competitive. The complexity of this phase moves far beyond the founder's original vision, and seems best served by extended teams working collectively to respond to a myriad changing customer demands. It is just at this transition point to maturity that Japan makes its massive inroads. Conversely — witness total quality groups, grid groups, sensitivity groups — work groups as a mere means towards individual ends have limited utility. Too much is extracted from them and too little is contributed. Such a self-interested attitude, also characteristic of a certain kind of achievement orientation, also leads to short-termism.

Corporate strategy

Anglo-Saxon corporate strategy is channelled towards the achievement of individual success, covering both the internally driven manager and the inner-directed organization. This individually competitive strategic orientation can be contrasted against the realization of a managerial or commercial status that has been externally ascribed by an outside party, be it by a government department in particular or by society in general. This kind of Anglo-Saxon achievement orientation leads, on the one hand, to prolific entrepreneurism and, on the other, to rampant short-termism.

Short-term gain supplants long-term benefit

Achieved performance rather than ascribed status   Achievement, Hampden-Turner argues, is close to being the cultural bedrock on which the USA is founded. The Puritans were distinguished by their insistence that the Kingdom of Heaven could be built on this earth. It followed that each soul was 'justified through works', through the visible signs of achieving part of the kingdom. Status by achievement is pragmatism and empiricism applied to progress, rewarding most who or what works best. Achievement therefore, in the USA, is the reality test for human potential. The ideal then is to mark out a universalistic playing field, carefully specify the rules and rewards, let all individuals compete through their inner commitment, and recognize the highest achievers. Within such a game-play, corporations attributing achievement to the sterling character of the individual allow themselves to avoid responsibility for more general improvement. It can hire, fire and 'hunt heads' instead of joining to educate the nation's workforce.

By way of contrast, an Eastern company, knowing that it must pay more as its employees age, may serve to ensure that they mature in all possible ways, as well as become more valuable to their company in the process.

Such cultures are not de-emphasizing achievement but are seeking it by indirection. In so doing, moreover, they are acknowledging the organic nature of their business and organization, something which tends to go across the Anglo-Saxon grain.

Corporate structure

In the Anglo-Saxon business world, equality is rapidly gaining ground over hierarchy, especially with the advance of communications technology, and the progressive de-layering of organizations. At the same time such reorganization is conventionally seen in sequential, linear cause–effect terms. American managers, despite many of their 'management gurus' arguing to the contrary, tend, when it comes to the proverbial 'bottom line', to view their organizations as 'mechanisms' rather than as 'organisms'.

Preferring mechanisms to organisms
Equality transcends supposed hierarchy   The accepted wisdom, based on considerable research, is that simple products and technologies can be run by steep hierarchies, because the total task can be encompassed by a single mind. Moreover, complexity requires many sources of knowledge and multiple authorities, all needing to be reconciled. Such an argument favours flat hierarchies.

Yet of potentially great importance, and little understood by Westerners, is the process Hampden-Turner terms 'organic ordering'. At its most primitive this is a form of semi-feudalism, in which those owning land and property are deemed to have rights over their subordinates. At its most sophisticated organic ordering mimics the hierarchical ordering of knowledge itself. By issuing diffuse instructions, senior Asian managers are offering generalities and abstractions for their subordinates to exemplify with specifics and concrete achievements.

This is not an hierarchy that issues precise orders but one which holds up ideals for interpretation. The reason so many thousands of suggestions move up Japanese hierarchies, steep though they are, is that generalities need examples. Those who pose problems need solutions, while quality programmes need high-quality products. Those at the top of the knowledge ladder can only establish the validity of their concepts with the help of those at the bottom, so the organization as a whole can learn. Moreover, there is an equality of a kind in such arrangements, since those near the bottom dealing with the specifics are the only people who can confirm or disconfirm the validity of the broader propositions ascertained by their superiors. This circular form of equality, though, is less clearly apparent than its linear counterpart, as embodied in 'flat' organizations.

Time as linear rather than circular   How, in fact, should we think of time: as a series of passing events or as past experience joined with future expectations to influence present decisions? For the Greeks, Chronos was the god of 'seriatim' or clock time, and Kairos was the god of time and opportunity. The USA places particular emphasis on universalisms, in the form of codified laws, and upon atomism, in the forms of sequentially ordered tasks and techniques, units and data. Japanese managers, however, prefer to start with particulars: that which makes a culture and its people unique. These particulars are then arranged 'synchronously' in holistic and harmonious patterns. Whereas for the sequentially ordered American mind, time is perceived as a threat, an expensive train of events that must be used fully, for the synchronously ordered Japanese time is perceived as a friend who keeps coming around, providing fresh opportunities for engagement on each occasion.

Similarly, for the Westerner, products are regarded as maturing over time, from novelty and profitability into lower margins and eventual death. For the Japanese, products are regarded as self-renewing over time, the genes of one product giving life to the next.

We now turn fully eastwards, towards Japan. What passes as universalism and particularism in the West is a championing of the whole against the parts, or vice versa. In Japan universals and particulars, atoms and wholes are all encompassed within a circle that ebbs and flows.

CAPITALISM JAPAN

Corporate philosophy

Whereas the Americans are culturally prone to segmentation, the Japanese are culturally predisposed to integration. In this respect, as in so many others, the two leading business nations, albeit still under the aegis of so called 'capitalism', are polar opposites. In terms of their respective and underlying business philosophies: the east, first, exhibits diffused awareness where the West is focused; Japan, second, is oriented towards seamless quality whereas America focuses on quality standards; third, the either/or Anglo-Saxon culture is supplanted by Japanese values in combination; most particularly and fourth, the exclusively competitive strategy of the Anglo-Saxon variety is supplanted by an inclusively cooperative competition in Japan; and finally, Western-style consensus is superseded by an eastern orientation towards harmony.

Preferring integration to segmentation

Diffuse rather than focused awareness   US culture, and much of north-west Europe, according to Hampden-Turner and Trompenaars, defines the world as consisting of objects located in 'public space' where all detached observers would agree on their description. The Japanese take the approach that all phenomena can be seen from multiple points of view and that these additional angles make reality more whole and comprehensive. 'Monocular' Western objectivity isolates and objectifies, as if a telescope had been focused. Yet the same focused lens that clarifies the distant object makes the foreground and background fuzzy and cuts off the object from its field. Characteristically, such a 'Western' manager 'cannot see the wood for the trees'.

The Japanese view, conversely, is 'polyocular'. Every member of a quality circle sees different aspects of an issue. Products and services are themselves multidimensional. The whole truth is always in the process of being discovered. There is no such thing as a completed product system to which no improvements are possible, since there is always another viewpoint to be taken into consideration. All employees can and must participate because each has another view to add. All customers must be listened to with rapt attention because they must have another valid reason for appreciating or not appreciating what is being offered.

The notion of a world that consists not of objects but of differences could be giving the Japanese a massive advantage in the knowledge revolution. Maruyama, upon whom Hampden-Turner draws extensively, argues that arranging particulars or differences is a variety-increasing process, while looking for universals among objects is a variety-reducing one. For example, a well-known method of the Toyota production system is the 'five times why?' process of investigation. Moreover, in the 'kanban' procedure every part in a factory bears a label that describes which particular one it is, and the place it has in the whole assembly. The quality of the whole ultimately transcends that of the part.

A general seamless quality supplants specific quality standards   Thinking in Japan moves from particulars to generalizations. When you think inductively every detail from the shopfloor gets included. Moreover, influence flows up from the workfloor to those responsible for the larger system. Deductive thinking works the other way, down from those who form the hypotheses to the manual workers who do what the theory tells them. This is the whole notion of Taylorism, which the Japanese see as America's fatal flaw. This hypothetic-deductive method does not tolerate personal knowledge or vaguely defined bonds of affinity among workers. In order to deal scientifically with data the human world must first be reduced to objective facts and hard units, resembling objects which yield to the mastery of physical science. The preference is for highly codifiable knowledge, preferably numbers. The Japanese, according to Hampden-Turner and Trompenaars, see 'prajna', an intuition of the whole, as the source of 'vijnana', reason. You first intuit a pattern of particulars; only then does reason go to work on this. It does not matter that skills are tacit, vague or indefinable. What matters is that they make a noticeable difference to the whole of the group or plant. The Japanese, for example, are not keen on questionnaires, but prefer to talk face to face with customers.

The Japanese approach to quality, therefore, is to create a seamless whole from an ever-increasing number of particulars. In this view, quality is integral to the whole process. It is everyone's responsibility. American quality, by focusing on separate pieces, often misses the gaps between, that is, the quality by which the whole is organized. This may not be the responsibility of any one group or person. Also the inspection of parts tends to cause adversarial relationships between inspectors and producers. Japanese quality is pushed higher and higher by the initiatives and learning of the workers themselves. Production and inspection are 'values-in-combination' rather than being valued apart.

Beyond either/or — values in combination   Americans, Hampden-Turner and Trompenaars suggest, tend to segment values into either/or. Market segmentation, niche marketing and price bands are all the rage. In Anglo-Saxon classical economics, moreover, choices are irrational and subjective. One consumer likes strawberry ice, the other raspberry. The only objective facts are the level of demand at particular prices. One choice typically obviates the other. The Japanese view would seem to be quite different. A product is as valuable as the number of particular human situations which have been wrought into the whole combination. The more values by the more people that have gone into a product's making, then the more satisfactions by the more customers that will go into its consumption. The larger the values combination, the more potentially valuable the product, the higher its quality, the more multifaceted and hence wider its appeal.

This 'polyocular' approach seeks to reconcile many points of view into a choice combination, rather than a choice between one thing or another. Of course, both approaches are valid, but the either/or approach is more for the ice-cream vendor and the choice combination is more for the purchase of computers, video recorders and fax machines, where the product becomes increasingly greatly complex over time. World market trends would seem to suggest that Japan is increasingly dominating those products that fit its thought patterns.

Polyocularity also shows up in the gradual and seemingly circuitous manner in which the Japanese build their business relationships. Hampden-Turner and Trompenaars characterize the difference between the Japanese and US approaches as following the 'letter of the law', in the Anglo-Saxon cultures and the 'spirit of the law' in the Japanese one. Westerners assume that the less ambiguous the terms are and the more literally they are enforced, the fewer will be the attempts by self-interested parties to interpret the law in their favour. Universal obligations attach to precisely defined contractual terms. In the Japanese view whole relationships develop and mature from particular and changing needs of partners.

Whereas the Americans say 'yes' to specific propositions, the Japanese, therefore, say 'yes' to a continued relationship. For Americans an orderly framework is being constructed out of specifically agreed points. These terms must be agreed first without equivocation, since without carefully defined parts you cannot build a whole. It is therefore crucial to know whether the Japanese agree or not, point by point. For the Japanese, many of the particular wants of both parties need to be accommodated through a whole relationship, preferably flexible, loose and friendly.

The actual points matter far less than building the relationship, since the greater the mutuality and trust, the more it will be possible to include the widest range of particulars sought by each party. Moreover, particulars are frequently interchangeable, there being many alternative ways of satisfying a particular want. Such 'many ways' are inclusive, moreover, of both competition and cooperation, rather than either one or the other.

Cooperative competition   The habit of Anglo-Saxon empiricism is to reduce concepts to their basic ingredients or atoms. Competition is pure to the extent that the sheer number of competitors has driven price down to the lowest possible level. In Hampden-Turner's eyes, the Japanese engage in cooperative competing — 'kyoryoku shi nagara kyosa' — whereby particular competitors harmonize their talents purposefully, and through sociable motives.

In the Anglo-Saxon model we start with separate atoms of product, or units of sale, and these become subject to the universal laws of supply and demand, otherwise known as the 'market mechanism'. This is a variation of Newton's perpetual motion machine, the central metaphor of classical physics, which did so much to shape Western consciousness. The Japanese view grows out of their own story and cultural preferences. It begins with a whole multitude of particular products being offered for sale and competing with one another, but from the seeming chaos there grow clusters of cooperation and harmony. Individuals cooperate. Organizations compete. The quality of the first increases the intensity of the second. The industry as a whole has requirements independent of competing with each other, and separated in time. It is the same as cooperating in basic research and competing in applications. It is important not to confuse cooperating with harmony, which, as we shall see, is a far more subtle and inclusive concept.

By competing we learn to differentiate, contrast and evaluate products and processes. By cooperating we learn to integrate, encompass and facilitate the adoption of what we found to be best. Japanese competition stops short of destruction, arising out of its inherent appreciation of harmony.

Harmony not consensus   The Americans, for Hampden-Turner and Trompenaars, have their framework all laid out in advance, and proceed to order their different blocks to fit the slots available. Workers have standardized skills, which vary by specialty, so you hire a specified skill to fit a predesigned job. The Japanese hire irregular lumps of stone — extending the metaphor of the bricklayer versus the stonemason — which the mason or manager then shapes so that they fit together harmoniously. The stones are not specialized, but have the capacity to be shaped for many purposes. This makes the concept of team and of teamwork quite different in American and Japanese cultures.

American teamwork begins with a demand for consensus. You must agree to put your paid specialty at the service of the overall framework. Your contribution is known in advance, is contained in your job description, and has a market price, dependent on its scarcity. So your labour is an atomistic thing, and is contained in your job description. The 'house' is thus constructed from 'bricks' of different shapes, sizes and functions, and is built up piece by piece according to a codified plan. The Japanese view of the team and teamwork is crucially different. It begins with the heterogeneity of unshaped 'stones' with a variety of potentials. Workers are encouraged to have multiple skills and are valued and paid for their versatility, the number of different roles they can play within the team. The work is more varied, flexible and challenging and may make whole levels of supervision unnecessary.

The difference between consensus and harmony originates in how Americans try to build an objective order out of predefined atoms of speciality, while the Japanese seek to create a harmony of the whole from many particular talents. Note also that the Americans need to reach consensus before work starts and do not like to deviate in the process. But the Japanese can leave open, until the task is complete, exactly how the harmony is achieved, and how the particulars are included. The basis of harmony is to be heterogeneous, to have skills which are complementary rather than substitutable. In a Japanese home — by opening partitions and changing interior configurations — the same space serves multiple purposes.

It would appear then, for Hampden-Turner and Trompenaars, that the Japanese derive some competitive advantages from their indigenously based corporate philosophy, whereby they give priority to configuring wholes from a host of particulars, in which patterns are seen or from which patterns are created. More specifically, and in summary, they seem to have:

- An ability to see more numerous points of view, and never to see a product or service as perfect or finished, so long as additional viewpoints can be brought to bear.
- A capacity to think inductively, thereby drawing upwards hundreds of details from the shopfloor and customers to constitute more elaborate products.
- A view of quality as multifaceted, a seamless whole from which the whole group's overlapping viewpoints and mutual supervision are responsible.
- A preference for forming strong and lasting relationships with business partners in the context of which contracts, terms and items can be changed, if necessary, to maintain mutuality.
- A view of value, and value creation, as formed from choice combinations rather than from either/or subjective choices. The more values and viewpoints encompassed within a product and service, the greater its potential appeal to customers.
- A preference for cooperative competition, rather than pure competition. Competing discovers which of several ideas are better; cooperating ensures these are swiftly learnt.
- A search for harmony among a large variety of particulars, as opposed to an *a priori* consensus on objectives. Values do not need to be the same. They need to be congruent with each other.

Similarly, the Japanese corporate 'culture', from an organizational perspective, is distinctly different from the Anglo-Saxon one.

Corporate culture

The Japanese, like the majority of the world's population notwithstanding the apparent triumph of individualism across the world's economic stage, are inherently group oriented. Interestingly enough, and with the demise of a 'statist' brand of Communism, we now have an autonomous form of 'communitarianism' to take its place. For the Japanese their company represents a community, in the most fundamental of respects. Moreover, the most successful individual companies are grouped together into a so-called 'kereitsu' or grouping of affiliated enterprises.

Preference for group over individual
Communitarian rather than statist   The seeming anomaly of failing and succeeding 'collectivists' is explained by Hampden-Turner and Trompenaars in the distinction they make between

statism, the belief that the government can and must 'command' the economy, and *communitarian* values. In the latter case, the whole organization, society and economy is assumed to be able to learn to act coherently, so as to nurture higher rates of economic development. The idea that governments can unilaterally plan and control an economy is indeed dead, and the ever-growing complexity and turbulence of the world economy guarantees against its resurrection. Yet the importance of communal values, the idea that in the midst of economic cyclones, the group, the organization, the whole economy and society is needed to sustain individuals, and that the group is more than the sum of these individuals, seems crucial to sustained economic development in the period of 'late capitalism'.

Kaisha as community rather than firm as enterprise   While the Anglo-Saxon-based corporation is a legal contractual arrangement between individual stakeholders and an institution, also conceived of as an individual, a Japanese corporation is based on the model of a community. Individual shareholders in Japan have a lesser influence than investment banks, and those suppliers, customers and 'friends' with cross-holdings in the 'kaisha', who can typically block any hostile takeover while facilitating friendly ones. The net result of this is that the Japanese are able to wait out a sustained profit squeeze, and fight for market share until the Americans give up. What matters most is that the kaisha continues to serve the larger community, not that the holders of capital must wait for their money.

There are natural bonds of interest and affection between a community of suppliers and a community of users. In the case of complex products these will typically extend the nervous systems of makers and customers alike. These are connections to grow with. The priorities of Wall Street and the City of London are quite different. Shareholders, Hampden-Turner and Trompenaars emphasize, are typically faceless aggregates until one or more of them tries to take you over, or 'greenmail' you. Conversely, in the Eastern world, as your market share expands you find yourself working for your community, your society and your nation. Your work is a gift to your culture, as opposed to a means to pay returns to someone unknown to you. Such an individual orientation vitally affects the way organization is construed.

M-Form rather than H-Form organization   William Ouchi, an American Japanese management academic based in California, has called Japan the 'M-Form Society'.[3] The reason for this, according to Ouchi, is because Japanese organizations like to form multidivisional corporations around a technological core. They typically share in the research, development and manufacture of, say, micro-electronic components and then use multiple divisions to reach various markets. Matsushita, for example, has divisions of consumer electronics, industrial equipment, business machines, home appliances, lighting equipment, system products and electronic components. The central learning core feeds numerous applications. Such organizations include Honda, Hitachi, Fujitsu, Sony, Matsushita and Mitsubishi. For Ouchi, Western corporations are more characteristically H-Form (Holding Company). Britain's ICI, for example, has recently disbanded its 'M-Form' structure to adopt more of an 'H-Form' one. While information flows easily throughout the 'clan' culture of the M-Form, only thinly codified information, mostly numbers, is the currency of the 'market' culture of the H-Form.

But Japan's major corporations have an additional communal advantage — most of them belong to a kereitsu, or economic grouping, organized around banks or trading companies. Unlike the holding company, the kereitsu is designed on principles of reciprocity and complementarity. These groupings have almost inexhaustible funds and the capacity to undercut foreign rivals in strategic technologies, regarded as key to future dominance. They can concentrate all their resources at one strategic point to make sure that, if necessary, the cost of capital, of material, or of information is lowest for themselves. Hence, in Hampden-Turner's terms, kereitsus are spider webs of extensive networks leading from the smallest job-shop to the pinnacles of the economy. Each is a microcosm of the larger economy, a whole within a whole. As in the 'diamond sutra', each jewel in the bracelet has facets that reflect the entire bracelet, yet each is also a separate stone.

We have seen, then, that the Japanese are substantially more communitarian than individualistic. Instead of believing that social benefit will be conjured up by the invisible hand, if individuals concentrate upon their self-interests, they believe social harmony will lead automatically to the benefit of individuals, both culturally and strategically.

Corporate strategy

The Japanese aim, strategically, is not so much to develop competitive technologies as to become a lynch-pin of an industrial community. Such an approach arises out of their characteristically circular process of reasoning, whereby circles progressively strengthen the elements of which they are constituted. This strategic approach, in its turn, fosters the development of knowledge-intensive enterprise, with a view to developing both employees and customers, rather than the Anglo-Saxon financially oriented one. Finally, and perhaps most evidently, Japanese business groups focus on market share rather than profitability, thereby facing outward towards society rather than inward towards the company's owners or managers.

Long-term benefit supplants short-term gain

Communal rather than competitive technologies   Japan, according to Hampden-Turner, does not pick winners, it picks 'teachers', key technologies whose influence will spread most diffusely through the economy. Japanese culture has a logic of community that asks which are the technologies that do the most to develop its economic infrastructure.

Electronics, semiconductors and microchips are all important to the Japanese, for example, for a number of reasons. They embody miniaturization in a country desperately short of space. They represent light as opposed to heavy industry and, barring the acid used to etch silicon chips, they are relatively non-polluting. To say they are knowledge intensive is an understatement. They literally insert tiny brains into physical products to make these extensions of human purpose. For a culture which has long considered nature as animate and dynamic microchips enliven the world of manufactured objects.

In fact the Japanese call microprocessors 'the rice of industry', feeding competitive advantage into every object with a mind of its own. If Japanese microchips were to supply the competitive edge for a thousand other Japanese products it would pay the kereitsu and the larger economy to develop these even at a financial loss, provided they contributed to thousands of victories. If you dominate the market you will make more chips for companies who, if they are wise, will not allow you to go under. Your safety lies in having a large market share of tools that make tools, being the lynch-pin of an industrial community. As a node in the network you are a crucial part of Japan Inc. Your future will be co-extensive with that of the nation itself. Your progress, as a business, as an economy and as a society will be wholly circular rather than partial and linear.

Circular reasoning versus linear reasoning   The word 'fire', to take one evocative example, is a celebration of cause-and-effect thinking in its purest form, a straight, logical progression. 'Bang, he's gone.' As such it makes the Japanese deeply uneasy, because for them the consequences return. As for the firers, what will they learn, that people they do not agree with can be made to disappear?

'Tai Chi' cyclicality is strongly imbued in Far Eastern patterns of thought, as the most sacred and ultimate reality. In fact it is not possible to visit a modern factory in Japan without seeing scores of feedback loops with virtually every important operation monitored electronically so that the machine shuts down automatically if malfunctioning. Waste and scrap are routinely recycled. But what concerns us here are not simply loops that are self-correcting and which learn, but circles that progressively strengthen the elements of which they are constituted, for this is how interdependent members of communities develop. For example, the group becomes increasingly responsible for — finding increasing numbers of errors — for which it holds individuals increasingly responsible — for making more and more corrections.

In his 'Mandala of Creativity', based on Japanese folk arts such as wood carving and flower arrangement, Sheridan Tatsumo, author of *Created in Japan*,[4] describes a self-transforming circle. In it he describes five elements of Japanese creativity, that is, *sairo* (recycling), *tansuku* (search), *ikusei* (nurturing), *hassoo* (breakthrough), and *kaizen* (refinement). This entire process is conceived of as a developmental helix, spiralling upwards to ever greater enlightenment. Every person in the creative group, moreover, is both subject and object, and there are many polyocular ways of perceiving as there are elements in the group. Development is an interdependent process of mutual, helical empowerment, in a process that imitates living nature.

Where time is seen as sequential, therefore, the hours, days and years stretch out in an endless line, which appears out of the future and disappears into the past. According to this view time is a sequence of events measurable in intervals through which they have occurred. Managers should create schedules and deal with tasks in strict priorities. The secret of mass production is to send as many standardized products down the line as possible in rapid sequence. According to the synchronic view of time the past keeps returning to the present to help nurture and create the future. Time is full of recurring features, the friends you learn from, seasonal fluctuations, generation after generation of new products, each building on the 'genes' of their forebears.

If managers see their future as already here, interacting with their past and present in an eternal now, they are going to take it much more seriously. It is concerned with seeds and seminal technologies, sown in the present, producing generation after generation of products in the future. Microchips, semiconductors, machine tools and robots, for example, are progenitors of future products. These, in turn, are products whose 'genes' eternally return — like the 'kami' or nature spirits returning from the past — and whose learnings fructify. Recurring Japanese products are like families which give themselves mutual support. Teachers earn a high salary because of their public role as circulators. Only if teaching and learning are seen as synchronized with the economy long term will adequate provision be forthcoming. Knowledge is not an eternal thing but the germinator of eternal rebirth.

US companies typically proceed sequentially from research to development, to process design, to manufacturing, to product — a push strategy. In contrast, Japanese companies may start the process anywhere, with a borrowed process design, with a product purchased from abroad which is then re-engineered, or with the refinement and development of an American invention. The advantage of 'pulling' everything together in one place, towards a deadline in the future, is that you design for better manufacturability. You research and develop for easier layout or quicker assembly. The customer's future requirements drive synchronized circles of improvement and rapid deployments of resources.

Knowledge-intensive enterprise   A fundamental principle of classical economics, Hampden-Turner claims, is that human wants are subjectively based, 'value empty', mere matters of taste. What this view fails to take into account is that producing and consuming certain products profoundly educates and develops all those involved. Consider the design, development and manufacture of a computer. The sheer volume of technical, intellectual and social learning involved in such processes is incalculable. But the challenges do not end there. The computer needs to be distributed and sold to those who can realize the machine's full potentials, or rather the full potentials of their own minds and the accumulated experience of their companies acting through the computers. Whole libraries of software must be transferred to those who need them and who know how to use them, along with the peripherals they need, all joined into a dense network of communications. All these levels of complexity are called knowledge intensity.

Only economies with high levels of educational attainment, plus continuous learning on the job, are able to supply products with high educational contents while educating customers in their use. Moreover, learning is progressive. The more you already know, the easier it is to learn. We may be less inclined to consume a fourth cream cake, but the appetite for knowledge feeds upon itself, so that the concept of 'declining marginal utility' in economics, Hampden-Turner argues, fails to take into account the reality of information and learning. You cannot eat your cake and have it, but you can sell your knowledge and keep it. Knowledge, love and growth defy the laws of physics. Whereas many nations can cut and shape leather to make shoes, very few can supply computers to companies in ways that make these more productive and effective enterprises. With cars the high value-added design, electronics and automatic gearbox will often be Japanese while the assembly, hubcaps, and seat cushions will be done locally.

The Japanese contribution is a seamless whole, a body of accumulated learning that extends from applied research, through development to complex manufacture. In the process thousands of people learn an interlocking set of sophisticated procedures. A better education and training of workers has to find its way into what they make in order to make their educations affordable by the economy. Only products which use and sell knowledge can pay back to their society the cost of educating their citizens. What the Japanese government has decided is that entering the 'high knowledge' contests will develop more of its people. The decision is made before the market mechanism is even encountered. It is a choice to engage markets at higher levels of sophistication and to win or lose the more educative challenges.

So Japan does not abandon textiles, but turns to specialized carpeting and ultra-suede; it does not abandon ships, but builds trawlers that can fish, process, preserve and export their catch on a single journey. The higher the knowledge intensity of goods, the more are the connections between these and related products, and the faster knowledge circulates. The mastery of, say, micro-electronics enables companies to supply hundreds of related applications. The knowledge revolution gives the advantage to those with closer social bonds. Such social bonds, interestingly enough, also lead to Japan's pre-emphasis, at least in part, upon the acquisition of market share.

The drive for market share rather than profit   While the return earned by an individual shareholder is the quintessence of Western individualism, what the corporation has done for society is captured in market share, and is the quintessence of Japanese communitarianism. Market share faces outward to society, while profitability faces inward to its owners. Market share measures what has been put into a relationship, while profitability measures what has been taken out, with all the perils attendant on exacting too much.

Market share is also a better gateway to learning. The more the volume of throughput and the greater the variety of customer needs which are satisfied, the faster the organization learns to improve quality and lower its costs. Those who would win a learning race need the largest possible share of the market from which to learn. Strategies that challenge close communities to fight for increased market shares are also valuable in encouraging corporations to 'stick to their knitting' and increase the skeins of learning around their key technologies and distinctive competencies. By getting increasingly larger shares of the market for, say, fax machines, your stakes in those technologies increase. But profit-maximizing strategies will often divert you.

Faced by a Japanese competitor that has taken the profit out of, say, copiers, Anglo-Saxon companies will diversify into more profitable fields, even when these are unrelated to their core competence, and thereby lose their 'technological integrity'. This can be contrasted with the tendency to think cybernetically, in self-developing loops which spiral helically. Knowledge and information encompassed in these loops systematically upgrade the knowledge intensity of goods and services offered for sale. Moreover, this process increases the value of such products, and sustains educational and cultural institutions around the country.

The relentless drive for market share, rather than profit, assumes that 'excessive' efforts on behalf of customers will come 'full circle' as customers reciprocate, if necessary saving the organization which has given them so much. The 'kaisha' is able to do this because it is first and foremost a community of employees trying to serve a community of customers, all organized around the integrity of the product or service.

This integrity of product is facilitated by the 'M-Form', multidivisional companies organized around a shared enthusiasm for a technological core. Around this, moreover, a clan-culture forms with intimate relationships capable of communicating complexities. These forms are themselves embedded in 'kereitsu', economic groupings, with billions of dollars of resources. Finally, the community as a whole is able to attribute greater status and priority to tools which make the tools, or cooperative technologies chosen to 'teach' the infrastructure of the economy to be more effective and productive. The Japanese will fight tenaciously for these technologies, even losing money on a per-item basis because this technology 'feeds' a thousand other products. This strategic orientation, moreover, is facilitated by the 'organic' Japanese organizational structure.

Corporate structure

The Japanese view is that the organization is an organism to be nurtured, facilitated and developed, through its people and products, its market and environment. Such an organization is prone to flexible manufacturing rather than standardized production, arising out of its synchronous mind-set. Such synchrony in approach also lends itself to a continual process of product or organizational renewal through the juxtaposition of social and technological roots and branches. Finally, the Japanese manager is more of a synchronizer–coordinator than a Western-style leader.

Organism rather than mechanism
Nurture over nature   For the English-speaking cultures the market mechanism works not only at the level of domestic and world economics but also within corporations which have 'internal markets', allowing the more successful profit centres to rise and the less successful to fall. The economy, for Hampden-Turner and Trompenaars, is conceived as an equilibrium machine, as nothing but the sum of its parts, operating by universal principles. The Japanese view the company chiefly as an organism to be nurtured, facilitated and developed. In a garden, every growth is unique and particular, yet it forms an ecological and aesthetic whole. The Japanese economy is

frequently regarded as a 'food-chain' with microchips as 'the rice of industry', feeding numerous other products 'seeded' with brains. This is facilitated by seeing the corporation as an organism, competing with other growing organisms, but also nurtured and sustained by the ecology as a whole. Such an ecological perspective lends itself more easily to flexible manufacturing than to mass production.

Flexible rather than mass production   As soon as a product approaches maturity huge markets for single lines no longer exist but subdivide, like the Nile, into thousands of niches and tributaries. Customers now need elaborate, customized variations upon a general theme. The problem is that varied products need frequent tool changes, large inventories of parts, a more skilled, alert and flexible workforce, and better information flows. The Japanese culture that invented flexible manufacturing from its own synchronous mind-set is likely to gain and retain its advantage as manufacturing grows complex.

Taichi Ohno,[5] the Japanese production 'guru', conceived the Toyota Production System as an integrated series of race circuits, mediated by a baton-passing zone, where one runner passes over the baton while overlapping and running alongside the next. He argued for the adjustment of each circuit, so that the speed and the stamina of each runner are adapted to one another. This is his definition of work flow as opposed to work-forced flow, which happens when you see a mechanical assembly line. Whereas in steel and paper mills (with 18 to 24 manufacturing steps), the Japanese and Americans had near-identical labour hours, in car engines, (with over two hundred steps), American companies, used 60 per cent more labour hours. The advantages of synchronous strategies which pull toward final assembly increase with the complexity of work. Such a synchronous approach also serves to align, as well as continually realign, roots with branches.

Roots before branches   Whereas the Western tradition sees creativity as a flash of insight, an individual 'ah-ha' experience, the Eastern way to create a prosperous future is to promote synchrony between two or more streams of technology. In one such case Seiko set out to challenge the Swiss watch industry long term. Electronics engineers, quartz specialists and jewellers were initially assembled and invited to synchronize their expertise. The Japanese think in terms of both hybrid technologies and inter-industry technology fusion.

Such cybernetically based thinking, unlike the deviation-reducing American variety, tends to be deviation amplifying. What can happen is that some happy accident, an idea or suggestion from the workforce, kicks off a small change which amplifies progressively to transform the entire system. Japanese kaisha seem to be able to proliferate multiple varieties of a basic product in a remarkably short time.

The Japanese may be unconsciously imitating evolution itself, albeit a much speeded-up variety, by employing high degrees of minor variation, discovering and colonizing the niches into which these penetrate. They thereby turn minor variations into major ones, wherever customers selectively reinforce this deviance amplification. This approach has the virtue of minimizing risk and expense, since the initial deviations are small.

A more organic metaphor for thinking about the future than the cybernetic circuit is the tree. Trees tend to grow slowly, reaching maturity in five to fifty years. For the Sharp Corporation, basic technologies like signal processing and symbol processing feed into the trunk of the tree, and from this grow PCM adapters, satellite receivers, microphone amps and so on. Instead of analysing each product separately, and asking whether it will reach the 'hurdle' rate for investment, all products, according to Hampden-Turner, are seen as outgrowths of knowledge and nutrients flowing up the trunk and drawn from the education-rich soil beneath. Upon the synchrony of these converging roots will depend the quality, quantity, and variety of products. The branches reach out to customers while the roots delve into the earth for knowledge, also spreading out and searching. This means that growth takes care of the future, and products are self-elaborating, with connections among connections and branches of branches. As a result, the supposedly hierarchical Japanese organization is more than at first meets the Western eye.

Coordinations rather than chains of command The Japanese hierarchy, in its organically ordered form, is less a chain of command than a series of more and more inclusive coordinations of synchronies. Managers act on behalf of the community to synthesize and configure all the contributions of those reporting to them. Superiors are more synchronizer–coordinators than leaders, responsible for what the subordinates do, but at a higher level of abstraction.

In summary, therefore, in comparing a 'mechanistic' type organization within an organically based Japanese one:

- The universalist 'law givers' are supposedly obeyed, while the managers with their hands on particulars can respond more easily to initiatives from below.
- Those who give specific atoms of instruction expect exact compliance, while those given vaguer and more holistic advice leave more room for subordinate participation.
- The individualist will, as leader, seek personal distinction, but the communitarian is more content to orchestrate others.
- Those directed from within will want to see the corporation stamped with their own characters, whereas those directed from without will welcome other contributions.
- Seekers after personal achievement will use leadership opportunities to make their mark, while those to whom status has been attributed may seek to reciprocate respect.
- A chain of command is a time-oriented sequence, while coordinating the contributions of lower levels is synchronous.

For Hampden-Turner and Trompenaars, finally, the three concepts of 'amai', 'sempai-kohai', and 'naniwabushi' help us to understand the strong emotional obligations placed on Japanese leaders by their subordinates. Amae can be translated only roughly as a 'reliance and dependence upon the indulgent love of an older person'. For the Japanese, work relations should be familial and affectionate. In a culture of accelerating complexity and runaway varieties of expertise, we are all increasingly dependent on each other's distinctive competencies.

CONCLUSION

As we continue our journey we are left with the feeling that America and Japan indeed present themselves to the traveller as dramatic contrasts (see Table 2.2). Moreover, and as readily becomes apparent, the American way is much easier for the traveller to assimilate than is the Japanese way. No wonder the East Europeans have been rushing helter skelter in a westerly direction. However, as we have seen, while the Western way has its attractions in the short term, it also exacts its price over a longer time frame.

The polar worlds of the East and West thus illustrate the tensions which exists across our transcultural world. Looking once more at the global businesssphere we visited in Chapter 1, these tensions now appear as a four-polar world of transcultural resources — the assets of the transcultural business traveller. This is illustrated in Figure 2.1.

We now set course, away from the primary economic field incorporating America and

Table 2.2   The primary force field

America	Japan
Corporate philosophy	
Universal codes of behaviour, underpinned by the competitive marketplace	Cooperative competition, underpinned by communal technology
Focusing on the part, with a view to gaining consensus	Diffuse awareness, harmonized through the particular
Segmenting business organization, reinforced by quality standards	Seamless quality, arising out of values in combination
Corporate culture	
Energy from within	Oriented towards outside, reflected in the group
Focuses on personality	The company represents a community
Favours the individual	A grouping of affiliated enterprises — kereitsu
Corporate strategy	
Individual achievement	Promote knowledge-intensive enterprise, through circular reasoning
Competitive strategy	Become the lynch-pin of an industrial community
Short-term profitability	Long-term market share
Corporate structure	
Creed of equality	An organism is to be constantly nurtured
Progressive de-layering	Prone to continuing organizational renewal
Sequential/cause–effect thinking	The manager is a coordinator–synchronizer

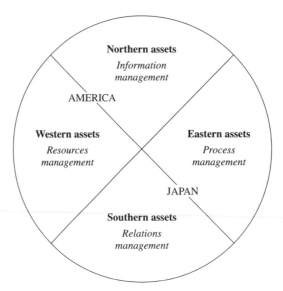

Figure 2.1 The global force field.

Japan, and move towards Europe, where we shall be adding further richness to our understanding of the complexity of our multicultural business world. Although this journey will add complications to our managerial lives, we would hope that the opportunity to move out of the field of Japanese–American dominance will be welcomed. Our guide on this part of the journey will be the extraordinary Spanish transcultural traveller, Salvador de Madariaga.

STUDY QUESTIONS

1. In what way do the Eastern and Western cultures differ in respect to their structural and strategic approaches to business and how does their relative individualism or collectivism impinge upon these considerations?
2. What are the principal differences between the Eastern and Western approaches to competition and how are these manifested in the ways in which businesses interact?
3. How are culture and market share linked and what are the implications of this linkage for international marketing strategies?

REFERENCES

1. Hampden-Turner, C. and Trompenaars, F., *The Seven Cultures of Capitalism*, Doubleday, New York, 1993.
2. Maruyama, M., 'New mindscapes for future business policy and management', *Journal of Technical Forecasting and Social Change*, **21**, 1982.
3. Ouchi, W. G., *The 'M-Form' Society*, Addison-Wesley, Reading, MA, 1984.
4. Tatsumo, S. G., *Created in Japan*, Harper & Row, New York, 1990.
5. Ohno, T., *The Toyota Production System*, Productivity Press, Cambridge, Mass., 1978.

THREE

A VOYAGE IN THE COMPANY OF SALVADOR DE MADARIAGA: EUROPE'S THREEFOLD IDENTITY

INTRODUCTION

Europe in a global context

The stem of the global tree

While Hampden-Turner's representation of American and Japanese management covers an important part of the global businessphere, a more complete view requires an understanding of Europe as an emerging economic entity. We are, however, somewhat hampered in our quest since much less is known about Europe's internal management diversity than is known, for example, about the differences between 'Eastern' and 'Western' management styles. Our European journey will therefore begin in the company of the remarkable Spanish diplomat, and founder of the College of Europe in Bruges, Salvador de Madariaga, who will take us on an expedition into Europe's literary and political worlds.

From the 1920s to the 1960s de Madariaga combined his profound understanding of European literature with his everyday appreciation of the European peoples, to uncover what he has termed *The spirit of Europe*. This European 'spirit' he first placed within a global perspective, before proceeding to focus, second, on the individual attributes of what were for him Europe's three most clearly identifiable European peoples: the English, the French and the Spanish.

De Madariaga uses the tree as his metaphorical cultural framework, whose roots he sees embedded in Africa, and whose stem he finds in Europe. The roots are the obscure part, composed of the vast commonality of our ancestors, and drawn from throughout the centuries of our family trees. Europe, most importantly in this chapter, is strongest in the one individualized part of the tree, the stem. This is the part on which the structure stands as a well-defined unit of life, the conscious mind and will. The foliage of humans is that light and airy part which seems able to draw inspiration and intuition from the light above. This is strong in Asia, where Europe has derived most of its religious experiences. 'While Asia yearns towards heavenly things and Africa remains sub-earthly, Europe disperses its being into myriads of separate human stems, and prefers to express its genius in terms of individuals.'[1] De Madariaga thus introduces the traveller to Europeans as the inventors of individualism, revelling in a synthesis of the Socratic and Christian traditions.

EUROPEAN UNITY IN INDIVIDUAL VARIETY

The chief virtue of Europe, for de Madariaga, and its main gift to the world, is its capacity for producing vintages of individual and national types with a strong spiritual and historical aroma of their own. Europe remains rich, above all, he says, in national characters, and for de Madariaga these are the true components of the European spirit. Significant differences of variety within a relatively narrow field of unity account for the typically European gift of quality. The essence of quality is uniqueness. Something, somebody has quality when he or she or it can be distinguished from the rest. Quality and distinction are naturally interrelated. These qualities must be tasted in order to be known. This has profound implications, of course, for total quality management, at least within a European context, a fact that has not yet been fully appreciated, so widespread is the American and Japanese influence in our business lives.

Unity, the stem, variety, the branches, quality, the flower, taste, the aroma, such — for de Madariaga — is the symbolic tree of the spirit of Europe. The variety of Europe, then, gives to each of the characters in its inner conversation enough definiteness and richness for the discussion to be lively. The unity of Europe, on the one hand, preserves enough common ground and reduces enough the distance between the inner voices for the discussion to be stimulating and fertile rather than conflicting and disharmonic. It is this perennial dialogue ever going on in the recesses of the European being which has determined the remarkable evolution of the European intellect; since the intellect, like all forms of life, is stimulated by exercise. Unfortunately, at least up until now, such a debate has not been conducted within the realms of European management.

While the Greeks made gods of the forces of nature, of the manifestation of fate that they could not master, de Madariaga's Europeans have given forth their gods by endowing with human features the tensions of their own complex and ever-labouring souls. Born of a mixture of bloods, carrying in his or her veins several collective memories, the European is a living debate, a permanent and never-settled argument. It is this argument which Europe's great creative artists have sublimated into an Olympus of European characters, Hamlet, Don Quixote, Faust, Don Juan, Ivan Karamazov, Peer Gynt. The great European management thinkers, alas, like Lievegoed in the Netherlands and Hampden-Turner in England, have not yet begun to follow suit, by debating among one another, across Europe east and west, north and south.

A European journey

With the demise of the old Soviet empire, we now visit the east/west divide afresh. Such a 'spiritual' and physical journey within Europe passes from the vast landmass of Russia, which for de Madariaga is sunk in a kind of 'natural Communism', to the land of the most clearly defined individual, France. Germany, meanwhile, occupies in the European spirit the same intermediate situation between Russia and France that it occupies in space. Just as the French feel in the German spirit an underworld of subconsciousness which evades the light of intellect, the Germans feel in the Russians an even deeper and primordial subconsciousness. The 'spiritual' journey from East to West is therefore also an ascent from the depths of human being, where forms melt into each other and the individuals sink into the mass, to the clear surface of the intellect. Interestingly enough it is the hitherto 'West' Germans, positioned midway between the depths and the surface, who are showing themselves to be profoundly adept in the modern business world. Perhaps, in de Madariaga's terms, this indicates that, in business terms, they have become fully evolved, or 'inviduated' (Figure 3.1).

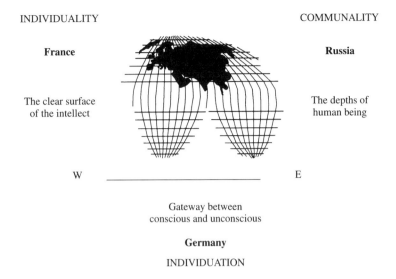

INDIVIDUALITY   COMMUNALITY

France   Russia

The clear surface   The depths of
of the intellect   human being

W   E

Gateway between
conscious and unconscious

Germany

INDIVIDUATION

Figure 3.1   Journeying east/west in Europe.

More specifically, as de Madariaga poetically describes, from the vast plain sea of Russia, a sea without shores, Europe sets itself in motion towards the West, passing through the rapids of Poland, to flow through the mighty river of the German soul. From the Black Sea, another current brings out its core the dark Balkan passions, to which Hungary imparts a vigorous rhythm, and these two currents, meeting in Vienna, endow the world with Mozart, Beethoven and Schubert. From the Mediterranean the spirit of Europe gathers to itself the divine light of Greece and Italy; from the Baltic and the North Sea, the colder and quieter light of the North; from Flanders and the Netherlands the light of homes and families. The spirit of Europe, ever more and more precise, reaches the West and branches into its three best-defined people. These three European nations — which Madariaga respectively characterizes as people of action, England, of thought, France, and of passion, Spain — interestingly enough flowed on to create America beyond the seas.

From Switzerland the Rhine takes the traveller on its northwards journey as it flows towards the sea. The Rhine and the Danube are thus the two axes of Europe. The Rhine divides the Teutonic world from the Latin world; the Danube brings Asiatic influences to the very core of Europe and enables European life to flow to the edge of Asia. The Rhine, then, is the spine of Europe, between the Germanic and Latin worlds. The Swiss, the Alsatians and Lorrainers, the Luxemburgers, the Belgians and the Dutch, all these regions are tough and stubborn, as was to be expected of frontier tribes. All speak their language with a particular accent of their own. All have left their mark on the chief European pursuits, mainly science and trade, having proved themselves well endowed in will and intellect.

European polarities

Having reviewed Europe as a whole, within a global perspective, de Madariaga proceeds to compare and contrast one part of Europe with another, focusing initially on transnational and subsequently on national attributes. He begins, intriguingly enough, by comparing the 'non-rational' with the 'intellectual' peoples of our continent.

TRANSNATIONAL POLARITIES

De Madariaga's European dance — the rational /non-rational duet

For Madariaga the three 'non-rational' peoples of Europe — English, Spanish and Russian — daring to venture out into the oceans and unlimited plains of the spirit which the intellect is unable to charter, provide Europe with its substance. Out of this substance the three most rational — France, Germany and Italy — provide the form (Figure 3.2).

The three rational countries are the critics, the legislators, the creators and keepers of rules, the born classics of the European spirit. To them we owe the categories and the forms. Without them, the Russians, the English and the Spaniards would have remained incapable of moulding their crazy lava into durable shapes. Where, for example, would Adam Smith have been without Henri Fayol? In their turn, without the Russians, the English and the Spanish, the three people of the intellect would have remained empty forms. Where would Fayol have been without Smith? Interestingly enough, as business advances from its pioneering to its more evolved and 'rational' form, so the 'rational' Europeans come into their own. They provide valuable support to the process of balancing individual interests with those of social need.

Individual–group

Hamlet and Don Quixote, for de Madariaga, are the two European symbols for the most European of problems — that of the balance between individual and social humans. Hamlet incarnates the tortured souls of people born free (Western), like a Clive Sinclair or a Steve Jobs, who have to live in a community too strong and too exacting for them. Don Quixote incarnates the equally tortured souls of people born social (south-eastern), like perhaps the Spanish prime

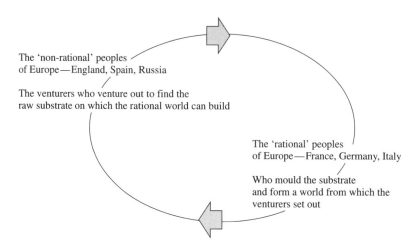

Figure 3.2   The interdependency of de Madariaga's European duet.

minister Philipe Gonzales, who have to live in a community too loose and rarefied for them. The European then seeks to retain both, in a balanced combination of individual freedom and social discipline. Whereas some European nations are tilted towards the individual, others are oriented towards the group.

NATIONAL POLARITIES

In the emerging European community Germany is increasingly perceived to be occupying pride of place, at least economically if not also culturally and politically. We would do well, therefore, with the help of de Madariaga, to compare the other major European nations with the Germans.

France–Germany

Germany, de Madariaga argued then (in the 1950s), as now, lies at the core of Europe. It stands at the centre of Europe's body, at the apex of its mind, in the innermost chambers of its conscious and subconscious being. Philosophy and music, science and technology, were unthinkable without Germany. If Germany falls, Europe falls. A thing in German is not done; it becomes done. This feature imparts to the language a kind of continuous motion, a sense of flow. The German language, therefore, reduces to its barest minimum the instant we call the present, merging it into instants before and after. Hence the avoidance of 'sein', to be, which the German discards for 'werden', to become, precisely in order to express that sense of fluidity which is the deepest feature of German life.

The tension between Germany and France — creative or otherwise — the strongest and most constant in the continent, is the main feature of the psychological landscape of Europe. To the east are the Germans, a people whose way of living had been for long that of warring tribes, and who were therefore apt to look at life as something ever in flux. To the west are the French, a people always ready to shape its life into concrete and definite forms. Life, which for the Germans is like a river, for the French is like a string of clear-cut crystals. Everything for the French, according to de Madariaga, is limited by hard and fast planes and can only change by sudden recrystallizations into equally set forms.

Italy–Germany

The tension between Italy and Germany is one of the oldest in Europe. It dates from the days of the Roman Empire when the Germans fell on the Roman cities. Little by little the Germans allowed themselves to be domesticated. This was the first victory of Italian creativeness over the formless fury of the Northerners, between the formless vigour of the North and the tradition of beauty, order and purpose in the South. Italy, de Madariaga claims, may therefore be said to be the mother of German civilization. Its influence, moreover, in German business today is more apparent in southern Germany than in the north. There is, however, between the two nations, as a whole, a common feature. Both Germany and Italy reveal a strange resistance to coalescence into big states. As a consequence both remained congeries of small states until the nineteenth century. Germany's, in fact, were more monarchical, Italy's more republican and unruly. But, in both cases, this feature led to a multiplication of small capitals and courts, which fostered intellectual life and turned people away from the international political struggle to the pursuit of ideas and forms. This in turn prepared the way for the mutual curiosity and respect the two people's have for each other on the cultural plane.

Germany–England

Both the English and the Germans are somewhat deficient in the sense of form; but for different reasons. In the English it is due to their predominant interest in action. The Germans, in contrast, neglect form to take refuge in their inner being. The deficiency of form in the English manifests itself as complication, accumulation, improvisation; in the Germans it leads to their dealing with a world of the fluid and nebulous. There is a world of difference between the well-articulated sets of concrete arguments in a Descartes or Spinoza and the stream of dialectics which flows from a Kant or Hegel.

The English take nothing for granted. They do not lose their will until they have carefully taken stock of things and people. The Germans live within themselves and it is there, within their inner laboratory, that they draw their plans and prepare their deeds. When they sally forth towards action their decisions are already made. Things do not resist them for they know them well and they are good technicians. But people do, for they are not skilful at handling them. Hence their failure as an imperial people. They are tenacious but, unlike the English, they are not elastic. Rigid without, they are fluid within. The mechanical discipline to which they long to submit and the military parades are but forms of their need for a strong social container, or business organization, to hold their soft being, or business strategy.

It is as if Germany corresponded more to physical nature and England to social nature. Just like Germany, physical nature is intelligent in an applied, infallible and mechanical way; but wholly indifferent to moral and social values. The English way is a sense of social nature, impure, empirical, growing little by little with time until it becomes a human society moved by moral values.

Germany–Spain

The English then — de Madariaga maintains — are akin to earth, the French to air, the Germans to water and the Spaniards to fire. The natural motion of water is along the line of the earth, as low as possible; while the natural motion of fire is upwards against all there is to block the way of the ascending flames. The Germans feel in touch with their source through the continuous flow of the river of their collective life; the Spaniards feel the beginning of things in the native and

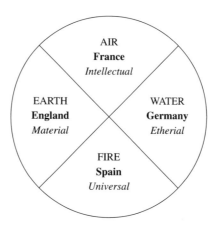

Figure 3.3 Europe's psychological force field.

pristine impetus of the fire that rises within them. Anarchist, disobedient Spain longs for the gregarious ways of obedient Germany. The Germans, too gregarious and nationalistic for the health of Europe in de Madariaga's view, would benefit from a blood alliance with the most individualistic and universal of all European peoples (Figure 3.3).

We now turn, more specifically, to consider the 'European trinity' that de Madariaga deems to personify, respectively, as action, thought and passion.

THE EUROPEAN TRINITY

Action/thought/passion

In a brilliant piece of analysis, upon which we shall meticulously draw, de Madariaga aligns the English, in particular, with action or doing; the French with thought or intellect; and the Spanish with passion or feeling (Figure 3.4). De Madariaga selects those three of the European nations because he believes they represent the purest form of each of those attributes. Other major European countries, such as Germany and Italy, can therefore be placed in appropriate in-between positions.

De Madariaga is not suggesting, moreover, that the English do nothing but act, the French nothing but think, and the Spanish nothing but feel (see Table 3.1):

'One character differs from another not so much in tendencies it contains as in their relative strength and mutual interplay. For stronger or weaker, all tendencies are probably in all people — hence the unity of the human race. Yet, when composed in one living total, all these differences in the quantity of the particular tendencies produce that difference in quality which we call character; just as quantitative differences in hardness, weight, and sensitivity to acids make up the qualitative difference between copper and gold'.[2]

It is merely, then, a question of emphasis. For in the final analysis we are all unified beings, potentially capable of a full spectrum of action, thought and passion. However, that potential can only be realized once we interact intensively with one another. Now it is time to follow de Madariaga's full line of argument. De Madariaga starts with a complete assessment of the Englishman before moving onto the Frenchman and finally to the Spaniard.

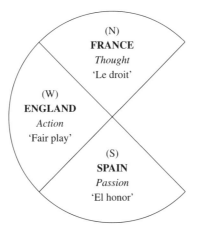

Figure 3.4   The European trinity.

Table 3.1   National tendencies

States	Action	Thought	Passion
Action	Action in the person of action	Action in the person of thought	Action in the person of passion
Thought	Thought in the person of action	Thought in the person of thought	Thought in the person of passion
Passion	Passion in the person of action	Thought in the person of passion	Passion in the person of passion

The English 'person of action'

English action — freedom constrained by responsibility

The English are preoccupied, mainly, with taking appropriate action. With this end in view they organize, discipline and control themselves. In fact, for de Madariaga's English, self-control is an essential requirement. This self-control is easily transplanted from the individual to the group. Such group control manifests itself in two ways. The first is in a strongly internalized tendency towards social discipline. The second is in the sense of social service that is deeply ingrained within the English psyche. Hence, for both the above reasons, voluntary organizations proliferate in Britain.

The individual lives in an atmosphere, de Madariaga adds, which is therefore imbued with moral and social responsibilities, divided into zones of different obligations. The individual is thus closely watched by his or her own social self, and acquires a self-consciousness through freedom constrained by responsibility. Alas, during the Margaret Thatcher years, the former served almost to eclipse the latter. Finally, though, interlinking innate insularity with a moral stance, the English person of action is prone to a sense of self-righteousness.

English thought — stored up experience

The allogic of the pragmatic English means that from one action to another the basics of their thinking may have changed. Why? The line of conduct of the person of action, for de Madariaga, is winding because the topography of action, like that of physical nature, avoids the straight line. At every moment, such a manager instinctively seeks and finds the line of least resistance which skirts around the obstacles and adapts itself to them. Hence the continuous and winding rhythm of thought and action.

The complex and vital character of English thought, therefore, demands a standard more complicated and at the same time more elastic than mere reason. This standard is wisdom. Wisdom is reason saturated with stored-up experience, continually adapted to the moving waters of life. Moreover, for de Madariaga's English, thought is inseparable from action, which it guides and fertilizes. In fact it is so 'reasonable' that it knows, whenever necessary, how to sacrifice reason! Thinking, as we shall see in its pure French form, implies a separation from the things thought, a distance which enables us to dwell on the ideas of things and not the things in themselves. Experience, on the other hand, is a stream of life which bathes us at every moment. In this stream the English swim, according to de Madariaga, with the same pleasure through which they bathe in the cool waters of their rivers and shores.

Empiricism, similarly, as a philosophical system to which the English are singularly prone, is the continuous mixture of thought and action. In other words, it involves the blending of each instant of action with the minimum of thought needed for putting into effect. Such empiricism comes in two guises. One is instantaneous, and the other is accumulated: a kind of stored-up treasure house of experiences, which an individual applies subconsciously at the moment it is required. The first is a direct result of the feeling for the complexity of life; the second is a substitute for the principles the person of action rejects under the influence of the feeling that life is unforeseeable.

From life, then, action borrows its complexity, its elasticity, its allogic, its detailed shading. It does not worry beforehand about form. When the outcome in hand, therefore, is that of inspiration, the neglect of form allows a greater freedom of the creative spirit. For the poet or innovator, for Shakespeare or for Faraday, as for the inventor of 'action learning' — Reg Revans — a kind of internal inspiration seems to guide the work, like the instinct that guides the root towards the rich layer of earth.

English passion — still waters run deep

The people of passion of England are its great poets and adventurers, from Byron to Shakespeare, from Francis Drake to Rannulf Fiennes, from Brunel to Branson. These inspired individuals tower over the quiet levels of the English soul, as testimony to the profound passions hidden under the crust of the nation's apparent calm. Properly observed, in fact, the English calm is by no means phlegmatic. On the contrary, it evokes an almost imperceptible vibration which shows that its immobility is not due to the absence of forces. Rather, it is the result of a continually renewed, static equilibrium between the opposing forces of a powerful passion and a usually more powerful self-control. In essence, the English lifestream is canalized in order to be utilized. Passion becomes polarized. Certain passions can be utilized and are therefore sources of power. Others cannot, and must be considered wasteful, or, worse still, antagonistic. This leads onto 'the English way', that is, the composite of that nation's actions, thoughts and feelings.

The English way — a sense of fair play

Spontaneous organization   How, then, does the English pragmatic approach to life and work manifest itself in the social, economic, political and cultural life of the nation? In every nook and cranny of English collective life cases will be found, de Madariaga emphasizes, of spontaneous organization. Charitable enterprises are the most obvious example, whether in the traditional form of Christian Aid or in the contemporary form of Bob Geldof's Live Aid.

The strongest feature of English social and political life, moreover, is liberty rather than equality. For liberty is the absence of political constraint, and such constraint is unnecessary and undesirable for a people gifted with the powers of spontaneous organization.

Class structure   In this atmosphere of liberty, accompanied by inequality, the English nation ironically adopts a hierarchical structure. In fact the English base their hierarchical structures on continuity and tradition rather than upon principles of organization. English society is therefore not homogeneous, but naturally divided into classes and sub-classes. A reflection of this structure in English educational life is the privately financed but so-called public school, which substitutes itself for the family as a character-moulding agency. It thereby introduces a powerful element of standardization at the top of the social pyramid, the English gentleman.

The most important items in the curricula of the public schools, moreover, according to de Madariaga, are the sundry types of sports which they cultivate. Their heroes are the captains of their cricket, football and rowing teams. Their true competitions are those in which those teams are pitted against each other. Here, through the play of muscles and not by any brainwork, the English cultivate the sense of fair play, the spirit of teamwork, the self-denial for the sake of the community to which they belong. They also demonstrate capacity for fighting with grit and determination, yet with detachment and good humour. In the majority of cases this public school education is completed through studies in classical languages, history and English, all providing information about human character. The person of action is now ready for collective activity!

Teamwork The virtues which characterize English collective units — stability, continuity, teamwork — are those of the national group, as of the family. Whatever there is that is stable and strong in the English family group is just so in the Civil Service or banking community. The 'father', in one word, is the 'governor'.

People of action are always on the move, knowing that they have a collective existence and that they need to go forward. They want, therefore, to be led. The people of action therefore train their leaders for this important task. It develops in them resolution, self-discipline, authority, knowledge of the law of things and knowledge of people. The empirical spirit of the English manifests itself in the unpopularity of the 'brainy' person.

Self-control develops rapidly in this closely watched environment so strongly dominated by group influences, and self-consciousness follows self-control. Like its public schools, de Madariaga finds England organized around an unwritten constitution that rests on tradition, convenience and rule-of-thumb practices. Local government is a spontaneous local growth, due to the same virtues that can be observed in central and national institutions.

Social consciousness English finally — according to de Madariaga — is a monosyllabic language, suited for the action person. The tendency to action, no doubt, also explains the aptitude of the English language, as in 'grease' or in 'iron', to turn anything into a verb. We know that the present is the tense of the person of action, and therefore we are not surprised to find that it is on the present that the English verb is built. Literature is in England eminently social. The novel is a direct reflection of the life of the people, woven with all the threads which cross in such a developed society.

An English artist, therefore, is a person in whom there is a permanent conflict between action and passion. Interestingly enough the Royal Society for Arts, in Britain, includes the 'arts of manufacture' within its overall remit. Similarly religion, for the English, is very much concerned with things of this world. 'Here and now' is the English motto in religion as in everything else. Religious bodies therefore take a strong interest in collective tasks. The YMCA and the Salvation Army are just two such cases in point. England's world philosophy, in conclusion, is that of the will. Britain wants to be 'at the heart of Europe', not to join in with some noble European ideal, but 'to exercise its influence'. De Madariaga's English live in action. They are busy. They move. For relaxation and rest they move again, passing from business to sport. They mix with people and things.

The French, in turn, are very different.

The French 'person of thought'

French action — the right way to proceed The person of action expects practical results from activities. The thinker, on the other hand, wants to create order. Order is the intellectualized outcome of action. It is the idealized projection of the world along the plane of intellect. This explains why the French, as people and as managers, are likely to excel in the preliminary stages of action, as well as in the routinized stages which follow implementation. Where they are likely to experience problems is in the thick of activity. For the intellect is a faculty which wants space and leisure, while the present is but a point and an instant.

While the English apply their thinking, therefore, to the solution of practical problems, the French see in practical problems the opportunity to exercise their minds. In fact the intellectuals in action tend to force a situation into categories pre-established by their minds. Their attitude in action, according to de Madariaga, is one of continuing protest against the illogical behaviour of life. Whereas, therefore, English organization tends to be simultaneous with action, French plans and structures often precede action, and involve a complicated system of written laws which aim at foreseeing all possible eventualities. This network of principles is 'le droit', the right way to proceed.

French thought — leaders in the art of method   French thought is therefore strongly analytical. It likes to burrow into ideas to find out their elements, and to classify them. While the English seek to safeguard the rights of life by surrounding their thoughts with blurred outlines, the French seek to guarantee the clearness of their intellectual vision by defining the knowledge with the neatest possible edge. French knowledge is cold, scientific and precise.

All the French qualities contribute to give them that sense of form, which is one of the manifestations of their instinct for clearness and a kind of discipline for their creative and representative minds. For form, in the eyes of the French, is not merely outwards elegance, ornament, or grace; it is a kind of inward elegance which results from the true balance of the parts, their harmonious arrangement, and the clearness and beauty of the whole.

In fact there is an aspect of spontaneous collaboration which distinguishes French intellectual life. In France intellectualism is general. The taste for things of the mind resides especially in the middle class. The French are acknowledged leaders in the art of method, and it is not by accident that their greatest philosopher, René Descartes, gave to his main work the title *Discours de la Méthode*. Thus, not surprisingly, the French are the leading European producers of computer software.

French passion — beautiful refinement   The intellectuals, instead of coming nearer to life, tend to get away from it by virtue, not of a decision of a conscious mind, but of an instinctive desire to draw apart from that which they want to understand. The French, according to de Madariaga, deeply feel the dignity of reason. It is out of respect for this reason that they supervise their life streams.

In the French, unlike their English counterparts, passion is not the enemy who is feared and watched but the natural phenomenon that is foreseen, and has its place. Passion has free access to the surface of French thought. What characterizes their pleasures, therefore, and their love of life is their intellectual appeal, their refinement. Whether it is food, wine, or song, it is the shades of difference, the elements of nuance — intellectually derived — that count. In the final analysis, the life of passion leads the French towards beauty. No wonder French window displays are such an art form!

The French way of life — knowledge, culture and ideas
Intellectual order   De Madariaga emphasizes, not surprisingly, that the social structure of France is more rigidly framed than its English counterpart. In it custom is an element of lesser importance than law, or, more exactly, 'le droit'. The framework of society has been and is constantly thought out, deduced from general principles. The main ingredient of French social life therefore, according to de Madariaga, is not liberty but equality. Equality is a geometrical plane

made up of human rights. It is beautifully level. It is also an intellectual rather than an instinctive construct that must be deliberately conceived. The order that prevails rests upon an assumption of equality intellectually established.

Therefore, the multifarious activities that are met in England by the free and spontaneous growth of private initiative must in France rely on the help and the leadership of the state. The movements of their collective life must be pre-arranged, and laid down beforehand by some foreseeing mind, well trained to anticipate the chessboard of possibilities.

French elites   The dominant feature in the French family is perhaps the 'mariage de raison'. The atmosphere of a French home is cordial in its calm. Family traditions are rich and complex to a degree sufficient to stamp the individual with a family seal. The family, in France, like the public school in England, may be considered as the field in which social and individual tendencies come to terms and compensate each other. Through it a sufficient standard of collective behaviour is maintained in the nation.

The French word 'elite' is the nearest approach to the English 'leader'. But whereas 'leader' implies leading, and therefore movement, 'elite' conveys more the idea of a position: it is static. All it suggests is that the persons it designates are the selected few, and therefore occupy the highest ranks in the hierarchy of established order. The French system differs from the English, then, in two respects: it is directed towards the cultivation of the intellect and it is organized by the state. The secondary schools and their teachers pass from one to the other as a major or colonel changes garrison. French secondary education, for de Madariaga, is specialized in the development of the brain. The education of the will and character is no special concern of the school. Thus the family has a stronger formative influence than in England. Beyond the secondary school the Ecole Polytechnique stands for a highly specialized education of the mind. Above all, 'les écoles' develop in their students a love of knowledge, culture and ideas.

Shades of opinion   The political evolution of France, not surprisingly therefore, is in typical contrast to that of England. In England it evolved slowly and empirically, with strong conti-nuity. In France the political mould of the country is broken now and then and a new cast made on the old mould. France is the specialist in constitutions among nations. Whereas the English constitution is always changing, and yet always the same, the French follow each other through sharp turns or revolutions in the political life of the country. The place which efficiency occupies in England is overtaken in France by intellectual honesty.

Thus the working of the French parliament differs profoundly from the English model. It is divided into interest groups representing a considerable number of shades of opinion. The French people, moreover, are interested in politics from an intellectual standpoint. Not surprisingly, therefore, the French language is a carefully pronounced one. Every letter receives its value and remains in place. The French do not tolerate the elastic attitude which makes English spelling the grammarian's despair. French pronunciation is accurate and precise, and it follows its own rules so precisely that it might even be viewed as a deductive science in its own right. In fact, turning from science to art, if you want to seek in France the equivalent of those popular manifestations of artistic life that are so abundant in Spain and Italy, you must turn — in de Madariaga's view — to the almost universal ability of the French to arrange material for life's use with refinement and taste.

Refinement and taste   The person or manager, therefore, involved in such artistic or industrial productions, is the artificer who, from the outside, works on material and gives it shape. Hence you find that sense of objectivity which forms a keynote of French art, as well as those 'isms', such as symbolism, romanticism and classicism, which the critical intellect assigns to a period of French artistic life. The analytical mind, finally, that is so closely associated with French art and science, business and management, also characterizes much of its attitude to religion, being both Catholic and sceptic in its beliefs. In conclusion, France's world philosophy is that of the mind. The French want to understand reality. Living for them consists of the development of their intellect and of the five avenues which lead to it, that is, senses. Refinement and enjoyment of his faculties is what life and work is all about. For the Spanish, people and things are very different, again.

The Spanish 'person of passion'

Spanish action — present with the whole self   From what we have seen, the essential, the immovable, the evident for the French is the idea, and for the English it is the act. Just as the French seek in action and in passion an intellectual result, the English seek in thought and in passion a practical result. The Spanish, however, seek in action and in thought a result in terms of passion, that is, according to de Madariaga, experience of life.

Just as the English select their passions, and only authorize the release of those which are useful to the group, the Spanish select their actions and only engage in those which enrich their experience. No longer do we witness the supple and continuous curve adapted to all forms of nature, which we have observed in the person of action of England. Nor do we see the series of straight lines successively correcting each other by sudden turns, as in the intellectual of France. Rather there is a kind of rest followed by an explosion of conquering will which, soon exhausted, falls back to the first indifference. In other words, in de Madariaga's view of his own country, there are a series of horizontal lines of action cut by abrupt peaks of overactivity. So the English struggle in order to do things; the French in order to possess them in knowledge; the Spanish to let off surplus energy.

This individual philosophy of the person of passion, moreover, implies a nature rebellious to the chain of collective life. Such collective life is seen by the Spanish as the connecting of individual lives to a system of gears. In such a gear only a small part of each wheel is actually connected at every moment, and playing an active role, while the person of passion is at every moment present with their whole self wherever they are.

Such a man or woman of passion lives and works in a highly personalized world. In fact the importance of personal contacts is well known wherever people of the Spanish race are concerned. Whether the question at issue is a trivial affair or the most important business, a person-to-person relationship is indispensable, according to de Madariaga, if results are to be obtained.

Spanish thought — let the stream of life pass through   De Madariaga described the English as taking from the object that which they think is useful to them. The French, conversely, investigate the object systematically with initiative and premeditation. The Spanish, finally, think by contemplation. They wait in an apparent passivity for the object to reveal itself. They let the continuous stream of life pass through them, until chance will suddenly imbue it with new light. In other words, the object contemplated reveals itself all at once in its essence, with all its connections and all the connections which attach it to the rest of life. Hence the inseparability of body and spirit which is a deep feature of Spanish thought.

It is at the moment when it emerges out of the subconscious that Spanish thought is strongest, most vigorous. It has all the vital freshness of natural facts. Free from all preparatory argument, independent of all dialectical plan, Spanish thought appears, in de Madariaga's terms, on the surface of the intellect still warm from the innermost folds of the soul in which it is formed. The very essence of the Spanish psychology, whether as a person or as a manager, is to set passion, not knowledge, as an ultimate aim. It follows that if and when the fire of passion deforms their instincts, knowledge in the Spanish becomes irretrievably warped. It fosters their tendency to arbitrariness and further curtails the efficiency and effectiveness of their intellectual work, founded upon the rich raw material with which they are endowed by nature.

Spanish passion — subjective vitality   While the psychology of the person of action develops mainly in the plane of his or her conscious will, and that of the intellectual may be easily observed in the sphere of the mind, the psychology of the person of passion is mostly subconscious. In effect, as de Madariaga puts it, such passion receives its first impulses from the life stream which reaches people straight from nature. At every moment, therefore, subjective vitality flows over the social will. With the same spontaneity with which we have seen the English people of action adapt themselves to 'the law of things', we see the people of passion in Spain force things to follow the law of the person. Nature is thus personalized, and obliged to follow the life stream which circulates in individual blood.

The popular language of Spain, finally, abounds in expressions of a strikingly synthetic nature, which sum up in a few words taut with sense, not the idea but the passion for wholeness which is the true substance of the soul of Spain. It is precisely when they are most egotistical that the Spanish are most universal. They seek universality without meaning to do so. For their egotism functions precisely in letting the life stream pass through them, in all its spontaneity and integrity.

The Spanish way of life — a person of the people
A person of the people   Not surprisingly, from what you have seen, Spain is lacking in all hierarchical sense, whether in the natural and instinctive form that it takes in England or in the outward and political form that it assumes in France. The sense of equality, which permeates all collective life in Spain, in de Madariaga's opinion, is different from the French idea of it. Spanish equality, being a living sense, is unconsciously assumed; French equality, being an idea, is aired and asserted.

Just as every Englishman, in de Madariaga's opinion, fashions himself after the aristocracy, and every Frenchman, whatever his station, is, in his heart of hearts, a petit bourgeois, the Spaniard, no matter what his class, is a person of the people. Thus the Spanish attitude to equality cannot foster an hierarchy of the English type, which implies a spontaneous recognition of inequalities. Nor does it provide the basis for the erection of a state hierarchy after the French pattern. For the sense of equality is subconscious, and does not level the people down to a flat plane of citizens. Spanish collective life, on a large scale therefore, has traditionally counted on superimposed cohesion, more often than not through the Church or Army. Cohesion, realized on a small scale, is more organic in its nature.

Family cohesion   The family in England is just one of the many forms which the spirit of teamwork takes in the people of action, and in France it is a kind of state writ small. In Spain, however, the family is the first collective sphere the individuals meet in their expansion as they travel out from their egocentric selves. It is therefore the strongest of the group units in Spanish life. While in England the nation is stronger than the family and in France the family is the meeting ground between individual and collective tendencies, in Spain the family is stronger than the wider forms of community.

Personal influence   Political allegiance is more personal and familial, therefore, than objective. The Spaniard is held by the vicissitudes of continual battles for power. For the Spaniard, therefore, the constitution is like an act in a play. It can be brushed aside.

Whereas the French revolutions are instigated by intellectuals, Spanish revolutions are crises in drama, in which the moving forces are not principles but personalities. Whereas at first sight the political structure of the three peoples of Western Europe is the same — they are three democracies organized under a parliamentary system — in reality they are as different as the three national characters would lead us to expect. In England, as we have seen, political institutions are the outcome of an empirical evolution. In France they resulted from a constitution carefully planned beforehand. In Spain, de Madariaga claims, politics is in a plastic state.

When passing from the English idea of leaders to the French idea of elites we lost the notion of movement but retained that of hierarchy. In passing now from the French elites to the Spanish 'minorias', the notion of hierarchy itself goes by the board. The *minorias* are merely a small number of people who happen to have reached a higher plane of development than the rest. That is all. When Spaniards speak convincingly of medicine, according to Madariaga, the chances are that they are artists. If they show an above-average knowledge of painting, they may be a colonel. Each individual seeks ideas and sensations by their own unaided effort, both because their own character as a person of passion requires them to do so and because the environment itself provides scanty food prepared, so to speak, for wholesale educational consumption. Exceptional individuals in Spain rise, as it were, from sea level, not from the highlands of a social culture already established.

Individual passion   The Spanish language, finally, is the one of the three that draws most on the inner person. You may drawl English, de Madariaga claims, and you may pronounce French trippingly off the tongue, but you must speak Spanish fully and frankly and fill up with your life's breaths the amplitude of its words. For its words are not like English monosyllables, snapshots or acts; nor like clear French polysyllables. They are the objects themselves full square, with all their volume, mass and colour.

Of the three countries, therefore, Spain is the only one in which an aesthetic attitude, at least in de Madariaga's opinion, is natural, spontaneous, innate and general. Hence the exceptional wealth of popular art, in different degrees. According to local climate, occupation, and economic conditions, it is one of the most potent manifestations of popular life, influencing directly the house, the dress, the language, the ceremonies and the religion. In Spain, in fact, religion is above all an individual passion, like love, jealousy, hatred and ambition. It consists of a relation between the individual and his or her creator. We now need to conclude with de Madariaga's overall European perspective.

SUMMARY

Englishness

Active English manager   For de Madariaga's English manager, characteristically engaged in *action*, such activity represents to him or her freedom constrained by responsibility. In the process, therefore, individual self-control is exercised in a self-conscious way, constrained by the social discipline of teamwork, duly exercised as a social service.

Interestingly enough, in recent years within Britain, the self-conscious action has raced ahead of the socially constrained service. It may well be that this imbalance is partly responsible for the UK's economic ills. Ironically, Margaret Thatcher's so-called economic miracle in the 1980s might have, over the long term, accelerated Britain's economic decline rather than halted it. By reinforcing the split between self and social interest, that is, freedom constrained by responsibility, Thatcherism cut across the natural English grain.

Thoughtful English manager   In drawing on his or her stored-up experience, the *thoughtful* English manager is a characteristically experiential learner. The wholesale import of MBA-type curricula from America have therefore done the UK a disservice. For the natural bent of the English is to learn, bottom up, from the experience of self and other. Unlike the French, as we shall see, the English predilection is inductive and pragmatic rather than deductive and rational. The UK is less famed for its industrial logic, for example, than for its commercial practicality.

Passionate English manager   The English manager characteristically restrains his or her *passions*, thereby keeping their feelings hidden. He or she has strong feelings — still waters run deep — but they tend to be polarized, and therefore rendered static rather than dynamic. Passionate commitment, on the inside, is restrained by social restraint, on the outside. The only managers who have managed to transcend that position of stasis are the inspired individuals that this nation has produced. The closest a British manager has come to such, in recent times, has been Sir John Harvey-Jones (see Table 3.2).

The English manager's way of life   The English are renowned, whether in business or in politics, for their sense of fair play. Of particular interest, in that overall context, is the combined emphasis upon both fairness and on play. To that extent, the British approach to the European Union is dictated by the need, on the one hand, to create a level 'playing' field and, on the other, to ensure that the twelve constituent nations play fair.

Linked with ethos is once again a philosophy of action, drawing upon acts of will circumscribed by reason, rather than the other way around. Fair play, on the one hand, is closely linked with teamwork, at all levels, and, on the other, with the class structure, in which 'everyone should know their place'. Finally, the English preference for spontaneous organization, as opposed to formalized bureaucracy, follows from an internalized sense of fair play circumscribed by an implicit class structure, as opposed to externalized rules and regulations circumscribed by an explicit meritocracy — as in France.

Frenchness

Active French manager   Action, for the French manager, is disconnected from his or her sense of individuality, which, as we shall see, is directly connected with freedom of thought. Responsible action for the French follows freedom of thought, that is, individual mental exercise resulting in a structured plan. Such an exercise is expected to create order, that is the right way to proceed. Whereas for the English such a 'right way' is pragmatically constrained by economic or social circumstances, for the French it is rationally dictated by logical necessity.

For the French bureaucracy, to the extent that it is seen to be a logical manifestation of rationality, is enabling rather than disabling, as it would be perceived to be by the English or by the Latin's. Similarly, thought is not antithetical to action but a necessary prelude for it.

Thoughtful French manager   It is not surprising, therefore, that the Frenchman Henri Fayol was the first person to classify systematically the functions of management, and the activities of

Table 3.2   European trinity — comparative management

Englishness	Frenchness	Spanishness
Action in the person of action	*Action in the person of thought*	*Action in the person of passion*
Freedom constrained by responsibility	The right way to proceed	Present with whole self
Self-control Self-consciousness	Creating order	Life experience
Self-righteousness Social service	Mental exercise	Activity peaks
Social discipline	Structured plan	Conquering will
Thought in the person of action	*Thought in the person of thought*	*Thought in the person of passion*
Stored-up experience Pragmatic	The art of method Strongly analytical Likes to classify	Stream of life Thinks by contemplation
Allogical approach	Scientific/precise Strong form	Tendency to arbitrariness
Experiential orientation	Able to balance body and spirit	Body and spirit inseparable
Passion in the person of action	*Passion in the person of thought*	*Passion in the person of passion*
Still waters run deep Hidden feelings Static feelings Polarized feelings	Beautiful refinement The dignity of reason Pleasures are intellectual Passion for beauty	Subjective vitality Subconscious feelings Nature is personalized Passion for wholeness
Way of life for the person of action	*Way of life for the person of thought*	*Way of life for the person of passion*
A sense of fair play Philosophy of the will Spontaneous organization Class structure Teamwork	Knowledge, culture and ideas Le droit Refinement and taste French elites Shades of opinion	A person of the people Personal influence Individual passion Natural equality Family cohesion

business and organization. In fact he followed in the footsteps of his great predecessor, Descartes, in applying the art of method. Such scientific precision, coupled with a strong sensitivity towards balance and form, results in a strongly analytical approach to management, for which French managers are noted. It also can result in the proverbial 'paralysis by analysis', for which rational managers are sometimes noted.

The passionate French manager   The French have a passionate commitment to the dignity of reason, rather than to action. Such a passion is reflected in the beautiful refinement reflected either in a software package produced by a systems house or by a display of pastries in a shop window. In other words, the French have a passion for beauty, which emerges from a combination of intellectual and emotional capacities. It is neither that raw passion of the Latin nor the restrained version of the Anglo-Saxon, but a channelled version, somewhat in between.

The French manager's way of life   The French manager, totally unlike his or her English counterpart, is driven by knowledge, culture and ideas. Refinement and taste, as we have already indicated, 'le droit' — that is, the right way to do things and an appreciation of manifold shades of opinion — are all part of the way of life of the French intellectual elite. Their top management cadre, moreover, are very much part of that elite, albeit that they will have reached that point of intellectual and managerial ascendancy through a meritocratic route. The Spanish way of life, finally, is very different.

Spanishness

The active Spanish manager   The Spanish manager, characteristic of those in more southern climes, have peaks and troughs of activity and are subject to alternate doses of 'conquering will' and managerial lapses. Moreover, like their Anglo-Saxon counterparts, they are liable to draw heavily on experience, albeit of life and work all wrapped up in to one. In fact, the overriding feature of their managerial being is the fact that they are present with their whole self in the workplace.

For, as Koopman has already indicated in Chapter 1, the southerners 'being' cannot easily be connected from their 'doing'. The fact that, in southern Africa, the northern approach to management has predominated, whereby the African way of being was separated from the European's way of doing, has had dire social and now economic consequences. The same division, though to a lesser degree, separates the southern from the northern European way.

The thoughtful Spanish manager   The Spaniards, for de Madariaga, think by contemplation. Having immersed themselves completely in the subject at hand, the managers enter into their work as into a stream of life. Physical activity and the spirit that underlies it are inseparable. Therefore the nature of the work and the mood of the person undertaking it are closely interconnected. As a direct result, moreover, there is a tendency among Spanish managers to act, at least at times, somewhat arbitrarily.

The passionate Spanish manager   The Spanish are most themselves when thinking and acting passionately. Such individual passion, within the person, is also manifested in passionate relationships with other people. Personal connections are therefore all-important in the conduct of managerial activity, as is the significance of family business and of family type affiliations. In the final analysis, for de Madariaga, a kind of 'natural equality' prevails in Spain, notwithstanding a history of 'imposed' inequality, usually by the Church or the military.

Ultimately, then, the southern style manager is a person of the people, at least if he or she is managing 'naturally', and in the process getting the best out of his or her employees. Koopman in South Africa, in effect, has termed this managerial orientation to be one of 'pragmatic human-ism'. Needless to say, such a style might prevail with a particular individual, in England or France, if he or she happens to have what might be termed a 'Latin temperament'. However, outside of his or her indigenous environment, such a manager will be something of an anomaly.

De Madariaga's European Trinity thus provides a dynamic world of cultural tension, within which its individual players move, develop and grow. Each of its three main representatives holds within its borders its own diversity, but that diversity is coloured in one direction and is thus unbalanced if isolated from its European partners.

As we leave the world of de Madariaga, we thus sense our journey moving us on, from a world of conflict to one of a vague and as yet unfulfilled synergy. We will now continue our European quest.

STUDY QUESTIONS

1. Compare and contrast the three main European management styles as defined by de Madariaga.
2. To what extent does Europe represent a microcosm of the world's cultural diversity?
3. What are the three main European 'spirits' and in what ways do these represent both assets and liabilities for the transcultural manager?

REFERENCES

1. de Madariaga, S., *The Spirit of Europe*, Hollis and Carter, London, 1966.
2. de Madariaga, S., *Englishman, Frenchman, Spaniard,* Oxford University Press, Oxford, 1922.

FOUR

THE EMERGING BUSINESSPHERE

INTRODUCTION

The European force field

In Chapters 1 and 2 the journey introduced the concepts of a four-polar global 'businessphere' with each point of the compass representing a different aspect of business competence. In the west, pioneering pragmatism, in the north, analytical rationalism, in the south, people-focused humanism and, finally in the east an integrative wholism seeing the parts recombined into a seamless whole. In Chapter 2 our travels in the east, and west provided evidence of the profound differences between businesses which emerge from these cultural roots.

In Chapter 3, in the company of Salvador de Maoariaga, we revisited Europe and began the process of sensing the origins and structure of its cultural diversity. Through the interplay of three of its cultural identities, de Madariaga shed light for us on the peoples of thought (N), of action (W), and of passion (S) and we began to see the emergence of Germany as our European gateway to the east.

We shall now set out to uncover more of this field of European management, both in theory and practice. The field is a unified sum of its varied parts, derived from contemporary European philosophies which have drawn, in turn, upon a classical Greek and Roman heritage. At the same time, moreover, it is important to recognize that business is now passing from an industrial to a post-industrial era, from what Harvard sociologist David Riesman has called a more 'outer-directed' to a relatively 'inner-directed' approach.

The time dimension   For the first time in its history western Europe is beginning to develop interdependently, drawing from within its own borders, rather than its constituent parts battling independently, without. This change coincides with a move from a physical labour-based economy to a more knowledge-intensive economy (electronics, biotechnology). Here human as opposed to financial capital, information rather than energy, philosophy rather than economy have become the primary business resources. It may therefore be prudent to evolve from a industrial era of free enterprise, marked by a spirit of self-help and move towards a more cooperative, post-industrial era where concepts such as those of the learning organization, characterized by self-development and knowledge sharing, become the backbone of our enterprises. That this should draw on our European cultural strengths should by now be self-evident.

The spatial dimension

Philosophical and managerial types   Of the four post-industrial factors of 'European production', pragmatism (W) is strongly rooted in English culture but has a clear affinity with the Dutch and the Scandinavians. Such empiricism has given rise to the experiential manager. While its positive manifestation is in free-spirited individualism its negative form of expression is in rampant materialism.

Rationalism (N) is strongly grounded in Gallic soils, and also in parts of Germany, northern Italy and also the French part of Switzerland. It has given rise, in its turn, to the professional manager. While its positive manifestation is that of a meritocracy its negative expression is in its stereotypical bureaucracy.

Wholism (E) has emerged out of a long-standing Germanic philosophical tradition, inclusive of Austro-Hungary and part of Switzerland. It has given rise to what may be termed a developmental manager. While its positive manifestation is wholistic, its negative expression is totalitarianism.

Finally humanism (S) is strongly rooted in Italian art and culture, whence came the first European Renaissance, while having distinct branches in Greece, Spain and Ireland. It has given rise to what may be called the convivial manager. While its positive manifestation is in its communal nature, its negative expression is in the form of nepotism and corruption.

Psychological types   These philosophically based factors of production are parts of a pan-European whole. In fact, Europe has been noted for the intense interplay between its diverse philosophical systems. Alas, until now, the same could not be said for our business and organizational systems.

The great Swiss psychologist Carl Jung, however, renowned in management circles through the Myers Briggs[1] personality inventory, established four personality types that can be identified with our philosophical domains. For his *sensing* type is empirically oriented, and his *thinking* type rationally disposed, his *intuitive* type is typically idealistic, and his *feeling* type characteristically humanistic. Moreover, we are all combinations of at least two personality types, albeit that one remains dominant (Figure 4.1).

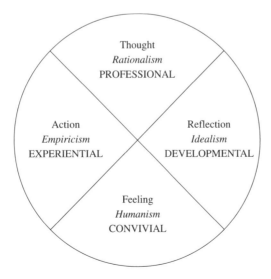

Figure 4.1   The force field of European management.

Interestingly enough, the European force field, as we can see above, constitutes more or less the learning cycle popularized by American organizational psychologist, David Kolb.[2] Following the basic methodology of scientific method, the European learner, depending upon his or her philosophical outlook, will start in one or other of the four positions, but will need to complete the cycle in order to learn 'fully' from the diversity of outlook offered and will become, in turn, a true 'European'.

Because in explicit management theory, if not in implicit business practice, it is the empirically oriented, competitively focused outlook which has predominated, our collective learning has been inhibited. The other three perspectives — rationalist, idealist, humanist — have been much less clearly differentiated, let alone integrated into an overall European, or even global, economic worldview. The result has been the overgeneralized, and hence ultimately destructive, as opposed to creative, tension between capitalism and communism.

Clear-cut differentiation is a necessary prelude to coherent integration. We start, then, with pragmatic empiricism.

PRAGMATISM

'Originating in or relying on factual information; relying on experience or observation rather than system or theory; the practice of emphasizing experience, especially of the senses, or relying on sensation rather than intuition, induction rather than other rationalistic means in the pursuit of knowledge' (*Webster's Third New International Dictionary*).

From free enterprise to learning community

Introduction 'Pragmatism', the doctrine which holds that all knowledge is acquired through experience, is firmly embedded in the 'empiricist' philosophical soils of Britain, most particularly in England. To some extent the Dutch and the Scandinavians within Europe, and to a greater extent the Americans and Australasians without, share this individually centred, experientially based philosophical outlook. Prior to the emergence of the Japanese as an industrial power with a rival philosophy to the Anglo-Saxon, it has dominated the global economic scene. It is also likely that it has profoundly influenced Britain's independent outlook at Maastricht (Table 4.1).

Pragmatism shares its analytical bent with rationalism, and its practical orientation with Italian humanism, but it stands, as Michel Albert had recently revealed in his book *Capitalism against Capitalism*, in polar opposition to 'Rhenish' idealism. Hence the great divide between Adam Smith's 'realistic' capitalism and Karl Marx's 'idealistic' Communism.

Table 4.1 Features of pragmatism

Aspect	Attribute
Kindred philosophies	Empiricism, utilitarianism
Unit focus	Entrepreneur, enterprise
Business outlook	Competition, transactional
Managerial orientation	Experiential
Psychological type	Sensing, action oriented
Path of evolution	Self-help — self-development; free enterprise — learning company

The idea of pragmatism   The seminal 'empiricist' philosophers Thomas Hobbes and John Locke, as well as the classical economists Adam Smith and Jeremy Bentham, were all of a pragmatic bent. Common law based on precedent, behavioural psychology based on directly observable phenomena, and classical science based on visible blocks of matter, all stem from this Anglo-Saxon 'feet on the ground' approach. Empiricism is eminently suited to the early, entrepreneurial phase of business, when it is essential to be 'close to the customer', and to have a 'bias for action'. In fact the popular American historian of philosophy, Will Durant, claims that

'English thought took its spirit from a life of industry and trade, and looked up to matters of fact with a certain reverence. This tradition had turned thought in the direction of things, mind in the direction of matter, the materialism of Hobbes, the sensationalism of Locke, the scepticism of Hume, the utilitarianism of Bentham were so many variations on the theme of a practical and busy life'.[3]

The Industrial Revolution in Britain, though born of a little science, was responsible for the emergence of a wealth of scientific knowledge. Take, for example, Robert Boyle and Humphry Davy, who opened up the treasures of chemistry, and Michael Faraday who made the discoveries that would electrify the world. These were all scientists who 'managed by wandering about', keeping their eyes and ears close to the ground. The world of the technician–craftsman and that of the scientist–technologist, moreover, was never far apart.

The experiential manager   The seminal influence on empiricism, from a managerial perspective, has interestingly enough been Francis Bacon in seventeenth-century England. His work on the inductively based *Advancement of Learning* did for the scientific revolution what Adam Smith's treatise *The Wealth of Nations* did for the industrial one. Following in the footsteps of Adam Smith, the Victorian biographer Samuel Smiles distilled from emerging nineteenth-century free enterprise the concept of individual self-help that underpinned it. Subsequently, drawing on Bacon's inductively based approach to learning, the contemporary and experientially based English management philosopher, Reg Revans, has distilled from it the emerging twentieth-century 'action learning' the concept of manager self-development that underpins it.

An empirical or experiential summary would be:

- The *subject* of European pragmatism has been the individual manager, duly evolving in orientation from self-help to self-development.
- Its *object* has been the independent enterprise, duly evolving in its structure from a free enterprise into a learning company.

RATIONALISM

'The notion that reason is in itself a source of knowledge superior to and independent of sense perceptions, as contrasted against sensationalism or empiricism; knowledge can thereby be deduced from *a priori* concepts; such rationality is opposed to non-rational emotion or intuition' (*Webster's Third New International Dictionary*).

From formal organization to requisite bureaucracy

Introduction   Where empiricism is inductive, rationalism is deductive. The seventeenth-century French philosopher, Descartes, was as seminal an influence on the latter as Francis Bacon was on the former. According to Durant: 'Beginning in philosophy with clearly perceived institutions

Table 4.2 Features of rationalism

Aspect	Attribute
Kindred philosophies	Positivism, scientism
Unit focus	Management, organization
Business outlook	Coordination, hierarchical
Managerial orientation	Professional
Psychological type	Thinking, analysis oriented
Path of evolution	Functional — structural; bureaucracy — requisite organization

which he regarded as comparable to the axioms of geometry, Descartes, a mathematician of the first rank, constructed by deductive reasoning his complete cosmic theory.'[4] Thought-centred rationalism shares with empiricism its functional orientation and with idealism its structural perspective, but it stands in polar opposition to Italy's feeling-centred humanism. While most strongly rooted in France, there are manifestations of such rationalism in so diverse European regions as Scotland and Prussia, in northern Italy and in Scandinavia. In many ways (northern) rationalism is the most quintessentially European of the four philosophies. Moreover, it is of particular applicability when a commercially based enterprise evolves into a managerially directed organization (see Table 4.2).

The rational idea   In the economic arena the Physiocrats, immediate predecessors of Adam Smith, were 'rationalists who set out to find self-evident truths in the light of reason rather than with the help of experience'.[5] However, the direct counterparts to the British classical economists were the French socialists. The best known is the nineteenth-century pamphleteer Henri Saint-Simon, who considered the forces of the market as conducive to anarchy rather than as instruments of discipline. However, he upheld private property in strong terms, but grounded it in social utility rather than as an absolute right. From each according to his capacity to each according to his works, Saint-Simon saw all producers, employers and employees united in a huge class of 'industrialists'.

For the rationalists, whether in Paris or Stockholm, 'dirigiste' style planning supplants free market economics, constitutional law transcends common law. Moreover, the social sciences become dominated by such structural/functionalists rather than empirically based behaviourists. What, then, of the rational management perspective, which is objectively depersonalized rather than experientially personalized?

The professional manager   The management thinker who followed in the functional line, with mechanical Descartian precision, was the redoubtable turn-of-the-century engineer and European industrialist, Henri Fayol. Rationalism has also found a home in certain parts of America. Here, where the economy at large has remained largely true to the empirically based free market, such people as Frederick Taylor and Henry Ford have brought a strong rational influence to management. More recently in Europe, a structural advocate who has drafted a general theory of bureaucracy is the French-Canadian, resident in Britain, Elliot Jaques. Where Henri Fayol deduced his clear-cut business and managerial functions, Jaques has subsequently articulated his requisite organizational and management structures.

A rational management summary would be:

- The *subject* of European rationalism has been depersonalized management, duly evolving in its orientation from a functional to a structural one.
- Its *object* has been the enterprise as an institution, dependent on the 'dirigiste' state, duly evolving in its structure from formal organization to 'requisite' bureaucracy.

WHOLISM

From closed to open system

'A conception of something in its highest perfection; a theory that affirms that mind, or the spiritual or ideal is of central importance in reality, asserting either that the ideal element in reality is predominant, or that the intrinsic nature of reality is consciousness' (*Webster's Third New International Dictionary*).

Introduction   Commercial realism, whether pragmatically or rationally founded, has all too often been contrasted against social idealism. In fact it has hitherto epitomized the capitalist–socialist divide. However, this oversimplified division has been challenged, in recent years, most noticeably by the Japanese. For, as Pascale and Athos[6] have written in their *Art of Japanese Management*, it has been Honda's or Matsushita's ability to unite matter and spirit, real and ideal, that has underpinned their success. It is relevant to our European journey that, more recently, Michel Albert has indicated that the Germanic and Japanese models of business and management are very similar (see Table 4.3).

The philosophy of wholism   Bacon in England, Descartes in France, Friedrich Hegel in Germany — there lies a formidable European trinity. For Hegel, the idealist: 'Every condition of thought or of things — every idea and every situation in the world leads irresistibly to its opposite, and then unites with it to form a higher or more complex whole. History is made only in those periods in which the contradictions of reality are being resolved by growth, as the hesitations and awkwardness of youth pass into the ease and order of maturity.'[7] Marx, in his turn, has also emerged out of this dialectical, developmental mould. Ironically, it was his very failure to follow through with this 'historicist' logic which led him, and his followers, towards their static state socialism.

In contrast, the German advocates of the social market, the so-called 'ordo-liberals', have tried to avoid the excesses of both Communist and fascist totalitarianism, while retaining, like

Table 4.3   Features of wholism

Aspect	Attribute
Kindred philosophies	Idealism, historicism
Unit focus	*Primus inter pares*, industrial association
Business outlook	Cooperation, systemic
Managerial orientation	Developmental
Psychological type	Intuiting, reflectively oriented
Path of evolution	Differentiation — integration; closed cartel — open system

the 'gestalt' school of psychology, the German sense for the social totality. Such a sense also underlies, at least in part, the Dutch notion of the civic economy, and the Scandinavian brand of social democracy. Idealism therefore shares with rationalism a notion of partnership between public and private interests, and with humanism a sensitivity for the interdependence between an organization and its environment. However, it stands directly opposed to the brand of economic freedom embodied in Adam Smith's *laissez-faire*, or in Charles Darwin's survival of the individually fittest.

The developmental manager   German management thinking, as we shall be seeing, has not been made accessible to the world at large. In effect the Dutch management thinker Bernard Lievegoed, following in Goethe's footsteps, has come up with an approach to the developing organization that is better known than any German version. It also systemically and organically represents a higher rationalism than the systematic and mechanistic bureaucracy which Max Weber himself articulated, and yet so despised because it cut across the developmental, idealist grain.

A developmental, industrial summary would be:

- The *subject* of European idealism has been developing groups of industrialists, duly evolving from differentiated bureaucrats to integrated organizers.
- Its *object* has been the industry, duly evolving in its structure from a closed cartel into an open industrial system.

HUMANISM

'Pertaining to the social life or collective relations of mankind; devoted to realizing the fullness of human being; a philosophy that asserts the essential dignity and worth of man, relating to the arts and humanities, to the "good" things of life' (*Webster's Third New International Dictionary*).

From family business to socio-economic network

Europe's cultural heritage is richly bestowed with not only the fruits of science and technology, strongly connected with its empirical and rational philosophies, but also with arts and artefacts, represented in 'the humanities'. Such humanistic elements are most strongly rooted in those south European climes — in ancient Greece and Rome as well as in modern Italy and Spain — where 'taste' is so important. It is also in those parts of Europe where passion, as opposed to mere thought or action predominates, and where sociability is so prized (see Table 4.4).

Table 4.4   Features of humanism

Aspect	Attribute
Kindred philosophies	Aestheticism, classicism
Unit focus	Family group; social community
Business outlook	Communal, networked
Managerial orientation	Convivial
Psychological type	Feeling, concretely oriented
Path of evolution	Patriarch/social architect; family business/ socio-economic network

The philosophical perspective

Renaissance humanism was first and foremost a revolt against the otherworldliness of medieval Christianity, a turning away from preoccupation with personal immortality to making the best of life in this world. For the Renaissance the ideal human being was no longer the ascetic monk, but a new type — the universal man — the many-sided personality, delighting in every kind of this earthly achievement. The great Italian artists, Leonardo da Vinci and Michelangelo, typified this ideal. The Humanist intellectual awakening consisted largely of a rediscovery and a return to the Greek and Latin classics.

Ferdinando Galiani, an eighteenth-century Italian abbot in diplomatic employment in Paris, condemned the dogmatic rationalism of the French Physiocrats, and he called for flexible policies in line with historical and geographical conditions rather than for adherence to immutable principles of allegedly universal applicability. Galiani's doubts about the power of reason to deduce eternal truths reflect the influence of Italy's seminal philosopher, Giambattista Vico, who opposed the antihistorical rationalism characteristic of French Cartesianism. In his approach to history Vico stressed the evolution of social institutions.

Galiani's historical sense made him see value not as an inherent quality of goods but as one that will vary with our changing appreciation of them. He recognized the effect of social forces and stressed the role of fashion as a determinant of our desires and thus our values. A historical perspective, for him, gave feeling-centred humanism a relativist connection with idealism, and a pragmatic link with empiricism, maintaining, however, its polar opposition to thought-centred rationalism.

The convivial manager   The flexible specialization cited by economists M. Piore and C. Sabel, is the direct antithesis to formal bureaucracy, and to large-scale mass production. As such it directly reflects Galiani's doubts over undiluted rationality. It also draws upon the aesthetic sensitivities, highlighted by Alberti in the fifteenth century.

Leon Battista Alberti (1404–72) was a humanist who had not yet lost his faith in our capacity to act effectively in human affairs. Alberti's confidence in our capacity to organize the world led him to assert that humanity achieves highest expression in two arts: plastic and political. In the former art we discover order and harmony in nature; in the latter we translate that order and harmony into social terms. A perfect example of the latter has been the industrialist and humanist Aurelio Peccei, who, as founder of the 'Club of Rome', attempted to bring a 'human quality' into the global business environment.

A humanistic, societal summary would be:

- The *subject* of European humanism has been the politically and artistically based impresario, duly evolving in orientation from patriarch or matriarch to 'impannatore'.
- Its *object* has been the community, duly evolving in its structure from a family business into a socio-economic network.

So we end our expedition into the philosophical worlds which separate and differentiate the European parts. We now need to step back and view the dynamically integrated European management whole — the European businessphere.

The European businessphere

Complementary forces   The combined western–eastern (empiricist–idealist) and northern–southern (rationalist–humanist) dimensions provide a basic template, a force field of creative tension, for European and for global management. Within this 'European businessphere' will be the adjacent countries; without lies the rest of the business world. Inevitably, and globally, they interpenetrate.

As we traverse such 'outer space' we shall, in Jungian terms, cross equivalent 'inner space'. In so consciously doing we move, in accordance with Jung's psychological types (popularized by Myers Briggs) from sensation-oriented (W) *empiricism* towards thought-centred (N) *rationalism*; and from intuition-based (E) *idealism* towards feeling-centred (S) *humanism*. The totality, albeit made up of differing degrees of emphasis, of light and shade, of colour and contrast, constitutes the whole of our transcultural personality.

For Carl Jung the fully functioning individual is able to move back and forth between his or her primary and secondary psychological types. In other words, an empirical (sensing type) orientation, for example, is often combined with (thinking type) rationality. Interestingly enough, this was the case for both Adam Smith and Isaac Newton, who effectively linked together induction with deduction.

Contradictory forces   In contrast, the fully functioning individual — or business, or economy — needs to come to terms with what Jung has called the shadow. The shadow side of our personalities stands in opposition to our primary selves, as empiricism does to idealism. In Jung's view, if we fail to acknowledge this opposing force it will unconsciously subvert our conscious purposes. For example, in the UK — in the absence of a healthy idealism — an ideologically based class war subverts its pragmatically based market economy. Conversely, the individualizing thrust of Anglo-Saxon influence on collectivist Germany, after the Second World War, helped that nation to regain a dynamic balance. Similarly, the relative success of middle Italy, *vis-à-vis* the north, but more particularly the south, is because it has succeeded in balancing, at least to some degree, the opposing forces of thought-centred rationality and feeling-centred humanism.

The Jungian analogy would also suggest that, should the shadow side of management, as with personality, be shunned it will assume its most primitive form. For example, while experientially based education for the individual manager is virtually non-existent in Germany and Japan, trade associations in Britain and America are of limited economic influence when compared to their multifaceted German and Japanese counterparts.

European management, as a dynamic whole, represents an interplay between the four psychological or philosophical types, albeit with different shades of emphasis in the various European regions. Whereas Michel Albert has identified a major east–west polarity separating the free market/empiricist Anglo-Saxons from the social market/idealist Japanese–Germans, we would argue that there is an equally important north–south tension between rationalism and humanism.

In the final analysis, all four philosophical factors have a role to play in the process of integrated managerial learning and organization development. Moreover, as and when space is transformed into time, experientially based enterprise develops into professionally based organization. Thereafter, and in turn, the developmentally oriented industrial association ultimately develops into the convivially networked economy and society.

CONCLUSION

The European management whole

While it may seem obvious that the Japanese and the British come from very different cultures, which in turn affect their management and business behaviours, it may not be so clearly apparent

Table 4.5   The European management whole

Generic philosophy	Management type	Process	Orientation
Pragmatism	Experiential	Competition	Transactional
Rationalism	Professional	Coordination	Normative
Wholism	Developmental	Cooperation	Integrative
Humanism	Convivial	Co-creation	Transforming

that different European regions and nations have fundamentally different philosophical tradi-tions. These, in their turn, radically precondition the European 'art of the possible', in management as in life as a whole. They may thus be seen as the generic factors of European production, its assets and its liabilities, to be harnessed to our benefit or to be ignored at our peril (see Table 4.5).

STUDY QUESTIONS

1. What are the four philosophical types which exist in Europe and how do these manifest them-selves in a managerial context?
2. Discuss the role of culture in defining the 'art of the possible' in a commercial setting.

REFERENCES

1. Myers Briggs, I., *The Myers Briggs Type Indicator*, Educational Testing Service, 1962.
2. Kolb, D., *Organizational Psychology*, Prentice Hall, Englewood Cliffs, NJ, 1974.
3. Durant, W., *Outlines of Philosophy*, p. 307, Benn, London, 1962.
4. Durant, W., *Outlines of Philosophy*, p. 261, Benn, London, 1962.
5. Poll, E., *A History of Economic Thought*, Faber, London, 1953.
6. Pascale, R. and Athos, A., *The Art of Japanese Management*, Penguin, Harmondsworth, 1982.
7. Lamb, D. Hegel, *From Foundation to System*, Martinus Nijhoff, Leiden, 1980.

INTERLUDE: THE MISTS OF SYNERGY

As we approach the end of the first phase of our transcultural journey we look back momentarily to find the mists beginning to clear. To the west we look out from Europe's shores to the worlds of the individualist 'people of action'. In this pioneering world, whose gladiators are its heroes, a sense of trial and error prevails, a pride in learning by the seat of the pants provides the fertile breeding ground for the self-made person.

To the north we sense a cooler more thoughtful world, a place where calm analysis prevails, where order and coordination preside over disorder and fragmentation. Northern heroes are its thinkers and its social architects, building dreams of a quiet and secure future for its peoples. To the south, as the mists roll back, we see uncovered a world of families and of friends, of passions and of pleasures. Our southern heroes are its fathers and its mothers, its artists and its musicians. Our southern world takes on the shape of a network of interrelated parts, each finding its own way within the context of its neighbour.

Looking finally to the east we see the world of integration, a world where parts are interwoven into wholes, a place where opposites are welcome partners in the building of a new tomorrow, a place where we are constantly becoming and never being, a world of ebb and of flow, a world of ideals and of ideal products. In this eastern world you can have your cake and you can eat it too.

As we look around we sense the beginnings in us of a new vision of our complex transcultural world, but there remains an uneasy feeling that we have taken in too easily this strange tale. We sense a need for proof, of practical means and measures, the yardsticks of rational thought. And so we must now head back to the northern and western worlds, to the worlds of analysis and of 'bottom-line' results.... .

MODELLING AND MANAGEMENT
OF CULTURAL DIVERSITY

A MEETING WITH DESCARTES: THEORIES OF CULTURAL DYNAMICS

This chapter introduces a number of key economic or institutional theories and their contributions to the comparative analysis of organizations within an international context. They provide a variety of views on the make-up and operation of the organization or firm, its emergence and its integration in the whole economy or society, the nature of the organization and its boundaries.

The point of the inclusion of this pluralist perspective is to provide an antidote to the growing segmentation of academic investigation: for instance, that in economics between markets and structures (macro approaches) and organizations/firms and agents (micro perspectives). We feel that an intermediary level of investigation, between macro- (nation- or whole economy-centred) and micro- (individual- or firm-centred) approaches, is missing and is essential to a realistic view of organizations and how they relate to the world in which they operate.

In this chapter we will look at three areas of research which have attempted to fill this gap. The first, known as market–organization duality, proposes alternative solutions to the issue of the coordination of social (economic) action. A second group of workers consider the possibility that differences in organizational make-up and operation result not from national cultural differences but from the interplay of the institutional framework in which they operate. A third, and more recent, area of research considers organizations within the broad economic and social context within which they operate, including the overt or hidden networks which exist within and between the organizations concerned.

THE MARKET–ORGANIZATION DILEMMA

It is traditional in economics to take either a macroeconomic or microeconomic perspective on your subject: the macroeconomic approach deals with market mechanisms and the formation of aggregates (GNP), the microeconomic approach is concerned with the behaviour of the individual agent and assimilates the firm to an individual agent (the entrepreneur). The two approaches have developed in an increasingly separate manner, so that each almost ignores what the other takes into account and, furthermore, the existence of large private economic organizations seems to be a blind spot to both traditional spheres of economics.

This section considers various economic theories which attempt to explain the existence and internal structure of organizations and looks at these from an international perspective. The common ground to the theories we will present is that there are two ideal types of coordination mechanisms: markets and organizations (or firms). The question which these approaches attempt to answer is: how can the preference for one mechanism rather than the other be explained?

The nature of the firm

In a seminal article written in 1937, Ronald Coase[1] initiated an alternative vision of economic organization, in which he challenged the established assumptions in economic theory — for instance, that 'the allocation of factors of production between different uses is determined by the price mechanism'. Coase claimed that such an assumption is not realistic because in the real world 'if a workman moves from department Y to department X, he does not go because of a change in relative prices, but because he is ordered to do so'.

More generally speaking, Coase postulated that, if production is coordinated by price movements, it requires no organization to be carried on. He proposed instead his 'transaction costs' concept, in which two systems of coordination exist, one outside the firm (market transactions) and one inside the firm (exchange transactions). 'Outside the firm, price movements direct production, which is coordinated through a series of exchange transactions on the market. Within a firm, these market transactions are eliminated and in place of the complicated market structure is substituted the entrepreneur-coordinator, who directs production'.

Coase thus proposed the market and the firm as alternative methods of coordinating production. He elevated the firm above that of an 'imperfection', some residual, to that of an object to be studied *per se*, whose characteristics must be defined within the framework of the marketplace.

Markets and hierarchies

According to Williamson,[2-4] who followed Coase, the nature of the environment and the behaviour of the decision makers are also relevant to the understanding of the emergence of the firm, an issue not covered in the transaction costs model. Williamson claims to provide an explanation of organizational forms in general, including hybrid forms (non-standard markets, government regulatory agencies, trade unions, etc.). His theory can thus be said to be rather more broad-ranging and systematic than that of Coase.

Williamson's framework is twofold. First, it is based on behavioural assumptions: human beings are characterized by bounded rationality and opportunism. Bounded rationality, originally the concept of Herbert Simon, suggests that there are limits to the extent to which human beings can make rational decisions. Bounded rationality is therefore the concept that, in addition to mental limitations, there are also limitations imposed by the fact that one cannot take into account every possible potential situation which may arise from a decision. This suggests that the rational market mechanism operates best for once only transactions and is poorly adapted to complex situations. Second, Williamson claims that the nature of the transaction varies along three dimensions — complexity–uncertainty, asset specificity and frequency — and suggests that these act together to determine the best 'arrangement' for the situation in hand. Williamson thus couples environmental factors, related to the nature of transactions, with behavioural assumptions in his model of organizational development.

Clans and treaties

Two other theories, also based on the transaction costs approach, provide further insight into organizational and inter-organizational relationships. First, in a sociological and eventually culturalist vein, the Japanese researcher Ouchi added a third mode of coordination, the 'clan' type, and offered empirical support drawn from Japanese companies. He also attempted to promote a new type of organization in the American context, which is intermediary between the traditional American mode of functioning, heavily relying on market and authority, and the efficient and more modern Japanese way, rooted in specific cultural traits.

Second, according to Aoki, the functioning of Japanese firms is not understandable through Williamson's framework, because it does not rely on explicit and formal coordination, such as those achieved through contracts. Aoki proposed that the concept of 'treaties' as a basis for understanding relational contracting, i.e. long-term and stable inter-organizational relationships, also provided a means of understanding the specific context and apparent efficiency of the internal organization of Japanese firms.

From clans to 'type Z' organizations   The contribution of Ouchi[5] (1980) is to apply the transaction-costs framework to a comparative approach to the understanding of organizations. According to Ouchi, besides the two principal mechanisms for mediating transactions — market and hierarchy (bureaucracy in his own terms) — the transaction-costs approach 'also suggests a third mechanism: if the objectives of individuals are congruent (not mutually exclusive), then the conditions of reciprocity and equity can be met quite differently'. He justifies this point by the example of Japanese companies where 'it is not necessary … to measure performance to control or direct their employees, since the employees' natural [socialized] inclination is to do what is best for the firm'. Ouchi states 'organizations can, in some instances, rely to a great extent on socialization as the principal mechanism of mediation or control, and this 'clan' form ('clan' conforms to Durkheim's meaning of an organic association which resembles a kin network but may not include blood relations) can be very efficient in mediating transactions between individuals'.

Most of Ouchi's reasoning focuses on employment relations. Compared in terms of efficiency within the market, it comprises two critical elements: he claims first, that the measurement of individual performance is ambiguous (related to bounded rationality) and second, that there may be more or less incongruence of employees' and employer's goals (similar to the possibility of opportunistic behaviour). The efficiency of market relations thus comes from the low level of ambiguity over performance, which makes relatively high levels of opportunism acceptable by each party, and the efficiency of bureaucratic relations results from moderately high performance, ambiguity and goal incongruence.

The clan type of relationship achieves efficiency in situations with high-performance ambiguity and low-goal incongruence and clan relations therefore contrast with contractual relations, because they primarily rely upon solidarity. As mentioned above, examples of the operation of clan relations can be found in Japanese firms.

Ouchi contrasts these three basic modes of control, which he terms his 'organizational failures framework'. This is shown in Table 5.1. It must be noted that the model is not, like Williamson's, stated in oppositional terms and that the clan form appears to be the most complete and complex form since it combines the three basic normative requirements.

It could seem rather paradoxical that traditions are presented as the root of the recent and enviable performance of Japanese companies. It is not clear, however, whether these traditions are local to the firm or are originated in a broader framework, such as national culture. In this respect Ouchi's approach is an important bridgehead to the subject of transcultural management with its roots in economics and its 'branches' in the transcultural world.

Ouchi's arguments are, in fact, more based on sociology than on classical economics. For example, his term 'bureaucracy' for authority refers to Weber, and his notion of clan derives from Durkheim's contrast between organic solidarity and contract. Ouchi's contribution has not

Table 5.1 The organizational failures framework

Mode of control	Normative requirement	Informational requirement
Market	Reciprocity	Prices
Bureaucracy	Reciprocity Legitimate authority	Rules
Clan	Reciprocity Legitimate authority Common values and beliefs	Traditions

Source: Ouchi.[5]

really been further developed in the area of organizational theory, although this merits some attention. A possible reason is that his model is highly general and that its empirical basis seems somewhat weak and controversial.

Ouchi is probably best known for his model of 'type Z organization', a hybrid between 'type A', the traditional American model (bureaucracy in his former terms), and 'type J', the model implemented by the Japanese firm (clan in his former terms), nowadays more efficient than the first one, but not fully transferable because of its roots in the Japanese culture. The 'type Z' organization would be the best compromise between the bureaucracy and the clan, notably with respect to the specific features of the American environment, and Ouchi identifies several American companies with such hybrid characteristics. By contrast, with 'type A', it would be mainly characterized by stable and long-term employment. Other specific features would be moderate career specialization, a lower need for explicit or formal supervision, coordination and evaluation, collective and consensual decision making, and the formation of cohesive work groups (Table 5.2).

Ouchi's contribution can be considered as having led to developments in the study of organizational culture. Curiously, later developments in the study of organizational culture strongly criticized economic and rationalistic biases in traditional models of organizational efficiency, a point that Ouchi seems to underestimate. It also provided some arguments and support to comparative approaches to management styles in terms of national cultures.

Discussing the alleged features of the Japanese management style (to the extent that considering that the functioning of Japanese companies could be understood and summarized in a single model is relevant) is beyond the scope of this chapter.

The firm as a nexus of treaties Whereas Ouchi proposes some refinements rather than a critical amendment of Williamson's approach, the work of Aoki, a Japanese economist, questions the basis of transaction-costs economics. He denies that hierarchy is the single alternative to market in terms of efficiency. He particularly focuses (unusually for an economist) on internal aspects of the firm: work organization at the shopfloor level and personnel management, and inter-organizational issues.

Aoki underlines the relevance of his reservations towards Williamson in the context of the Japanese firm and supports the necessity for a different perspective through a comparison of

Table 5.2   Characteristics of type A, type J and type Z organizations

	Type A	Type J	Type Z
Employment	Short term	Lifetime	Long term
Promotion	Rapid	Slow	Slow
Control system	Explicit and formal	Implicit, informal	Implicit, informal, with explicit measures
Appraisal	Frequent	Infrequent	Moderately frequent
Career paths	Specialized, functional	Non-specialized, cross-functional	Moderately specialized
Decision making	Individual, top-down	Participative, consensual	Consensual
Responsibility	Individual	Collective	Individual
Concern for employees	Segmented	Holistic	Wholistic

Adapted from Ouchi[6] and Ouchi and Jaeger.[7]

Table 5.3   Characteristics of the A firm and the J firm

	A firm	J firm
Information structure	Vertical	Horizontal
Personnel management	Decentralized	Centralized
Employees' mobility	Rapid or inter-firm	Slow and intra-firm
Career paths	Specialized	Multiskilling
Work organization	Job description	Teamwork
Industrial organization	Vertical integration	Quasi-integration

Adapted from Aoki.[8]

large Japanese (J) and American (A) firms. This is shown in Table 5.3. The two major elements in the internal organization of the J firm are the information structure and the personnel management. The former is horizontal, i.e. decentralized, and the latter is centralized, in the joint purpose of coordinating individual actions and providing incentives.

The consequence of the J firm's horizontal information structure is a better response to unusual events (specifically termed 'shocks' by Aoki). In the A firm, the worker has to notify his or her superior and wait for an order, whereas in the J firm, problem solving is achieved at the lowest possible level, through wide information sharing and group knowledge. Information sharing is facilitated by the lack of job demarcation and a wide use of job rotation and on-the-job training, so that considerable knowledge of the production process is developed at the team level. At the level of departments (R&D, manufacturing, workshops, etc.), the same principles are applied. These elements result in a very flexible way of organizing based on teamwork, able to deal with various internal or external uncertainties: changes in demand, failures in machinery, and also enhance productivity.

The functioning of this system requires a specific personnel management system. The A firm relies heavily on hierarchy, but as regards personnel management, it is decentralized and most personnel decisions are made at operational levels: assignments, recruitment and redundancy — in other words, they rely widely upon hierarchical and market mechanisms. The J firm, in order to achieve commitment and firm-specific learning, offers long-term employment and non-specialized career paths. Staying in the firm is thus encouraged: the learning of skills and cooperation will only be compensated after many years of service, in terms of salary and/or promotion. Because learning is specific to the firm, skills and ability to cooperate are not transferable to another company, and the outgoing employee will at least suffer a loss in salary (not to mention reluctance on the part of prospective employers to take on outsiders). The management of the employment system thus requires centralized personnel management.

In contrast to a widespread image, the Japanese life-long employment system is not a 'paternalistic' one, based on the equality of each employee (loyalty measured by seniority being the single basis for pay), but a competitive system where personnel efforts are appraised and are taken into account and compensated in a differential manner. The salary system is based upon seniority *and merit*. In some respects, seniority may thus be thought of not simply as a measure of the length of service but of the (slow) acquisition of new skills, will of learning, team spirit, zeal, and conformity to the firm's values and culture. Seniority appears in this respect to be a relevant measure of merit in that it is a measure of validated and proved performance (defined in terms compatible with work organization).

A further element of Japanese management is that the salary ranks of workers are not linked to specific jobs and agreements between the firm and its company union specifies the minimum and maximum speed of upgrading from a rank to the upper one. Within these negotiated limits, the appraisal of supervisors plays a critical role in decisions related to salaries and promotions. In the terms of Aoki, this rank hierarchy is a crucial device of the incentives system of the Japanese firm.

According to Aoki, the centralization/decentralization of information structures and the decentralization/centralization of personnel management are tightly coupled and represent a basic principle for any organization. The relations between the firm and its environment consist of alliances with public sector, company groups ('keiretsu') and labour market (technical schools and colleges) and bilateral contracts with suppliers. These alliances and even contracts involve implicit dimensions and enable Japanese companies to diminish uncertainty.

Aoki contrasts the vertical integration of the A firm with the quasi-integration of the J firm. In the J firm the relations with subcontracting firms are long term and stable, so that the latter are able to make investments but are still submitted to market incentives. Inter-firm learning is achieved through mutual knowledge, technology sharing and narrow cooperation beyond standard buyer–seller relations. Aoki also provides a basis for the subtle analysis of inter-firm relations which transaction-costs economics does not provide for.

Aoki questions the role of culture, such as group-orientation, in management practice. Though he accepts that they are an integral part of Japanese culture, he contends that these cultural elements are neither a sufficient nor necessary condition to the efficiency of the J firm. Aoki considers therefore that some J firm practices can easily be adopted by Western firms, in a manner compatible with a reinforcement of mutual relations between individuals educated to a certain type of socialization. He also considers that the Japanese firm can progressively accept the developing individualism of its younger generations, and suggests that, thanks to the development of communication technology, this can be achieved without critical loss of its main characteristics.

More recently, Aoki *et al.*[10] developed the concept of 'treaties', in a perspective which was also critical towards Williamson. Treaties are a less restrictive concept than that of contracts: contracts cannot embrace the much less formal implicit or explicit alliances which are the stuff of business life. In other words, the concept of treaties can also include looser forms of governance structures.

Some criticism has been made of Aoki's approach, not least on the question of the specificity of the J firm: is it fully Japanese? Because of the isomorphism between personnel management, relational contracting and alliances with banks and the public sector, the performance of the Japanese firm could be difficult to replicate in another economic setting. A second criticism is that, more recently, such isomorphism seems to be challenged, especially in the area of life-long employment.

Aoki also seems to overestimate the horizontal dimension of the internal and external information structure and appears to undervalue the need for control over employees or subcontractors. Even the scope of the participatory decision making might be narrower than what Aoki thinks. Because of the acceptance of the firm's rules and values, some kind of conformism makes opportunistic behaviour, conflicts or divergences of opinions, rather unlikely. It could be assumed that this mostly consists of wide information sharing and thus a feeling of collective responsibility, even if decisions are made in a conformist manner.

Possibly, as Aoki focuses on the Japanese firm he may underestimate its institutional environment, especially its historical conditions of emergence and its regulatory and political context. His contribution may therefore lie mainly in the microeconomics of the firm, or even the 'nanoeconomics', to the extent that he makes an economic analysis of shopfloor level.

While Williamson and the tenants of the transaction-costs economists assume that the market is the primary economic institution, Aoki shifts the focus away from the market as giving way to organizations towards a greater interest in organizations and firms *per se*.

ORGANIZATIONS AND INSTITUTIONS

The second section of this chapter looks at theories which consider the complex interplay between the characteristics of organizations and the environments in which they exist. The research underlying this section comes mostly from the world of sociology and relies heavily on various international comparisons which constitute their primary focus.

Two contributions will be examined, the first, that of the French 'school of Aix',[11] and the second and most recent, that of Whitley.[12,13] Generally, they both consider that institutional arrangements are at the root of national differences in the functioning of organizations. These groups therefore consider that an organization's national specificities cannot be ascribed to the cultural values of each country (a far too blurred notion, according to these authors) but rather may be ascribed to the institutional elements within which social relations are built and make sense.[14] According to Amadieu,[15] these elements can be defined as a set of rules with its own consistence and coherence.

The 'societal' effect

The societal approach has been developed by a French research group, known as the Aix group in the English-speaking world. Their starting point was an empirical comparison of firms, comparable in all respects (sector: petrochemicals and metallurgy, size, technology, performance, etc.) in France and Germany. As an originally comparative perspective, the first merit of this approach is to challenge the thesis of a single model, or similar models of development in industrialized countries.

According to the Aix group, in the same country, firms display similar characteristics, but from country to country, salient differences become evident. The specificities of these firms must, they claim, therefore be related to the broader *institutional* environments in which they operate (rather than the overall national cultural value systems of the country concerned).

The three dimensions of the societal effect   From their empirical work, the authors identified three major institutions or systems which they felt played a role in organizational development:

- The educational system.
- The organizational system.
- The industrial relations system.

Educational system   The group claims that, because of the type of education favoured in the recruitment and promotion of employees, the educational system has a visible influence on the functioning of firms. In France, for example, the educational system mostly provides a general education (in contrast to the less favoured vocational one), so that about 70 per cent of male employees had no vocational education. By comparison, this was about 30 per cent in Germany, where vocational education is more recognized and encouraged. As a result, French workers acquire their specific skills within firms and, because these skills are not transferable, it hinders their capacity to leave for another employer.

In Germany, by comparison, a worker's mobility is much greater, because their professional skills are widely recognized through public certification. The German apprenticeship system, better known as the 'dual' system, is organized by a close cooperation between employers and technical schools.

Organizational system   The organizational system defines occupational categories, job structures, employment patterns and hierarchy systems. In Germany, for example, workers and clerks have a strong professional autonomy and hierarchy is based more on professional skills than authority. Under these conditions, managers have a high level legitimacy and cooperation between departments and workshops is made easier as a result. Because there are only a limited number of basic professions and because a number of workers have been through a similar education, the set of skills is relatively homogeneous and the development of polyvalency is made easier. Moreover, German foremen are free to organize tasks in their units so that jobs are defined in relation with worker's skills rather than in a prescribed and formalized manner. According to Amadieu,[15] the skills of workers shape the contents of jobs and the work organization is adapted to the available competencies and it aims at making the best use of them.

By contrast, in France, the employees have to adapt to the jobs previously designed by employers. Whereas a German employer will recruit employees according to their potential, and then find them jobs to do as a second priority, a French employer seeks employees to fit a given job profile. Furthermore, in Germany, foremen are promoted according to their professional skills, not to their loyalty, so that the rate of managers promoted from within the ranks of foremen is higher than in France. This difference is compounded by the fact that wage differences between managers and workers are smaller in Germany than in France.

In France, wage determination and promotion is made on the basis of impersonal rules of administration, such as the weight of seniority, and emphasis is on job classification systems and job contents rather than on the individual skills of workers. Hierarchy is a matter of authority rather than professional skills. Career opportunities for workers are scarce, unless they join white-collar workers, for whom upward mobility is easier. In contrast, in Germany, a continuum exists between workers and managers. The critical segmentation or cleavage between employees is vertical (hierarchical) in France, whereas it is horizontal (according to differences between office and manufacturing work) in Germany.

Competence and performance play a major role in German firms and inter-firm mobility is higher than in France, so that seniority is less critical in wage determination. Pay structures are more egalitarian in Germany: the wage differentials between hierarchical levels are significantly higher in France. Moreover, because German workers have easier access to an external occupational labour market (due to the wide recognition of their professional skills), they are less dependent on their employers in matters of earnings than is the case for their French colleagues.

In France, promotion and earnings depend on loyalty and assignment to better jobs. Job assignment is thus a sensitive matter and a prerogative of personnel departments because of its consequences on the paybill. Unionization appears to be more alternative than complementary to the allegiance to employer and this confers a more conflictual orientation to industrial relations.

Industrial relations   The industrial relations system consists of the patterns of relations between employers and trade unions, of conflicts, and in labour and employment law. The German firm is better integrated to the society than is its French counterpart. For instance, the dual system (apprenticeship) owes its success to the close cooperation between technical schools and firms.

Industrial democracy has seen significant developments in Germany, as shown by the co-determination system. Trade unions and works councils are more recognized, powerful and legitimate and a number of matters are permanently negotiated. Efficiency, professional values and a spirit of co-responsibility prevail and are shared by both employers and workers' representatives so that when conflicts occur, each party is motivated to reach consensus and mutual advantage through negotiation.

In France, mutual recognition and legitimization of each party is not sufficient for the establishment of stable patterns of cooperation or contest. Trade unions are weak and display internal oppositions according to their ideological origins and positions. They challenge the employers' right to operate on the basis of harmonious and fair economic development.

The Aix group propose that these three systems combine to generate the specificities of each country's firms. Amadieu illustrates this point as follows:

> 'A given educational system, for instance in Germany, with a rule such as "alternate" education (apprenticeship joined with vocational education) provides a professionalized workforce. This "professionalism" ("professionalité") is recognized by a wage system where the rule is to pay for individual skills not for the job occupied. With such a wage rule, work organizations are designed so that they make use of the professionalism of workers, because it is paid for whatever it may be'.

These rules are congruent and consistent and they constitute what the authors of the school of Aix call the 'societal effect'.

The articulation of these elements and their specific dynamics is of particular interest: 'there appears to be a close interaction between factors in different spheres of society, which follows a logic upon which the identity of a particular society is built.'[16] 'Interaction or reciprocal conditioning occurs between societal institutions, on the one side, and what they [Sorge and Warner] term "material conditions for the survival and well-being in society".'[17]

Further developments   The Aix group later extended its comparison to Japan (see, for instance, Silvestre[18]). Most elements earlier mentioned (see the section on Aoki in this chapter) can be interpreted according to the specificities of the Japanese educational system and industrial relations.

The authors emphasize the following points. In Japan, general education prevails but the educational system is not stratified as it is in France, the only distinction being made is that between high school and university education. The notion of the individual job does not exist in Japan: there is an intensive job rotation coupled with on-the-job training, which highly favours the development of polyvalency and learning by doing. Seniority is taken into account in Japanese companies and there is a strong company identity. At key moments (introduction of new technologies, equipment failure, recruitments, etc.) this identity finds expression by a quick mobilization of the various hierarchical levels.

The social construction of business systems

Whitley[13] started with a rather similar viewpoint: 'there are a number of different ways of organizing economic activities' which 'result from, and are efficient within, particular institutional environments'. He proposes that 'the development and success of managerial structures and practices in different contexts require explanation in terms of those contexts'. Whitley[12] puts more emphasis on the socially constructed nature of business systems. As social constructs, Whitley holds that firms and markets 'are meaningful entities whose nature and operation vary according to differences in meaning systems and dominant rationalities'. According to him, these dominant rationalities are essentially of an economic nature.

The identification of business systems   Whitley proposes three fundamental issues for consideration:

- The coordination and control of economic activities and resources.
- The organization of market connections between authoritatively coordinated economic activities.
- The organization and direction of activities and skills within firms through authority relations.

A business system can thus be defined as 'systematic, interrelated responses to the three fundamental issues of any market-based system'.[19]

Whitley proposes an analytical framework in order to understand the essential nature of what he calls 'business systems' (earlier termed 'business recipes') (see Table 5.4). He considers that these elements are often interconnected, thus restricting the number of typical configurations. For instance, it is highly likely that strong owner control is associated with a low level of formalization of coordination and control procedures, and with highly personal connections between firms. These interconnections 'constrain, but do not determine the development of distinct hierarchy-market configurations'.[13] Thus distinct configurations, resulting from these interconnections, have become established as successful forms of business organizations. Whitley's ambition is thus to identify these distinct configurations and the way they become established according to a particular institutional environment. He then applies this framework in order to compare business systems in East Asia (Table 5.5).

Are institutions overwhelming?   Compared with that of the Aix group, Whitley's contribution is one of a broadened perspective comprising European and Asian countries. The third facet of his framework is very similar to the Aix group's approach, but the innovative contribution of Whitley lies in his attempt to clarify the relations of organizational processes and structures with the more economic aspects of organizational development. In this respect, he asserts that issues traditionally tackled either by strategists and industrial economists, on the one hand, and organization students and labour sociologists, on the other, are interconnected and should not be considered in isolation from each other.

Table 5.4 Characteristics of business systems

1. *The nature of the firm*
- The degree to which private managerial hierarchies coordinate economic activities
- The degree of managerial discretion from owners
- Specialization of managerial capabilities and activities within authority hierarchies
- The degree to which growth is discontinuous and involves radical changes in skills and activities
- The extent to which risks are managed through mutual dependence with business partners and employees

2. *Market organization*
- The extent to which long-term cooperative relations exist between firms within and between sectors
- The significance of intermediaries in the coordination of market transactions
- Stability, integration and scope of business groups
- Dependence of cooperative relations on personal ties and trust

3. *Authoritative coordination and control systems*
- Integration and interdependence of economic activities
- Impersonality of authority and subordination relations
- Task, skill and role specialization and individualization
- Differentiation of authority roles and expertise
- Decentralization of operational control and level of work group autonomy
- Distance and superiority of managers
- Extent of employer–employee commitment and organization-based employment system

Source: Whitley.[13]

Between institutions and agency

In contrast to the institutional school, Stewart Clegg[20] refers to

> 'Granovetter's[21] conception of economic embeddedness … and makes reference to culture but seeks to context and locate it in its institutional specificity. In organizational terms culture works through framing the assumptions that agencies are able to operate with. It frames and it enables; it enables and it constrains… Action is never unbounded. It is framed within more or less tacit understandings, as well as formal stipulations, which enable different agencies to do not only different things but also the same things distinctly in diverse contexts.'

This perspective is very similar to the so-called constructivist perspective, and was, among others, developed in the field of social theory by Anthony Giddens.

Amadieu builds a framework in terms of rules in which he acknowledges the interest of institutional perspectives which succeed in revealing overarching rules but at the same time he assumes that these rules mostly shape the various (macro) organizational features which in turn are influenced by the value systems of the individuals who make them up. According to the French sociologist Jean-Daniel Reynaud,[22,23] institutions as well as organizations (the top management) yield and spread general rules, which ensure a 'control regulation', whereas the implementation of these rules in an operational manner (daily individual or subgroups interactions in various social situations) involves adjustments, negotiations, bargains or compromises, which form the necessary but less visible 'autonomous regulation'.

A limitation of institutional rules is that they cannot foresee any kind of situation or problem

Table 5.5   Configuration of hierarchy-market relations in East Asia

Characteristics	Kaisha	Chaebol	Chinese family business
Economic actors			
● *Owner control*	High	Low	Low
● *Managerial homogeneity and similarity of activities*	High	Low	High in firms, medium in families
● *Strategic change*	Incremental	Discontinuous	Opportunistic
● *Growth focus*	Sector share	Vertical integration and diversification	volume expansion and opportunistic diversification
● *Integration of different activities*	Minority shareholding	Authority, hierarchy	Personal ties and ownership
● *Risk management*	Extensive mutual dependence	Diversification and state support	Limiting commitment and maximizing flexibility
Market organization			
● *Interdependence of firms*	High	Low	High
● *Long-term commitment to particular exchange partners*	High	Low	Restricted outside family-like connections
● *Reliance on personal knowledge, reputation and networks*	Low	Limited	High
Employment and personnel practices in East Asia			
● *Employer commitment to, and dependence on, core employees*	High	Limited	Medium
● *Formalization of procedures*	High	Limited to white-collar staff	Low
Authority and control systems			
● *Importance of personal authority and control in hierarchy*	Limited	High	High
● *Delegation to middle management*	Considerable	Limited to operational decisions	Low
● *Managerial style*	Facilitative	Authoritarian	Paternalistic

Adapted from Whitley.[12,19]

(the typical tragedy of bureaucracy), i.e. they can never be self-sufficient and omnipotent or cannot extensively cover every dimension of social action, and therefore they must provide or leave some looseness or ambiguity. Thus at the same time as they are at least formally respected, they allow the course of social action to unfold with some limited free way in a satisfying manner, according to institutional, organizational, group and individual interests. Control rules yield less strong constraints and commanded ways of working than a framework which establishes (even if fuzzy or ambiguous, and thus open to various interpretations) boundaries between what is acceptable and what is not and defines a space within which some autonomy is possible or even necessary.

NETWORKS AND CONVENTIONS

The approaches presented in this section attempt to build further on the material presented so far, overcoming, in part, some of the shortcomings identified. The first considers that networks based on trust constitute a third basic type of economic organization. A second line of enquiry considers social relations as being at the root of market organization. A third approach asserts the co-existence of several worldviews, or several possible worlds which would shape the processes and structures of collective action. This is supported by research asserting that four models can account for company diversity in the manufacturing sector.

Networks beyond markets and hierarchies

Networks have been paid increasing attention by organization researchers, leading to best-sellers, 'how to' recipes books and articles, and a range of academic works. Two broad types of networks have been extensively studied: inter-organizational networks and internal networks (good introductions and developments can be found in Thompson *et al.*[24] and Nohria and Eccles[25]). The first type of network includes industrial districts, centralized networks (composed of a core company and a constellation of peripheral subcontracting companies) and various arrangements such as alliances, partnerships, cooperative ventures. The second type covers highly decentralized multidivisional companies (for instance, organized into profit centres), clans and informal or personalized ways of organizing.

Powell's[26] starting point doubts the utility of a continuum (namely market-hierarchy) view of economic exchange, holding that this view 'blinds us to the role played by reciprocity and collaboration as alternative governance mechanisms'. Powell contends that some organizational designs cannot be understood within the hierarchy-market framework, even softened, as intermediary or hybrid form (as he formerly described them[27]). He proposes that it is 'meaningful to talk about networks as a distinctive form of co-ordinating economic activity'. Powell asserts that 'all forms of exchange contain elements of networks, markets and hierarchies' and encourages us to interpret his work as supportive of the premise that 'there is merit in thinking of networks as an empirically identifiable governance structure'. He then contrasts the three basic types of economic organization as in Table 5.6.

It is worth noting that in contrast to Ouchi (see above), Powell more specifically focuses on networks of organizations rather than internal networks, or clans, in Ouchi's terms. Powell[26] states that 'in network modes of resource allocation, transactions occur neither through discrete exchanges nor administrative fiat, but through networks of individuals engaged in reciprocal, preferential, mutually supportive action'. Networks are especially made both stable in the long term, in opposition with market relations, and adaptable to changing situations, in opposition with hierarchical relations, because 'reputation, friendship, interdependence and altruism become integral parts of the relationship'. For instance, the information passed through networks

Table 5.6 Stylized comparison of forms of economic organization

Key features	Market	Hierarchy	Network
Normative basis	Contract — Property rights	Employment relationship	Complementary strengths
Means of communication	Prices	Routines	Relational
Methods of conflict resolution	Haggling — resort to courts for enforcement	Administrative fiat — supervision	Norms of reciprocity — reputational concerns
Degree of flexibility	High	Low	Medium to high
Amount of commitment among the parties	Low	Medium to high	Medium to high
Tone or climate	Precision and/or supervision	Formal, bureaucratic	Open-ended mutual benefits
Actor preferences or choices	Independent	Dependent	Interdependent
Mixing of forms	Repeat transactions Contracts as hierarchical documents	Informal organization Market-like features: profit centres, transfer pricing	Status hierarchies Multiple partners Formal rules

Source: Powell.[26]

is both more dependable (less likely to be sensitive to opportunistic behaviour) than that obtained in the market, and more independent (less authority-biased) than that communicated through hierarchy. 'Networks are, then, especially useful for the exchange of commodities whose value is not easily measured'. Trust appears to be a kind of social lubricant because it 'reduces complex realities far more quickly and economically than prediction, authority or bargaining'. Networks both serve normative social standards because they rely on a community of shared values, and enhance individual interests through cooperation because they provide efficient and reliable information and increase the ability to learn and transmit new knowledge and skills. In contrast to the hierarchy and market model, networks increase the mutual dependency of the parties to the activities of others. Their dependency is lower than in a hierarchy and higher than in a market, because it is in fact an interdependence resulting from more or less formal negotiations within an agreed framework.

Empirically, Powell's approach is based upon the observation of high-tech start-ups in the United States and craft-based firms in northern Italy, 'which do not follow the standard model of small firms developing internally through an incremental and linear progress'. Similar examples can be found within the Route 128 Area and bio-technology industry (extensively described and analysed in Nohria and Eccles[25]). The case of northern Italy has been extensively studied in terms of industrial districts, the most famous one being Prato's (for some recent accounts see Clegg,[20] Inzerilli,[28] Locke[29] and Piore[30]). In contrast to these latter studies, Powell does not develop a comparative perspective.

Powell proposes an interesting theoretical framework. However, it is as yet uncertain to what extent it is realistic to assume that each form of economic organization may be governed by a single control mechanism. A number of studies have shown that most markets are far from being solely governed by purely economic mechanisms such as prices (for a review see Swedberg[31]). The same criticism could be made to this model of hierarchy, which is similar to Weber's and begs the question as to whether today's firms can be properly described and analysed as pure, or even mixed, Weberian bureaucracies.

The trouble with most network studies, including Powell's contribution, is that 'the term is used normatively: to advocate what organizations must become if they are to be competitive in today's competitive environment'.[32] According to Powell, networks are more flexible and effective than hierarchies in responsiveness to changing conditions.

The level of analysis used by Powell is also an issue: networks are inter-organizational designs, and it may be inappropriate to envisage firms and networks on the same level. Networks are constituted by firms, but what about the internal organization of these firms? Could their internal organization be based on hierarchy? This as-yet unanswered issue is common to a number of studies comparing firms with networks.

Back to trust and social networks

Other authors suggest that it is not necessary to identify networks as a specific organizational form controlled by a single coordination mechanism because, they argue, no organizational form is actually governed by a single or even dominant control mechanism. Bradach and Eccles,[33] for example, deny that coordination mechanisms are mutually exclusive. According to them, the three basic control mechanisms (price, authority and relational contracting) are always mixed, and thus can be found in any real organizational form (market, firm or network). These control mechanisms, however separate, are often intertwined. As mentioned above, markets display traits of hierarchies and hierarchies exhibit properties of markets. These authors thus consider that what matters in the analysis of economic organization is an understanding of the ways in which these various attributes act in concert with each other. They emphasize the importance of trust and they contend that 'transactions are embedded in a context of *other transactions* as well as in a social context'. Trust 'does not replace market and hierarchy: frequently it complements the two forms'. They advocate an analysis in terms of plural forms. In this respect, they contend, in contrast to Powell, that 'transactions controlled by one mechanism are profoundly affected by the simultaneous use of an alternative control mechanism'. In order to overcome the difficulties involved in the use of a single control mechanism, the simultaneous use of two mechanisms creates, in essence, competition between them. Plural forms are composed of two distinct control mechanisms, operated simultaneously for the same function by the same firm.

This assertion is supported by empirical evidence: some firms permanently rely on both arm's-length contracts and authority structures. For example, franchising systems are composed of company-owned units and franchise units. The former are managed by authority structure, but elements of price control mechanisms are introduced by management incentive programs and profit centres. The latter are managed by independent business persons, bound by a long-term contract to the company which specifies in detail how the franchise is to be run, so that, in this case, hierarchy permeates market mechanisms.

Though Bradach and Eccles hypothesize that the choice of a control mechanism is not really explained by efficiency or control considerations, the extent to which a company uses franchisees rather than company-owned units, or third-party distributors rather than a direct salesforce, is also not clear. Bradach and Eccles have contributed to fill the gap between a strictly economic perspective and a sociological approach but their account of the way 'control mechanisms are grafted on to and leveraged off existing social structures' is, we feel, not fully convincing. Finally, they do not seem to draw inferences from their analysis of trust (see below) as a control mechanism complementing hierarchy and market, and established in a wider social context.

Granovetter,[21,34] whose approach is presented below, offers a more profound analysis of trust in economic action. Granovetter's approach stems from sociology and is an attempt to lay the foundations for an 'economic sociology'. Though it does not focus on organizations, his contribution is well respected and has inspired a number of network researchers. Three basic assertions lay the foundation for this approach:

- The co-existence of economic and non-economic goals in economic action.
- The embeddedness of social action.
- The social construction of economic institutions.

Traditionally economists and sociologists only focus on the set of goals consistent with their own discipline, thus, we feel, losing a comprehensive understanding of social or economic action. In this respect, Granovetter is especially critical of Williamson's approach. His first assertion therefore is that the pursuit of economic goals cannot be separated from that of non-economic goals such as sociability, approval, status, and power.

His second assertion is that economic action is embedded in ongoing networks of personal relationships rather than carried out by autonomous actors. This suggests that looking at individual motives alone cannot help to explain economic action because it is performed in a social context. By this assertion, Granovetter overcomes the shortcomings of both deterministic approaches which solely focus on the dictating of individual actions by social structures (classes, culture, institutions, etc.), norms and values, and individualistic approaches which envisages social action as simply resulting from the aggregation of individual actions.

His third assertion is that economic institutions are socially constructed rather than being shaped by external circumstances such as historical forces beyond the reach of actors. This statement implies that a dynamic perspective on institutions is necessary to shed light on the complex historical interplay between the actors involved doing things and the social structures that shape, and are shaped by, their ways of doing things.

This approach was originally developed in a study of the process of recruiting.[35] According to Granovetter's results, impersonal sources of recruitment such as agencies and advertisements are more used in the case of technical (in contrast to managerial) jobs and those with lower pay. Jobs with higher uncertainty, i.e. managerial ones and those with higher pay because of greater responsibility, tend to be filled through the operation of personal networks: contacts between members of the organization and potential recruits. These jobs tend to be liked better by recruits, because personal networks provide better information on which to make their job choice decision. Granovetter also indicates that very often the ties that constitute these networks are weak, in the sense of being based on casual acquaintances rather than on family connections or years of contact.

More recently, Granovetter has undertaken a study of business groups in terms of networks, with particular reference to Japanese keiretsu and Sonta Korean chaebols. In this case, groups of businesses rather than individual organization or firm is here the relevant level of analysis. Though some examples, especially from East Asia, are well known, according to Granovetter a systematic study of business groups has never been made, and, he claims, is a necessary and a critical aspect of the understanding of modern capitalism.

Viewing organizations as social constructions, he contends that institutions can be conceived as crystallized or 'congealed' social networks; once established, a network follows a given path: a number of industries appear today as very stable and even natural, but a historical study of their constitution show that at various points they could have taken radically different institutional forms. An emergent industry is therefore seen as a result of the interaction of a constellation of networks and, in this respect, is partly a social construction.

Granovetter's approach has been applied to business groups and sector analysis, with results very different from those of most economists or sociologists. In this respect, there are also similarities to Whitley's approach except that Granovetter provides a more interactionist perspective.

Providing a general theoretical framework, Granovetter's approach has applications in the area of organizational theory. In his programmatic introduction to a collection of research works on networks, Nohria,[25] with a notable influence from Granovetter, brings to light the five basic premises that underlie a network perspective on organizations. The first is that organizations should be viewed as patterns of recurring relationships, whatever the level of analysis (from workgroups to economies). This means that, rather than considering networks as an organizational form in its own right, they are considered here as a constitutive component of any organization (as well as markets). This has two important consequences. First, networks become themselves a form of analytical tool and thus a network perspective is fundamentally relational. Second, it holds that a complete view of organizations should go beyond traditional features such as prescribed relations, formal structure and official charts and statements, and should look, in addition, at the informal, emergent, and hidden networks of relationships.

The second premise is that organizational environments should be conceived as networks of organizations. In this respect, these environments are characterized more broadly than they would be through general and abstract features such as environmental uncertainty, resource dependencies and institutional pressure.

The third premise is that actions of actors can be better understood according to their positions in networks of relationships than by their individual attributes. In this respect, this approach provides a new and interactionist approach to organizational dynamics.

The fourth premise is that networks constrain actions and, in turn, are shaped by them. Networks demarcate a field of action, making some courses of action, some opportunities, some patterns of relations, more likely to actors, and through the recurring patterns of relationships, networks are in turn reproduced or changed. This is very similar to the approach proposed above and clearly refers to the pioneering work of Granovetter.

The fifth and final premise is that a relevant comparative analysis of organizations requires their network characteristics to be taken into account. Such comparative analysis is often made by measuring abstract and general variables, for instance the degree of decentralization. This premise asserts that this approach cannot capture the actual configuration of organizations.

In a similar vein, Biggart and Hamilton[36] have made an innovative analysis of business networks in Asia. They criticize 'the Western bias of neo-classical economics' which conceptualizes markets and firms from a generalization of characteristics probably only relevant to Western countries, such as individualistic institutional structures. In Asian economies, social relations between economic actors, far from impeding market functioning, actually promote it. Here the notion of network is useful because of the assertion that neither the notion of market nor that of firm is able to give a relevant and realistic view of these economies: 'Asian nations have institutionalized networks and built economic policies around the presence and presumption of social relations among market actors.'

As noted above, the critical point is to identify the relevant unit of analysis, or, in their terms, the principles of social action on which Asian economies are based, and to understand the development of these principles through the historical experience of Asian nations. In Western countries, market self-regulation and firm autonomy have been historically jointly institutionalized and thus have become invisible or natural to observers. These authors claim that, far too rooted in Western experience, neo-classical theory cannot account for Asian societies and economies.

The various worldviews of collective action

At the heart of the approach of Boltanski and Thévenot,[37] lies a reflection on the production of agreements, or the accomplishment of coordination between persons. Because the notion of convention is central, the term has become generic to this stream of research, usually referred to as 'economics of conventions' (see especially Eymard-Duvernay,[38] Favereau[39] and Salais[40]). Nonetheless, despite a number of points of agreement, Boltanski and Thévenot, concentrating more on social theory and philosophy, prefer to call their approach 'economies of greatness'.

These approaches attempt to tackle the question of how the juxtaposition of heterogeneous principles can explain the functioning of a human group; what it is that makes it hold together. Emphasis is put on the manner in which compromises and agreements are made, not through the actions of the actors but in the justifications which underpin these agreements.

The notion of agreement is used in order to treat the problem of the necessity, in any society, to harmonize the various principles that individuals and groups appeal to in their action, or, more precisely, of how the constraints generated by these requisite agreements are dealt with. The benefits of these constraints can be related to the possibility of an adjustment between actions which they provide. According to these authors, an appropriate analytical framework for organizations must comprise an understanding of rules and play (in the French meaning: including some slack)[41] and how the actors act within this framework of the certainty/uncertainty it provides.

They propose to reconcile traditionally antagonistic views of economists and sociologists: they claim the firm is simultaneously a place where goods circulate and are exchanged, and where rules are enacted and implemented.[42] Compared with that of neo-classical economists, their scope is broader: an agreement between individuals, even if it is restricted to a market contract, is not possible without a common framework, a constitutive convention. Convention is a more general, more open-ended and less bounded notion than that of contract: it permits the coordination of contradictory interests which derive from competing logics, but which require to be kept together in order to be met.[40]

According to these authors, conventions are envisaged as a form of common knowledge, a cognitive model.[43] As suggested by its semantics, the term convention designates both the device constituting an agreement of wills as well as the product of this device, so the notion must be understood as the interaction of individual actions and also the framework which constrains them.

This position is thus rather close to that of Granovetter and suggests that relationships between persons require shared systems of equivalency, such as common conceptions of 'greatness', permitting each person to find references or landmarks that will guide his or her relations. These must underlie some process of ordering what matters the most and the least. These notions of greatness are deployed within six 'worlds', each governed by its own set of principles. These worlds, which characterize the universe of relations, should be understood as ideal-types, in the sense given by Weber. The basic features of the six worlds are summarized in Table 5.7. The comments below are drawn from Livian and Herreros.[42]

Inspired world   In the world of inspiration, the most valued objects are those which refer to the creative genius they bear. In an inspired world, artists will not worry about the market value of their work, creation and the lights of inspiration only matter to them. The creative staff in an advertising agency, the researcher and colleagues in the laboratory, the architect and assistants exist in this world. Reference to market constraints is totally alien to it.

Domestic world   The domestic world draws its references from family and tradition. Relations are in accordance with the rules of honour and with duty towards peers or family figures such as that of the father. Greatness stems from the position occupied in kinship, not from skills and knowledge. The efficiency in this world lies in the capacity to follow elders. A paternalistic and benevolent style of management in a small family business, the relationships between the boss and his or her team of assistants, resident medical students and nurses in a hospital department, strongly rely on recognized traditions and rules and fall into the domestic world.

World of opinion   The world of opinion is centred around the opinion of others or the fame one can draw from action. In this world, behaviour aims at gaining the recognition of a large audience. A project whose purpose consists of obtaining renown is rooted in this world.

Civic world   In the civic world, collective interests prevail over individual interests. People within this world invoke the notions of equity, freedom and solidarity. Law is central to this world and the right for expression, of each person or his or her legal representative is sovereign. Because it favours the defence of citizenship, in this world industrial democracy in organizations matters more than anything else. Friendly or cooperative societies have long responded to an objective prevailing collective solidarity. The notion of public service, often appealed to in state-owned companies, can be associated with this world.

Merchant world   The merchant world is focused on principles usually defining market laws. Aims such as being efficient, capturing customers, having the best price, reaping advantage from a transaction, making a success of a business, all illustrate what matters in such a world. Salespeople in a company may disagree on methods and tools when they have to sketch together a sales strategy, but their quarrels cease if one appeals to the very basic principle of this world: being the best in one's market. If opportunism favours winning, selling, then it will not mean losing one's prestige or standing, but it will show one's capacity to act in a responsible manner according to the values of this world.

Industrial world   In the industrial world, technological performance and science are at the root of efficiency. Investments in equipment or in training the employee in charge of running it, measurements of productivity by scientific tools, are typical actions in this world. The firm with heavy equipment, modern manufacturing methods, highly skilled professionals, appears as a perfectly functional system and thus is a pure image of this world. In case of conflict between persons (engineering professionals, ... etc.), this will be managed through by technical tests and rational and scientific analysis, which will permit to seal a new understanding.

Because these worlds are constructed as ideal types, they only have a theoretical existence and each real situation will be a mix of worlds. So, for instance, a company may comply with both domestic and industrial worlds (paternalistic companies), or opinion and merchant worlds (an advertising campaign made by a business group before some stock exchange dealings). The critical step then becomes the identification of the relevant worlds in order to make the necessary coordinations possible. The set of criteria in Table 5.7 provides a basic format for the identification of reasons for and solutions to conflicts which have arisen between co-existing worlds.

Several criticisms can be made of this approach. First, the authors focus on the process of reaching constructive agreement and perhaps underestimate the issues of conflict and power Second, since problems develop from the co-existence of several worlds which each have their own view of greatness, the question arises as to why should actors share an interest in clarifying a confused situation and in removing the uncertainty related to the relative greatness of the persons involved in this situation. The authors consider that through the process of negotiation, the situation is 'purified' (in their own terms), that is, in order to settle a litigation, a higher principle is appealed to and this approach is accepted by all players: some will become greater and some authors smaller, but each will accept one's new qualification. All conflicts, negotiations, bargaining, resistance, seem to be excluded from the field of analysis.

The authors draw on various sources, from political philosophy (Hobbes, Rousseau, Saint-Simon), to economics, including handbooks of public relations. Such sources are inevitably heterogeneous and it may be argued that it is inappropriate to create such strong linkage between historically differentiated theories. While this framework is innovative and stimulating for empirical research, we feel it nonetheless still requires substantial validation.

The conventional basis of economic organization

Salais's approach[40, 44-46] can be said to complement and extend that of Boltanski and Thévenot: first, because he concentrates especially on issues of labour economics (with elements from industrial, international and macroeconomics); second, because he supports his observations with empirical investigation (especially see Salais and Storper[46]).

In order to deal with both internal and external uncertainties and to manage conflicting but bound interests, Salais claims that employment relations are ruled through a double convention: the convention of productivity and the convention of unemployment. The first convention is the organizing principle through which an agreement is made between actors, regarding the relationship between supplied working time and amount of money. It is rooted not in an equation relating wage with actual or anticipated productivity but in minimal norms, normal averages and leads to habits, routines, customs, which are dealt with in the long term. The convention of unemployment contributes to the management of the permanent uncertainty over the acceptance of the products of the performed work by the market (more simply stated, on sales). Salais proposes the existence of four 'worlds of production' on the basis of criteria such as economic uncertainty, the type of ideal worker, the assessment of work quality (convention of productivity), the wage system, the nature of the firm (how the firm is conceived) and the type of adjustment to external uncertainty (convention of unemployment). Table 5.8 summarizes the salient characteristics of Salais' four worlds.

Table 5.7 The common worlds

	Inspired	Domestic	Opinion	Civic	Merchant	Industrial
Utmost principle	Eluding measurement, rising from inspiration	Personal relations, hierarchy tradition	Opinion of others	Pre-eminence of communities	Competition	Technology and science, efficiency, performance
State of greatness	Spontaneous, unusual escaping from reason	Benevolent, circumspect	Well known	Representative, official	Desirable, valuable	Performing, efficient, functional
Dignity	Love, passion, creation	Ease, common sense	Desire for respect	Freedom	Interest	Work
Basic subjects	Children, artists	Superiors, subordinates, ancestors	Stars	Communities	Competitors, clients	Professionals
Basic objects	Spirit, body	Precedence, gifts	Names, brands, messages	Legal forms	Wealth	Means
Type of investment (price to be paid)	Risk	Duty	Renouncement of secret	Renouncement of claims for particularity, solidarity	Opportunism	Investment, improvement
Relation of greatness	Unusualness, singularity	Subordination, honour	Identification	Membership, adhesion, delegation	Possession	Mastery
Natural relations	Dream, imagination	Education, reproduction	Persuasion	Gathering for	Business collective action	Running, working relationships
Harmonious figure	Imaginary	Family, social sphere	Hearing	Republic	Market	System
Model ordeal	Inner adventure	Family ceremony	Presentation of event	Demonstration for a right cause	Deal, striking bargain	Test
Expression of judgement	Flash of genius	Appreciation	Judgement of opinion	Result of poll	Price	Actual, correct
Form of conspicuousness	Certainty of intuition	Example	Success, being known	Text of law	Money, profits	Measurement
State of smallness	Routine	Unconventional, vulgar	Commonplace, trite, unknown	Divided, isolated	Loser	Inefficient

Adapted from Boltanski and Thévenot[37] and from Livian and Herreros.[42]

Table 5.8 Labour conventions and production worlds

MERCHANT LABOUR

Type of uncertainty:	on demanded quality
Identity of worker:	person, member of a work community
Assessment of work quality:	market price of product
Wage:	person, based according to product
Firm:	voluntary gathering of persons in a network
Adjustment:	personal responsibility

Interpersonal production world

UNSPECIALIZED LABOUR

Type of uncertainty:	local, on demand
Identity of worker:	available and autonomous individual
Assessment of work quality:	availability
Wage:	task-related
Firm:	gathering of individuals
Adjustment:	variability of *labour* quantity

Merchant production world

IMMATERIAL LABOUR

Type of uncertainty:	on future
Identity of worker:	expert
Assessment of work quality:	rules of professional or scientific conduct
Wage:	skill- and knowledge-based, as an investment in persons
Firm:	small groups
Adjustment:	mobility of knowledge and skills

Immaterial production worked

INDUSTRIAL LABOUR

Type of uncertainty:	predictable
Identity of worker:	job holder
Assessment of work quality:	work description, job classification
Wage:	hourly, job related
Firm:	internal labour market
Adjustment:	unemployment

Industrial production world

Adapted from Salais[44] and Salais and Storper.[45]

The industrial world   The industrial world can be roughly defined as comprising medium-sized or large companies dedicated to mass production. The characteristic products in this world are standardized and generic and it is faced with short-term uncertainty on the global economic situation. The producer relies on forecasts in demand and profitability, all the more as these forecasts are taken into account in decision making regarding heavy material investments.

In relation to these features, the work organization is designed in a highly pre-established, prescribed and routinized manner, within strongly hierarchical procedures. Seniority in the firm is beneficial to the learning of these routines by personnel so that internal labour markets are developed. What matters regarding work is thus the qualification of tasks and their dispatching according to hierarchical principles. In this highly impersonal world, the person is only taken into account as having social rights: the person is identified to a job which supports and ensures the rights acquired because of the type of economic uncertainty. Insurances then allow some protection of income against the effects of uncertainty (reduced working time, unemployment).

Merchant production world   In the merchant production world, the economic uncertainties dealt with by the unspecialized labour convention are essentially price and quantity. Since the product is standardized, there is no need to mobilize any specialized knowledge normally 'withheld' by employees. Employees can thus be treated as ordinary individuals within the context of spot relations. The demands made on workers are expressed in objective terms, inscribed in organization and technology, to which the individual must respond without delay. Employees therefore tend to be organized by and associated with subcontractors who are in charge of a specific task, and are thus reduced to suppliers of available working time. This world displays the greatest variety of atypical employment forms (temporary employment, fixed-term contracts, multiple subcontracting, etc.).

Interpersonal world   The interpersonal world is governed by the merchant labour convention. In this world, the firm mostly confronts uncertainty in the area of product quality. The products are both specialized (based upon know-how) and dedicated (adjusted to the particular needs of a given demander). Thus the producer must have both the quality of work and the polyvalency of equipment at his or her disposal in order to securely deal with a diversity of product quality. As the necessary knowledge is mastered by employees, the quality of their work is directly assessed by the desire of others for the product, and the price it commands in the market. For this reason the labour convention is called merchant (not to be confused with the merchant production world) but differs from the 'pure' economic market, because goods and work are personalized among a community of persons.

The productivity convention is based upon equity, approached through common knowledge. Wage is thus both ruled by customs and immediately reflects the price of the product. Wages are determined according to the handiwork of teams often composed of craftsmen. Because of the specialized skills of the workers, in this world the unemployment convention is based upon the mobility and knowledge base of the worker.

What matters most is that the status of autonomy and competence is maintained, and that belonging through a shared history is perpetuated and respected in everyday interactions. So the typical firm in this world appears to be integrated in networks in which persons can move without threats to their identity. According to Salais[44] it is rather similar to Aoki's J firm.

The immaterial production world   In the immaterial production world, the firm faces total uncertainty: that of newness. Uncertainty is thus tentatively overcome in work interactions by a scientific pragmatism. The productivity convention is based upon internal methodological rules of work and upon trust. The critical investments are 'immaterial' (knowledge, know-how) and thus concern the people themselves. The quality of work cannot be assessed through the intermediary of the product, nor by the satisfaction of a person: there is no market ordeal. In this world the unemployment convention only consists of the mobility of the persons' knowledge and of its applications within a given field. In contrast to the merchant labour convention, this knowledge is not made of (secret) manufacturing methods but of concepts, and general empirical methodologies. In other words, it is based on scientific principle. Because there is no market ordeal and demand, most often, these activities are performed in services or branches of a large company, or in a small collective organization with some financial security, for example from specialized public funds.

In the conclusion to their extensive study of the economic identity of France compared with Italy and the United States, Salais and Storper[46] propose elements of diagnosis and prospects for each economy. The French study is dominated by references to the industrial production world, so the major issue, according to its industrial structure and the constrains of international economy, is how to improve the access to the merchant and immaterial worlds. There appears to be a search for a new recombining, both merchant (through technological flexibility) and immaterial (through investments in R&D), and this is the most likely path for economic development according to the conventional characteristics of the French economy (especially the role of the state, of the public and private elites, of the local actors). A prerequisite seems to be the maintaining of a social consensus around a conception of employment: jobs must be both highly productive and socially protected inside the firm.

According to this study, the economy of the United States is characterized by a lack of interpersonal and immaterial foundations, because its international advantage has been for long based upon Taylorization and mass production; features progressively given up because of international competition from countries with more flexible and innovative firms. Public policies have strongly organized the rules of the game (financial markets, competition policy, tax policy, labour markets), in other words have reinforced merchant principles, so that economic actors had no choice to act according to other principles and this constitutes, the authors claim, a major barrier to innovation.

They also propose that the success of the Italian economy (especially the north-east and central regions) was based upon interpersonal coordination (for instance, through the famous industrial districts). This industrial structure seems now less successful, with a stagnation and sometimes a decline in employment and the number of firms, because their market niches are less secure, competition is stronger, with larger European firms using more flexible technologies. The future of this interpersonal sector is uncertain because its traditional basis (entrepreneurship initiated by former agriculturists or unemployed skilled workers, local political conventions, strong regional identity) becomes slowly but steadily less available and relevant. A possible solution would be the return of hierarchy, for example through a stronger formalization of manufacturing networks.

Though their analysis is mostly economic, the importance of the work of these authors lies in the way they strive to articulate the characteristics of organizations in a dynamic manner, especially regarding internal organization and employment relations, inter-firm relations, groups of actors and institutions.

SUMMARY

This chapter provides a basis by which the reader may begin to gain a broad theoretical perspective on organizational dynamics and provides a means by which this can be seen in a multicultural/multinational context. We believe the comparative potential of the models we have reviewed has not always been fully exploited, and would provide a useful foundation for further research. While we accept that this review is not exhaustive, we hope we have shown that a comprehensive understanding of organizations requires an interdisciplinary approach, and that this may require the researcher to go beyond the traditional boundaries of organizational analysis.

STUDY QUESTIONS

1. Describe the principal differences which exist between the eastern and western views on the market–organization dilemma.
2. Discuss the arguments for and against the view that culture is a contributory factor to national differences in the functioning of organizations.
3. Discuss the extent to which theoretical models of the separation of the 'worlds' of culture correspond to the geographical segmentation of the societies which have been studied.

REFERENCES

1. Coase, R., The nature of the firm (1937), in Williamson, O.E. and Winter, S.G. (eds), *The Nature of the Firm — Origins, Evolution, and Development*, Oxford University Press, New York 1991, pp. 18–33 (1st edn. in 1937, Economica, **4**, pp. 386–405).
2. Williamson, O.E., *Markets and Hierarchies: Analysis and Antitrust Implications*, Free Press, New York, 1975.
3. Williamson, O.E., *The Economic Institutions of Capitalism: Firms, markets, Relational Contracting*, Free Press, New York, 1985.
4. Williamson, O.E., The logic of economic organization, in Williamson, O.E. and Winter, S.G. (eds), *The Nature of the Firm — Origins, Evolution, and Development*, Oxford University Press, New York, 1991, pp. 90–116.
5. Ouchi, W.G., Markets, bureaucracies and clans, *Administrative Science Quarterly*, **25**(1), 1980, pp. 129–41.
6. Ouchi, W.G., *Theory Z: How American Business Can Meet the Japanese Challenge*, Addison-Wesley, Reading, MA, 1981.
7. Ouchi, W.G. and Jaeger, A.M., Type Z organizations: Stability in the midst of mobility, *Academy of Management Review*, **3**, April 1978, pp. 305–14.
8. Aoki, M., *Information, Incentives and Bargaining in the Japanese Economy*, Cambridge University Press, New York, 1988.
9. Tyrni, I., *The Japanese Management Structure as a Competitive Strategy: the Importance of a Nexus of Long Term Treaties, Common Knowledge and Firm-Specific Learning*, in Schutte, H. (ed.), *The Global Competitiveness of Asian Firms*, Macmillan, London, 1994, pp. 35–47.
10. Aoki, M., Gustafsson, B. and Williamson, O.E. (eds), *The Firm as a Nexus of Treaties*, Sage, London, 1990.
11. Maurice, M., Sellier, F. and Silvestre, J.J., *Politique d'éducation et organisation industrielle en France et en Allemagne*, PUF, Paris (translation: *The Social Foundations of Industrial Power*, MIT Press, Cambridge, MA, 1986).
12. Whitley, R., The social construction of organizations and markets; the comparative analysis of business recipes, in Reed, M. and Hughes, M. (eds), *Rethinking Organizations*, Sage, London, 1992a, pp. 120–43.
13. Whitley, R., Societies, firms and markets: the social structuring of business systems, in Whitley, R. (ed.), *European Business Systems — Firms and Markets in their National Contexts*, Sage, London, 1992b, pp. 5–45.
14. Livian, Y.F., Du bon usage des comparaisons internationales, *Personnel*, **337**, 1992, pp. 72–5.
15. Amadieu, J.F., *Organisations et travail — Coopération, conflits et marchandage*, Vuibert, Paris, 1993.
16. Sorge, A. and Warner, M., *Comparative factory organization. An Anglo-German comparison of Management and Manpower in Manufacturing*, WZB Publications, Gower, 1986.

17. Lane, C., *Management and Labour in Europe: the industrial organization in Germany, Britain, France*, Edward Elgar, London, 1989.
18. Silvestre, J.J., Système hiérarchiques et analyse sociétale — Une comparaison France–Allemagne–Japon, *Revue Française de Gestion*, **77**, January–February, 1990, pp. 107–14.
19. Whitley, R., *Business Systems in East Asia — Firms, Markets and Societies*, Sage, London, 1992c.
20. Clegg, S., *Modern Organizations*, Sage, London, 1990.
21. Granovetter, M., Economic action and social structure: the problem of embeddedness, *American Journal of Sociology*, **91**(3), 1985, pp. 481–510.
22. Reynaud, J.D., Conflit et régulation conjointe — Esquisse d'une théorie de la régulation conjointe, *Revue Française de Sociologie*, XX, 1979, pp. 367–76.
23. Reynaud, J.D., *Les règles du jeu: l'action collective et la régulation sociale*, Armand Colin, Paris, 1989.
24. Thompson, G., Frances, J., Levacic, R. and Mitchell, J. (eds), *Markets, Hierarchies and Networks — The Coordination of Social Life*, Sage, London, 1991.
25. Nohria, N. and Eccles, R. (eds), *Networks and Organizations — Structure, Form and Action*, Harvard Business School Press, Cambridge, MA, 1992.
26. Powell, W.W., Neither market nor hierarchy: network forms of organization, *Research in Organizational Behaviour*, **12**, 1990, pp. 295–336.
27. Powell, W.W., Hybrid organizational arrangements: New forms or transitional development, *California Management Review*, **30**(1), 1987, pp. 67–87.
28. Inzerilli, G., The Italian alternatives: flexible organization and social management, *International Studies of Management and Organization*, **20**(4), 1990, pp. 6–21.
29. Locke, R.M., The political embeddedness of industrial change: corporate restructuring and local politics in contemporary Italy, in Kochan, T.A. and Useem, M. (eds), *Transforming Organizations*, Oxford University Press, New York, 1991, pp. 28–42.
30. Piore, M. J. Work, Labor and Action: Work experience in a system of flexible production, in Kochan, T. A. and Useem, M. (eds), *Transforming Organizations*, Oxford University Press, New York, 1991, pp. 307–18.
31. Swedberg, R., *Introduction à la sociologie économique*, Desclée de Brouwer, Paris (translated from *Current Sociology*, Sage, London, 1987).
32. Nohria, N., Is a network perspective a useful way of studying organization?, in Nohria, N. and Eccles, R. (eds), *Networks and Organizations — Structure, Form and Action*, Harvard Business School, Cambridge, MA, 1992, pp. 1–22.
33. Bradach, J.L. and Eccles, R.G., Price, authority and trust: from ideal types to plural forms, *Annual Review of Sociology,* **15**, 1989, pp. 97–118.
34. Granovetter, M., Economic institutions as social constructions: a framework for analysis, *Acta Sociologica*, **35**(1), 1992, pp. 3–12.
35. Granovetter, M., *Getting a Job — A Study of Contacts and Careers*, Harvard University Press, Cambridge, MA, 1974.
36. Biggart, N.W. and Hamilton, G.G., On the limits of a firm-based theory to explain business networks: the Western bias of neoclassical economics, in Nohria, N. and Eccles, R. (eds), *Networks and Organizations — Structure, Form and Action*, Harvard Business School Press, Cambridge, MA, 1992, pp. 471–90.
37. Boltanski, L. and Thévenot, L., *De la justification — Les économies de la grandeur*, Gallimard, Paris, 1991.
38. Eymard-Duvernay, F., Conventions de qualité et formes de coordination, *Revue Economique*, **40**(2), pp. 329–59.
39. Favereau, O., Marchés internes, marchés externes, *Revue Economique*, **40**(2), 1989, pp. 273–328.
40. Salais, R., L'analyse économique des conventions de travail, *Revue Economique*, **40**(2), 1989, pp. 199–240.
41. Thévenot, L., Les entreprises entre plusieurs formes de coordination, in Reynaud, J.D., Eyraud, F., Paradeise, C. and Saglio (eds), *Les systèmes de relations professionnelles*, CNRS, Paris, 1990, pp. 347–70.

42. Livian, Y.-F. and Herreros, G., L'apport des économies de la grandeur: une nouvelle grille de lecture des organisations, *Revue Française de Gestion,* **101**, November–December 1994, pp. 43–59.
43. Dupuy, J. P., Eymard-Duvernay, F., Favereau, O., Orléan, A., Salais, R. and Thévenot, L., Introduction, *Revue Economique*, **40**(2), 1989, pp. 141–45.
44. Salais, R., Incertitude et interactions de travail: des produits aux conventions, in Orléan, A. (ed.), *L'analyse économique des conventions*, PUF, Paris, 1994, pp. 371–403.
45. Salais, R. and Storper, M., *Les mondes de production*, Editions de l'Ecole des Hautes Etudes en Sciences Sociales, Paris, 1992.
46. Salais, R. and Storper, M., The four worlds of contemporary industry, *Cambridge Journal of Economics*, 16, 1993.

FURTHER READING

Cazal, D. (1993), Ethique et management interculturel: le confucianisme en Extrême-Orient, in Bosche, M. (ed.), *Le management interculturel*, Paris: Nathan, pp. 181–192.
Coase, R. (1988), The Nature of the Firm: Origin, Meaning, Influence, *Journal of Law, Economics and Organization*, **4**, 3–47.
Hamilton, G.G. and Biggart, N.W. (1988), Market, Culture and Authority: A Comparative Analysis of Management and Organization in the Far East, *American Journal of Sociology*, **94** (Supplement): pp. S52–S94.
Orléan, A. (ed.) (1994), *Analyse économique des conventions*, Paris: PUF.

SIX

CULTURE'S INVISIBLE FILTERS: CROSS-CULTURAL MODELS IN SOCIAL PSYCHOLOGY

INTRODUCTION

This chapter takes the traveller on an expedition into the world of social psychology and takes a look at its contribution to the understanding of 'national culture' at a comparative 'macro' level. We will be guided by the work of three influential writers on national culture, namely Hofstede, Trompenaars and Schwartz, who have contributed to our understanding of national culture and its influence on work and organizations; all have provided models enabling national cross-cultural comparisons relevant to the workplace.

To light our way, examples are cited throughout the chapter contrasting Western and Eastern cultures and specifically comparing Britain and Hong Kong. These areas and countries are selected because of their substantially different cultural characteristics according to the models provided by all three of our 'principal writers' and due to identifiable differences in economic performance between many countries (like Hong Kong) in the East which have experienced remarkably high growth compared to some (like Britain) in the West.[1]

Impressive economic development in the Pacific Rim has coincided with a growth in the application of the concept of 'culture' to organizations, management and economic development. When economies like Japan and Hong Kong have experienced decades of high growth in comparison to economies like the UK, which has been *relatively* stagnant, culture as a partial explanation of the difference becomes a variable worthy of closer examination. Initially, the success of Japanese industry prompted studies like Ouchi's Theory Z,[2] which we met earlier, which ascribes this success to social policies and management methods originating in Japanese culture. More recently the 'Overseas Chinese' have come under scrutiny to identify cultural reasons for the phenomenal success of Hong Kong, Taiwan and Singapore. This is not to say that culture is *the* single determinant of economic growth, but in relation to Hong Kong and other Overseas Chinese societies it has been argued that economic success is at least partly due to the economic and wealth-orientation of the culture. As such, national culture warrants inclusion as a contingency variable founded in the environment within which organizations operate.

Gordon Redding[3] proposes that culture is particularly influential in the economic sphere within Overseas Chinese communities and he describes their culture as an *economic culture*. The implication is that national culture is a fundamentally important influence on the economic behaviour of Overseas Chinese organizations. It is, however, dangerous to regard the concept of *economic culture* as deterministic as, according to Redding, 'The Overseas Chinese have an apparent distinct economic culture, that is describable, and the outline of its determinants can be drawn. It is still necessary to place it in a larger framework of explanation if the question of macro-economic performance is to be a consideration' and 'it is necessary to reassert that it [culture] is not seen as *the* dominant cause of economic success, obliterating or ignoring other factors like economic policy. Culture is one of several key features deserving a respectable place in any account.'

WHAT IS CULTURE ?

Lack of consensus in the study of 'culture' begins with the initial problem of definition. Thus, the problem is in answering the question 'What is Culture?' and the answer will influence all subsequent questions arising from a more detailed examination of the subject. In describing and explaining culture we are faced with considerable difficulties[4] resulting in a tendency for researchers to provide a selection of definitions which best capture its essence. This has generated a plethora of definitions. This is reflected in a survey of definitions by Kroeber and Kluckhohn[5] suggesting that definitions may be classified into six major classes which cover the many (hundreds) of definitions proposed. The rising number of definitions has not, however, been matched with a growing consensus as to the answer to the question 'What is Culture?'. Hofstede[6] characterizes culture as a type of 'mental programme' which is specific to groups and distinguishable from other 'mental programmes' like Human Nature and Personality (Figure 6.1).

Among social psychologists, and within psychological study with a particular emphasis in the comparative examination of culture, which we may term cross-cultural psychology, there appears to be some consensus as to what culture is and does. First, there seems to be a general acceptance that culture is something peculiar to the human species and its unique ability to *learn* principally through *communication*, mostly via language. The learning occurs through formal socialization and informal 'enculturation' which are social (collective) vehicles through which we understand a 'reality' which in turn configures behavioural parameters. Culture does not concern individual behaviour as it involves a shared system of meanings about this 'reality' learned among groups. Seen this way, culture may be regarded as an invisible filter of values and norms which acts as an intervening variable between the environment and human behaviour. Reflecting this perspective is the definition of cross-cultural psychology as 'the study of similarities and differences in individual

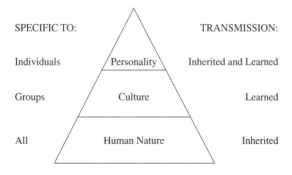

Figure 6.1 Levels of mental programming (adapted from Hofstede[6]).

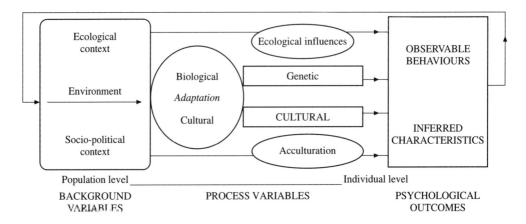

Figure 6.2 Conceptual framework for cross-cultural psychology (adapted from Berry *et al.*[1]).

psychological functioning in various cultural and ethnic groups; of the relationships between psychological variables and sociocultural, ecological, and biological variables; and of current changes in these variables'.[7] This view is represented diagrammatically in Figure 6.2.

Cross-cultural psychology is consequently an interdisciplinary subject acting between and synthesizing mostly collective-level, phenomenological, naturalistic analyses (such as anthropological study) and mostly individual-level, positivistic, experimental analyses (such as psychology). The subject also attempts to identify and synthesize both nomothetic and ideographic or 'emic' approaches and maintains a position of non-ethnocentric *cultural relativism* while engaging in a search for some universally applicable 'laws'. It is therefore the modern equivalent of a set of fundamental questions asked by scholars for several centuries.[8]

This general approach is analogous to the Indian fable of the elephant and the blind men. The fable tells of the blind men who, when independently examining the elephant by touch, could not understand what the animal was until they combined their experiences and, through cooperation, finally understood the object of their examination. The sentiment is therefore that different types of 'blindness' (i.e. anthropology and psychology) in social science require interdisciplinary cooperation of individually 'blind' social scientists in order to understand and see the subject better.

Although the interaction between the environment, culture and behaviour is a two-way affair (behaviour can affect the culture and the environment and vice versa), the emphasis of most studies is on the effect of the environment on culture and hence on people's behaviour. A central idea is that of cultural systems operating as providers of solutions to problems[9] faced by human groups. Such systems have social structures related to the form of social control used (using socialization, enculturation and the law) to enforce norms of values which delineate the parameters of acceptable behaviour. Culture therefore involves processes of nurturing, through social stimuli, a set of broadly held expectations of behaviour — thereby forming the basis for the behaviour of individuals.[10]

A crude but helpful analogy is with computers which need an operating system to tell them what the environment is like and what they are able to do. In human terms, therefore, culture can be likened to 'software of the mind' in the form of 'collective mental programmes' which configure our understanding of the environment and the parameters of acceptable behaviour.[6]

FOUNDATION MODELS

Here we take a short detour to look at some of the historical foundations of cross-cultural psychology, which have clearly provided the 'principal authors' with a basis upon which to build.

Kluckhohn and Strodtbeck's variations in value orientations

This anthropological study[11] has been widely quoted and used in cross-cultural research. The samples were of individuals from separate communities within rural south-eastern USA and the research instruments used were short stories that posed problems and alternative solutions. From the responses Kluckhohn and Strodtbeck were able to classify value orientations into five dimensions. The emphasis of this model is upon the idea that cultures respond to their environment through cultural assumptions which provide a framework for problem evaluation by combining cognitive, affective and directive dimensions. There are five basic common human modes of action reflecting orientations to human nature (evil–mixed–good), nature (subjugation–harmony–mastery), time (past–present–future), activity (being–being in becoming–doing) and relationships (lineality–collaterality–individualism) with corresponding cultural assumptions 'designed' to deal with them. Usunier[12] synthesizes Kluckhohn and Stodtbeck's model with Hofstede's, implying basic compatibility and synergy between the two, and thus supports the validity of both models.

The main problem with the 1961 study by Kluckhohn and Strodtbeck is that it is empirically supported by field research within a region of a single nation state among five small communities and as such is 'ethnic psychology'.[7] To assume that findings from such a limited sample can be extrapolated to all human societies as cultural universals must be regarded with suspicion. The value of the study is principally in showing that 'some general characterisations of cultural groups were possible using standard values measures'.

The Rockeach Value Survey (RVS)

Rockeach[13] in studying values in psychology using a US sample of about 1400 respondents distinguished two types of individual-level values; namely instrumental and terminal values (see below). Instrumental values are those concerning the modes of behaviour considered appropriate as the means to attain 'terminal' values, namely the idealized end-states of existence. Eighteen instrumental and terminal values were ranked by respondents some showing clear value differences with age. Examples of the RVS values are given in Table 6.1.

Ng *et al.*: RVS in Pacific Rim countries

S. H. Ng and his colleagues used a modified RVS in nine Pacific Asian countries[14] to a sample of 100 students in each of ten cultural groups. The outcome added four additional values relevant to developing societies and discriminant function analysis revealed two dimensions. The first opposes prosocial values to self-oriented values relating to hedonism and self-indulgence and the second opposes self-oriented values relating to inner strength with materialistic values.

HOFSTEDE'S MODEL OF NATIONAL CULTURE

Here we meet the legendary cross-cultural researcher Geert Hofstede[6,15] who has been by far the most influential scholar in the development of a theory of national work-related culture in the post-war period.

Table 6.1 RVS values

Instrumental values	Terminal values
Honest	Self-respect
Polite	Equality
Courageous	Freedom
Responsible	Salvation
Cheerful	True friendship

Hofstede's definitions of culture

Definitions of culture range from the very broad to the very narrow reflecting the extent to which culture permeates human experiences at different levels. Hofstede[6] recognizes the levels of culture by providing a narrow and a broad definition. The former concerns 'civilization' or 'refinement of the mind' and the concomitants of education, art and literature. The broader definition, which is derived from social anthropology and deals with more fundamental human processes (including those within the narrow definition), is the main concern for Hofstede. This broad definition is given as 'the collective programming of the mind which distinguishes the members of one group or category of people from another'.[15]

Levels of mental programmes

Culture manifests itself at different levels with the most apparent aspects like 'symbols', 'heroes' and 'rituals' which Hofstede collectively labels 'Practices'[6] in an 'onion diagram'. These practices are visible to outsiders but their meaning is only interpretable by insiders. At a deeper level are 'Values' which are at the cultural core and which are invisible; with those who hold them not being conscious of them. The 'onion diagram' representing the layers of culture is shown in Figure 6.3.

Values are defined by Hofstede as 'a broad tendency to prefer certain states of affair over others'. Values are attributes of individuals and collectivities (Hofstede refers to *norms* in the latter case), they are non-rational but determine our 'subjective definition of rationality' and are developed in the family, in schools and at work.

Values have both intensity and direction, they are distinguishable between the *desired* (phenomenological) and the *desirable* (deontological). Hofstede warns against the 'positivistic fallacy' of equating the *desired* and the *desirable* which 'leads to a confusion between reality and social desirability'. Values are central to Hofstede's study who views them, along with many social scientists (e.g. Schwartz[16]) as criteria affecting how actions are selected and justified, how people and events are evaluated and how reality is socially constructed.

Studies conducted by Kluckhohn and Strodtbeck,[11] Rokeach,[13] Ng *et al.*[14] Schwartz and Bilsky[17] and Schwartz,[16,18] emphasize the centrality of values in the study of culture and individuals. It seems clear, from these perspectives, that values and culture are interrelated and interdependent as 'values are among the building blocks of culture'.[15] Culture confers *identity* on a human group at a macro (societal / national) level. Hofstede uses the term 'sub-culture' to describe micro-level cultural systems like organizations or ethnic groups. Culture, for Hofstede, therefore concerns societies as social systems in homeostatic, quasi-equilibrium with societal

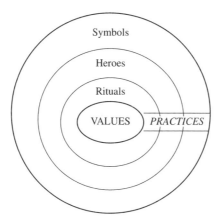

Figure 6.3   The onion diagram (adapted from Hofstede[6]).

norms or value systems at the centre interacting with 'ecological' origins and institutional 'consequences'.[15]

Hofstede contends that analyses of values at the individual level cannot be equated simultaneously with analyses at the 'ecological level' (defined by Hofstede as collective, societal, cultural) and to do so is an 'ecological fallacy' which confuses two separate and incompatible levels of analysis. This proposition is challenged most frequently by other psychologists concerned that 'the ecological or culture level approach [of Hofstede] does not yield individual level dimensions of values'[19] and challenged by Schwartz finding 'in contrast to Hofstede's findings, the dimensions derived at the two levels in our research appear to be closely related'.[16]

It is also suggested by Hofstede that mental programmes are intangible and exist as 'constructs' which are terms we use to define them into existence. This is fraught with problems as constructs are vulnerable to subjectivity and to the values of their creator and his or her own cultural background. Consequently we have the situation in cross-cultural studies of 'blind' researchers, with their own subjective perspective, trying to measure the subjective reality of individuals and organizations in another culture. To avoid research results which are meaningless, except to the researcher at the time of writing, it is therefore essential for social scientists examining culture to use research methods which are drawn from several sources, each providing a new perspective on the issue under study.

National cultures in Hofstede's terms

Travelling between the contrasting cultures of Hong Kong and Britain, we now look at Hofstede's model of national cultural differences and its relevance to work-related values. In a study of workers in over 40 countries Hofstede[15] initially categorized cultures on the basis of four dimensions: 'Power Distance', 'Uncertainty Avoidance', 'Individualism–Collectivism' and 'Masculinity–Femininity'.

Power Distance   Power Distance involves the universal issue of human inequality to which different societies have different solutions. It concerns inequality in power in a society, in families, at school and particularly at work. The central question in Hofstede's Values Survey Module administered to HERMES (IBM) employees internationally distinguishing differences between countries in Power Distance concerned *subordinates'* attitudes towards fear of expressing disagreement with managers.[20] Power Distance informs us about *vertical dependence relationships*. In countries with large PDI scores (i.e. Hong Kong) subordinates feel dependent on their superiors and are afraid to express disagreement. The result will either be a preference for an autocratic/ paternalistic boss or an outright rejection, but there is little indifference since the relationship is *morally* based. In contrast, within low-scoring PDI countries (i.e. the UK) there is less of a dependence and more of a *contractual* relationship between subordinates and superiors, resulting in a preference for a consultative rather than autocratic style of leadership. Power Distance therefore can be defined as 'the extent to which the less powerful members of institutions and organizations within a country expect and accept that power is distributed unequally'.[6] The source of PDI differences in the workplace is, according to Hofstede, in earlier periods of socialization when 'attitudes towards parents, especially fathers, and towards teachers, which are part of our mental programming, are transferred towards bosses'. The influence of Power Distance on organizations and work is pervasive according to Hofstede. The most significant influence is the effect of Power Distance on organizational structure as 'PDI is clearly related to the Aston dimension of "concentration of authority".'[15] By this Hofstede is proposing that PDI will affect the degree of centralization in an organization and the number of hierarchical levels present. The implication is that organizations in high Power Distance countries (e.g. Hong Kong) will tend to prefer greater centralized organizational structures than those in low Power Distance countries (e.g. the UK). Other consequences for organizations and work proposed by Hofstede are summarized in Table 6.2.

Individualism–Collectivism (I / C)   This dimension concerns the degree of *horizontal dependence of individuals upon the group*. Hofstede[6] provides a definition as:

> 'Individualism pertains to societies in which the ties between individuals are loose: everyone is expected to look after himself or herself and his or her immediate family. Collectivism as its opposite pertains to societies in which people from birth onwards are integrated into strong, cohesive in-groups, which throughout people's lifetime continue to protect them in exchange for unquestioning loyalty'.

The distinction between individualism and collectivism may be characterized by the difference between the 'I' or 'Me' society with the 'We' society, between what Tönnies[21] characterized as *Gemeinschaft* and *Gesellschaft*.

The survey questions on which the IDV index, which is Hofstede's measure of I/C, is based belong to a set of fourteen 'work goals' relating to the 'ideal job' for respondents. Individualist cultures placed emphasis upon a job allowing independence through 'personal time', 'freedom' and 'challenge' at work whereas collectivist cultures emphasize dependence upon the organization in providing 'training', good 'physical conditions' and enabling full 'use of skills'. This dimension tends to be negatively correlated with power distance and both dimensions were correlated with economic development. In terms of the two countries being used as examples here, Hong Kong is collectivist and the UK is individualist. In the workplace this dimension *fundamentally* affects the relationship between the employee and the organization. In highly individualistic societies this relationship is largely *contractual/transactional* and work is mostly organized and controlled with reference to the individual and his or her assumed economically rational and calculative self-interest. In contrast, in collectivist societies, the employment relationship is more *morally based* and management of groups is salient with personal *relationships* prevailing over the task with trust being the essential requirement for successful cooperation.

Table 6.2   Consequences of national PDI score differences for work and organizations

Low PDI (e.g. the UK)	High PDI (e.g. Hong Kong)
Decentralization	Centralization
Lower concentration of authority	Higher concentration of authority
Flatter organizational pyramids	Taller organizational pyramids
Hierarchy involves inequality of roles, established for convenience	Hierarchy reflects existential inequality between superiors and subordinates
Smaller proportion of supervisors in workforce	Higher proportion of supervisors in workforce
Narrow salary range between top and bottom. Lower differential in qualifications and status	Wide salary range between top and bottom. Higher differential in qualifications and status
Consultative relationship between superior and subordinate	Autocratic style of management
Ideal boss is resourceful and democratic	Ideal boss is benevolent/paternal
Mixed feelings about employee participation in management	Ideological support for employee participation in management
Informal employee consultation possible without formal participation	Formal employee participation possible without informal consultation

Adapted from Hofstede.[6,15]

Principal consequences proposed by Hofstede of national differences in the IDV index on organizations and work are summarized in Table 6.3.

Hofstede maintains that apart from East Asian communities which 'seem to have retained considerable collectivism in spite of industrialisation' because of the 'influence of the teachings of Confucius' and the *jen* philosophy, this dimension is the most likely area of international convergence.

Masculinity–Femininity   This dimension concerns the extent to which values are more 'masculine' (assertive, *competitive*, tough, results/performance oriented) in contrast to more 'feminine' (modest, *cooperative*, nurturing, tender, equity oriented). The different values an emphasis on work goals to satisfy 'ego' such as 'advancement' and 'earnings' on the masculine pole as opposed to interpersonal goals to satisfy the 'social ego' such as 'friendly atmosphere' and

Table 6.3   Consequences for differences in national IDV scores for work and organizations

Collectivist (e.g. Hong Kong)	Individualist (e.g. the UK)
Particularist relationships based on personal trust is basis for moral nature of work and business life	Universalist contractual transactions determine work and business activity
Promotion usually on ascriptive criteria	Promotion on 'merit' as defined by market criteria
Private and work life diffusely related	Private and work life specific and separate
Organizations protect well-being and long-term interests of member Policies and practices based on loyalty and sense of duty	Organizations not intensively involved with long-term welfare of member Policies and practices based on promotion of individual initiative
Underlying philosophy is Traditionalism	Underlying philosophy is Modernism
Management of groups Relationships prevail	Management of individuals Task prevails

Adapted from Hofstede.[6,15]

'cooperation'. The fundamental consequence for the workplace is in attitudes to work centrality in that the work ethos in 'masculine' cultures tends towards 'live in order to work' rather than in 'feminine' cultures where the ethos is more inclined towards 'work in order to live'.[6] This has consequences for how conflicts are resolved (by combat or compromise), types of motivation likely to be used (achievement/goal or welfare/socially oriented) as well as differences in the likely characteristics of 'heroes' (assertive/ decisive or intuitive/ consensus seeking). Principal consequences proposed by Hofstede for work and organizations of differences in national scores on the MAS index are summarized in Table 6.4.

In terms of the countries being compared as contrasting cultures in this chapter, namely the UK and Hong Kong, both score as moderately masculine on the MAS index. However, Confucian/ Taoist/Buddhist-influenced societies have a self-concept which is traditionally oriented, reflecting collective interdependence and social control based upon 'face' which is a 'social ego' more akin to feminine value systems despite the prevailing higher MAS scores in these countries. Logically therefore masculine values differ between the East and the West since their interaction (in the East) with Collective values and high PDI would seem to modify masculine values to a more benign form than the more interpersonally aggressive, competitive Western equivalent. This is reflected in the findings of a 'Chinese Values Survey' suggesting values in Hong Kong 'suggests "feminine" valuing more than "masculine"'' when measured on a scale constructed by Chinese minds.[22]

Uncertainty Avoidance   This dimension concerns 'the extent to which the members of a culture feel threatened by uncertain or unknown futures and situations. This feeling is, amongst

Table 6.4   Consequences of differences in MAS scores for work and organizations

High MAS	Low MAS
Managers have leadership, independence and self-realization ideals	Managers relatively less interested in leadership, independence, etc. More of a service ideal prevails
Managers expected to be decisive	Managers use intuition to strive for consensus
Belief in individual decisions, equity and competition	Belief in group decisions, equality and solidarity
Appeal of job restructuring permitting individual achievement	Appeal of job restructuring permitting group integration
Strong achievement motivation Achievement defined in terms of wealth and recognition	Weaker achievement motivation Achievement defined in terms of service, human contacts and living environment
Company interference in private lives accepted for legitimate reasons	Company interference in private lives rejected
Higher job stress More industrial conflict Conflict resolved by 'combat'	Lower job stress Less industrial conflict Conflict resolved by compromise
Gender-based occupational segregation	Less gender-based occupational segregation
Big is beautiful Growth more important	Small is beautiful Conservation more important
Fewer women in qualified jobs Women in such jobs highly assertive	More women in qualified jobs and not particularly assertive

Adapted from Hofstede.[6,15]

other things, expressed through nervous stress and in a need for predictability: a need for written and unwritten rules'.[6] In countries with high scores on the Uncertainty Avoidance Index (UAI) there is a greater willingness of employees to stay working for the company, reflecting a cautious approach to risk and a high degree of angst in the face of uncertain futures. The need for predictability and rules leads to a greater likelihood of bureaucracy as a means of structuring activities. In low UAI countries there is less anxiety about the future and, as a result, bureaucracy will be less apparent and job mobility will be higher.[23]

Organizations in societies with different ways of coping with uncertain environments themselves cope with uncertainty differently through the domains of technology, rules and rituals. The differences reflect a fundamentally different attitude to the environment or that which is 'usually taken to include everything beyond direct control of the organization'.[15] In dealing with uncertainty differently in different cultures, organizations will acquire and use technology differently and for different reasons. They will also employ rules and rituals differently in that these are likely to be more numerous, rigid and important in organizations within countries with higher UAI scores. A summary of Hofstede's proposed consequences for work and organizations of different UAI scores is shown in Table 6.5.

Hofstede[15] maintains that theories dealing with how organizations deal with uncertainty are divided into scientifically based normative theories assuming rational behaviour and descriptive theories assuming non-rational behaviour. Non-rational approaches have now begun to challenge scientific theories, which have proven increasingly brittle in the light of increasingly chaotic and turbulent environments. In the emergence of theories rejecting scientific approaches there is

Table 6.5   Consequences for work and organizations of differences in UAI scores

Low UAI	High UAI
Less structuring of activities	More structuring of activities
Emotional need for fewer written rules	Emotional need for more written rules
Relativism, empiricism	Absolutism, theoretical purity
More generalists	More specialists and experts
Organizations can be pluriform	Organizations standardized
Managers more involved in strategy, interpersonally oriented and flexible in style	Managers more involved in details, operations, tasks and consistent in style
Managers more willing to make individual and risky decisions	Managers less willing to make individual and risky decisions
High labour turnover	Lower labour turnover
Less ritual behaviour	More ritual behaviour
Smaller organizations	Larger organizations
Motivation by achievement	Motivation by security
High need for achievement determined in terms of recognition	Achievement determined in terms of security
'Hope of success'	'Fear of failure'
Less emotional resistance to change	More emotional resistance to change

Adapted from Hofstede.[6,15]

increasing attention to the importance of the perception of uncertainty in organizations and the focus upon strategy formulation as itself a cultural process.

In the original 4-D study the UK and Hong Kong were both classified as low scoring on the UAI. It should, however, also be pointed out that UAI (and therefore low UAI scores) may not be significant in Chinese societies as indicated by the construction of a values survey by Chinese rather than Western minds in The Chinese Values Survey (see below).

The Chinese Values Survey

More recently a fifth dimension has been added to the original 4-D model.[6] This new dimension is derived from the construction of a 'Chinese Values Survey' by The Chinese Culture Connection group.[22] It is directly relevant to our example of Hong Kong as it concerns 'Confucian Dynamism' which principally relates to the degree of long-termism inherent within a society. This dimension was named in this way since the research indicates that societies influenced by Confucianism (such as China, Hong Kong, Taiwan, Japan and South Korea) all share markedly high degrees of long-termism relative to all other countries. Hofstede points out that the Chinese Values Survey resulted in identification of three out of four of the dimensions identified in his own 4-D study. *None of the CVS factors, however, were correlated with uncertainty avoidance.* This is explained as a fundamental difference between Western and Eastern (particularly Chinese) cultures which means that Western cultures have a fourth dimension (uncertainty avoidance) related to different degrees to the search for 'Truth' whereas Chinese societies are more concerned with 'Virtue' — which gives rise to a different cultural dimension than that of uncertainty avoidance, termed Long-Term Orientation (LTO). It has been suggested that this is one of the fundamental reasons for the relative success of countries in the Pacific Rim influenced by Chinese culture as 'by showing the link between Confucian Dynamism and recent economic growth, the CVS research project has demonstrated the strategic advantage of cultures that can practice Virtue without a concern for Truth'.[6] It may also be that 'Confucian Dynamics' is an inappropriate label for this dimension since Confucian values are evident in both opposing poles and the term negates the contribution of other influences such as Taoism and Buddhism. Hofstede's adapted term for this dimension of Long-Term Orientation (LTO) will be used from now on. Its suggested significance in terms of comparative advantage is in cultivating a pragmatic synthesis in management where it seems 'What is true or who is right is less important than what works and how the efforts of individuals with different thinking patterns can be co-ordinated towards a common goal'. This dimension also emphasizes the inherent virtues of respect for tradition and ordered social structures based on status. The Chinese dimension of 'Human-heartedness' on the CVS correlates (negatively) with Masculinity and is characterized by values of kindness, courtesy and social consciousness. 'Integration' correlates (negatively) with Power Distance and is characterized by cultivation of trust, tolerance and friendship. 'Moral Discipline' correlates ($r = 0.54$) weakly with Collectivism and is characterized by group responsibilities as well as moderate, adaptable and prudent behaviour.[22,23]

Critiques of Hofstede's study

In reviewing Hofstede's 4-D study, Triandis[24] is largely complimentary with a few reservations. His principal objection is that in concentrating upon work-related values within IBM Hofstede limits understanding of cultural differences in depth and extent. Triandis suggests a fuller coverage of the topic in depth requires the inclusion of other levels of cultural difference involving perception, cognition and action as well as inclusion of further dimensions totalling twenty 'including the ones presented by Hofstede'. Triandis is also critical in more specific terms of Hofstede's 4-D study in suggesting 'severe limitations' due to the problems of:

1. The answers not being responses to questions derived from unstructured interviews with the respondents.
2. The meaning of the factors not being independently checked in each country.
3. The lack of checks needed to identify possible response styles in the data of members of each culture.
4. The absence of multimethod procedure for the measurement of each factor.

Other 'supportive opposition'[6] is provided in two reviews of Hofstede's 4-D study by Leonard Goodstein[25] and John Hunt.[26] The criticisms of Hofstede's methodology in these reviews reflect the most common misconceptions about Hofstede's work which relate to the appropriateness and size of the samples.

Most concern has been expressed about the use of IBM as the vehicle for this study which may cause 'some kind of built-in bias in the original sample because all individuals are employees of a single multinational'[25] or on the same point 'a sample of employees from one multinational organization inevitably raises questions when those results are generalized to entire societies'.[26]

In defending his sampling methods, Hofstede defends the use of IBM and the narrowness of his samples. He emphasizes that IBM was used to satisfy the principal requirement in cross-cultural surveys for functional equivalence and points out that the measures focus upon the *differences* between the samples rather than the absolute numbers. The implication is that the differences between these narrow, functionally equivalent samples reflect differences between the populations they represent. Sample sizes do not, therefore, need to be very large as 'The smallest sample, obviously determines the reliability of the study. However, if a sample is really homogeneous with regard to the criteria under study, there is very little gain in reliability over an absolute sample size of 50.'

SCHWARTZ'S MODELS

Schwartz and Bilsky[17,27]

These psychologists also used the RVS as a basis for a cross-cultural study of values involving seven countries including Hong Kong. They constructed seven motivational domains evident in all seven countries and discovered consistent oppositions and compatibilities. These proposed universals in value systems are the basis upon which Schwartz was able to develop a theory of universals in content and structure of values.

Schwartz's universals in the content and structure of values

Schwartz[16] provides the most recent research of note and the most substantive challenge to Hofstede's model in that, if further validated, it is likely to become regarded as a refinement of Hofstede and a seminal work in the field. The study does not confine itself to work-related aspects of culture but its potential as a unifying model warrants its inclusion here.

Schwartz proposes that in addition to formal features the primary content aspect of a value is the motivational concern it expresses. A universal typology of the different contents of values is derived by reasoning that values represent, as conscious goals, three universals of human existence concerning individual, social interaction and group needs. Eleven distinct universal motivational types of values (at the individual level) are proposed and ten are derived from the empirical data using Smallest Space Analysis. A set of dynamic relations among motivational types of values in terms of compatible or conflicting consequent actions is proposed and supported by the results. The individual level analysis shows some interesting findings. The value types are shown to form a circular *motivational continuum* rather than discrete entities. Thus partitioning into discrete value types is recognized as an expediency to facilitate research. The theorized dynamic relations amongst value types proposes *two higher-level dimensions* which are contiguous regions of compatible value types. These two dimensions 'organise value systems into an integrated motivational structure'.[16] The motivational continuum at individual-level proposed by Schwartz can be shown diagrammatically in Figure 6.4 .

The first higher-level dimension is labelled 'Openness to change versus Conservation' Openness to change bias results in a tendency to Self-direction and Stimulation value types (motivating people to follow their autonomous inner-directed interests in uncertain directions), whereas Conservatism leads to elements of combined Security, Conformity and Tradition (motivating people towards outer-directed avoidance of uncertainty to preserve the status quo in embedded relationships with close others, institutions and traditions). This dimension appears to resemble a combination of Hofstede's UAI and IDV but, as we shall see in the examination of the second of Schwartz's higher-level dimensions, there is sufficient reason to believe that it is substantially different or that UAI and IDV are perhaps the work-related context to Schwartz's trans-situational and abstract dimension.

The second higher-level dimension is labelled 'Self-Enhancement versus Self-transcen-

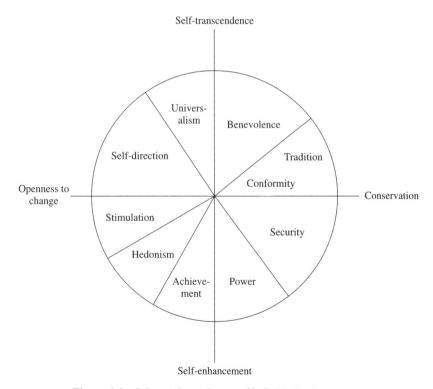

Figure 6.4   Schwartz's continuum of individual value sytems.

dence' and opposes Hedonism, Achievement and Power value types (motivating people to enhance their individualistic interests) against the combination of Universalism and Benevolence value types (motivating people to enhance the welfare of others and transcendence of selfish interests). At a broader level an individual interest region (Self-direction, Stimulation, Hedonism, Achievement, Power) and a collective interest region (Benevolence, Tradition, Conformity) are linked to complete the continuum by boundary regions that serve mixed interests (Universalism, Security). Schwartz emphasizes that the above 'interests facet' is not the same as Hofstede's Individualism–Collectivism (although clear similarities exist) since this is analysis at an individual and not a collective level of analysis. 'For example, the values wealth, social power, and authority, which primarily serve the interests of the individual person in our current analysis, tend to receive greater cultural priority in collectivist cultures in a culture-level analysis.'[16]

Accordingly, the implication is that clustering of values, as in Hofstede's study, is considered arbitrary by Schwartz since values exist relatively within a continuum defined by adjacent compatibles and opposite conflicts. Further, Schwartz suggests that Hofstede's method of standardizing scores to construct an index is flawed since 'standardizing changes the patterns of inter-relations among values within groups' and proposes an alternative procedure which, it is claimed, does not distort the structure of value relations in the same way. *Schwartz is proposing, with due respect to Hofstede, that the individual and the collective level dimensions of value systems are closely related structurally.* The configuration of values and value types between the individual and cultural level shows some content variation but the main differences between cultures is in terms of value priorities or in the hierarchical ordering of the relative importance afforded to values and value types.

Schwartz also finds at the individual level of analysis important differences in how PRC Chinese respondents construe the relations among collective and mixed interest values. The Chinese samples deviated from the universal or 'ideal' structure in that the values that constitute Universalism, Benevolence, Tradition, Conformity and Security could not be partitioned into regions representing each type. Instead they were partitioned into *three uniquely Chinese value types* consonant to the major 'religious' influences in Chinese culture: Taoism, Confucianism and Buddhism. Schwartz reports that Hong Kong was 'closer to the ideal structure and did not show this alternative pattern' although Hong Kong was among those samples that deviated most from the ideal structure.

Because Schwartz sees universality in the structure of values anchored in two higher-level dimensions he proposes hypotheses based upon this structure about the relations of value priorities with other variables. 'Two statements summarize the implications of the inter-relatedness of value priorities for generating hypotheses: (1) any outside variable tends to be similarly associated with value types that are adjacent in the value structure; (2) associations with any outside variable decrease monotonically as one goes around the circular structure.' As a result, the whole pattern of associations regardless of statistical significance rather than the significance of single correlations or mean differences is considered to reflect the validity of the theory. Predicted associations between outside variables and value priorities are represented graphically with a sinusoid curve.

For the purpose of this chapter the most interesting prediction using this method is the hypothesis regarding differences in value priorities between persons from *communal* societies versus *contractual* societies. Schwartz hypothesises that Tradition, Conformity, and Benevolence are more important in communal societies (such as Hong Kong) in contrast to the higher importance of Self-direction, Stimulation, and Universalism in contractual societies (such as the UK).

Schwartz compares his Taiwan (communal) sample with New Zealand (contractual) and finds the highest priority afforded to Security followed by Power and Conformity in Taiwan with the emergence of Benevolence as an unexpected priority in the New Zealand sample. Schwartz concludes that it may be preferable to compare the value priorities of cultures on value types derived from analysis at the cultural level as they are configured slightly differently from their individual equivalents. In doing so Schwartz is effectively conceding that Hofstede's cultural-level approach, designed to avoid the 'ecological fallacy', is more appropriate in this case, suggesting that even if the individual and cultural levels are structurally similar they should be regarded as separate for purposes of analysis of content.

Schwartz's two higher-level dimensions are useful bases upon which to examine principal themes in how culture influences work and organizations. The first higher-level dimension, 'Openness to Change versus Conservation', could equally be termed 'Modernism versus Traditionalism' in terms of concomitant ideology since the value structures represented appear to correspond to differences between modern and traditional societies (*Gemeinschaft* and *Gessellshaft*) particularly with regard to their *attitudes to the environment*.

The second higher-level dimension, 'Self-enhancement versus Self-transcendence', reflects opposing individual as against collective interests which also involves power and is reflected in the frequency with which this issue arises in cross-cultural studies. It is particularly influential in understanding differences in relationships with and *attitudes towards people* in that collective cultures are more relationship and people oriented whereas individualistic cultures are more atomistic, contractual and transactional. These higher-level dimensions are pervasive in all aspects of life and particularly influence management.[28] They must therefore be understood within that broader context.

Schwartz's culture-level analysis

Schwartz more recently[18] extends his individual-level analysis to the cultural level and supports a view of 'culture as a complex, multi-dimensional structure rather than a simple categorical variable'.[29] In recognition of the seminal status of Hofstede's work values suitable for uncovering Hofstede's dimensions are included in the analysis which serves as a 'check on the replicability of the Hofstede dimensions with a different method of measurement'.[18] The claim is that a more exhaustive examination of values based upon the 1992 study and a more adequate sample of nations will enable the determination of a more universally inclusive model of cultural dimensions which, by implication, will provide a more refined model than Hofstede's.

Schwartz used two types of matched samples to enable a check on the robustness of the value dimensions generated. The respondents included schoolteachers and university students and data was collected between 1988 and 1992 from 86 samples drawn from 41 cultural groups in 38 nations. Schwartz argues that 'there are cultural reasons to expect culture-level and individual-level value dimensions to be related conceptually' and proposes four hypotheses predicting the distinct types of values likely to be found in a culture-level analysis and the structure of relations amongst them based upon his own individual-level analysis and upon the work of Hofstede, Kluckhohn and Strodtbeck and Triandis.

The first hypothesis is presented thus:

'1. There is a broad dimension interpretable as a more sharply defined version of I/C. This dimension can and should be defined into more specific types of values to reduce confusions in the literature (Schwartz, 1990). Loosely defined, I/C has received considerable support in culture-level analysis. Its apparent usefulness for discussing cultural differences suggests that it does reflect an aspect of reality.'

The implication is that the extensive literature in the discussion of Individualism/Collectivism from Triandis and many others[30,31] emphasize multiple contrasts which Hofstede's dimension does not accommodate. Two major themes are identified in the contrasts mentioned. The first is the main focus of Hofstede's IDV index as it concerns whose interests take precedence in the conflict between personal and group interests (in parallel to Self-enhancement/Self-transcendence at the individual level of analysis). The second, which Schwartz contentiously considers more appropriate for defining the culture-level dimension related to I/C, concerns the autonomy or embeddedness of a person in relation to the group (in parallel to the individual-level dimension Openness to Change/Conservation) and is labelled *autonomy/conservatism* (A/C). The implication of this assumption appears to be that Schwartz considers I/C (A/C) to be principally concerned with group *embeddedness* in contrast to Hofstede's dimension which emphasizes priorities between individual and group *interests*.

The second hypothesis is presented as follows:

'2. In every society, people must manage their interdependence with one another. There is a culture-level value dimension that reflects the way societies procure and/or enforce the necessary consideration for the welfare of others and coordination with them in the course of coping with interdependencies. One pole of this dimension is related to the use of power.'

This hypothesis incorporates Hofstede's Power Distance with values associated with the Power value type identified at the individual level. In terms of I/C it is more closely identifiable with Hofstede's dimension. The implication is that Schwartz considers PDI and IDV to be indistinguishable. Schwartz predicts that this dimension will be closely related (e.g. adjacent) to *conservatism*.

The third and fourth hypotheses are framed as :

'3. There is a culture-level value type that emphasizes actively mastering the environment and changing the world (expressed in such values as success, ambition, daring). This recalls the mastery pole in Kluckhohn and Strodtbeck's (1961) man-nature orientation and is related to Hofstede's masculinity dimension. It is the societal response to the problem of eliciting individual productivity, reflected at the individual in the achievement value type, that emphasizes assertive achievement and success. Mastery is likely to be adjacent to the power/hierarchy type, with which it shares a broad concern for self-enhancement.
4. There is a culture-level value type that includes values that express concern for the welfare of others and emphasize harmony with nature (e.g. social justice, equality, protecting the environment). This type is the societal response to the problem of eliciting prosocial action. The existence of such a type is suggested by the existence of individual-level value types — benevolence and universalism — that are responses to the same issue. This type is also suggested by the femininity pole of Hofstede's masculinity dimension. Benevolence, universalism, and femininity all emphasize caring for the weak and the quality of life. Kluckhohn and Strodtbeck (1961) distinguish one component of this type, harmony with nature, which they postulate to be opposed to mastery. These approaches taken together suggest that this set of values forms a broad self-transcendence value type opposed to mastery and hierarchy.'

These four hypotheses are reframed into two broader hypotheses regarding the relationship between the content and structure of values. It is proposed that the content (of the higher-order value types) and structural organization of values into competing types is conceptually similar. Specifically it is hypothesized that:

'1. Autonomy versus Conservatism (parallel to individual-level Openness to Change versus Conservation and closest to the core idea of I/C).

2. Hierarchy and Mastery versus Egalitarian Commitment and Harmony With Nature (parallel to individual-level Self-Enhancement versus Self-Transcendence).'

In short, Schwartz proposes a cultural continuum based upon some of Hofstede's dimensions plus some of Kluckhohn and Strodtbeck's dimensions and which draws heavily upon the findings of his individual-level study with regard to the content and structure of values. The values included in the analysis are those identified in the 1992 study to have culturally consistent meaning for individuals and the principal statistical techniques are virtually identical to those used in the individual-level study.

   In reporting the results Schwartz reports 'As hypothesized, culture-level values are organized into the same two basic dimensions that organise individual-level values'. These relationships are presented in Figure 6.5.

Conservatism versus Autonomy   Conservatism reflects sociocentric values primarily concerned with security, conformity and tradition. It is negatively correlated with Hofstede's IDV and so reflects 'collectivism' in Hofstede's terms. Intellectual and Affective Autonomy opposes Conservatism. Autonomy reflects values primarily concerned with egocentric values concerned with self-direction, stimulation and hedonism. It is positively correlated with Hofstede's IDV and so reflects 'individualism' in Hofstede's terms. This supports Schwartz's first (narrow) hypothesis which seeks to refine I/C since 'when the loose I/C concept is narrowly understood as Autonomy versus Conservatism, a polar opposition may exist that is not found for broader definitions of the I/C concept'.

Self-enhancement versus self-transcendence   Hierarchy and Mastery form a broad region of interests relating to self-enhancement. Hierarchy emphasizes the legitimacy of hierarchical role and resource allocation. It is not correlated with Hofstede's PDI which probably 'reflects a difference between the concepts. The Hierarchy values emphasize the legitimacy of using power to attain individual or group goals in general. The PD items refer quite narrowly to legitimacy of

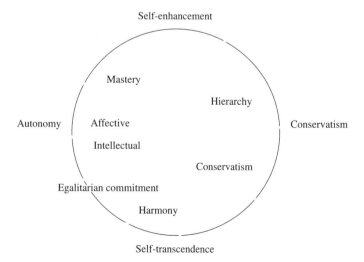

Figure 6.5   Schwartz's continuum of cultural values.

power inequality in employee-boss relations.' Mastery values emphasize active mastery of the social environment through self-assertion promoting active efforts to modify the environment to get ahead of other people and Mastery is positively correlated with Hofstede's MAS scores. Opposing Hierarchy and Mastery are dimensions of values promoting self-transcendence; namely Egalitarian Commitment (EC) and Harmony. EC values exhort voluntary commitment to promoting the welfare of others which is a necessary social requirement promoted in a society of autonomous individuals and more inherent in collective/conservative cultures.

The pattern of intercorrelations with the other value types is interesting. EC is negatively correlated with Hierarchy and Mastery as well as Conservatism and positively correlated with Intellectual and Affective Autonomy. This means that 'valuing emotional attachment and promotive interaction with others is not the unique hallmark of societies in which so-called collectivist values are given priority over individualist values'. In other words, prosocial action is a socialized value in individualist cultures and an inherent consequence of collectivist cultures which does not require promotion through value systems. In terms of Hofstede's dimensions EC is weakly correlated with UAI on both samples.

Harmony emphasizes harmony with nature and is found opposite Mastery and Hierarchy. Harmony concerns values such as 'World at peace' and 'Social justice' and is orthogonal to the autonomy/conservatism dimension. In terms of Hofstede's dimensions it correlates positively with UAI.

Schwartz's Continuum of Cultural Values may thus become regarded as a refinement of Hofstede's model. Hofstede's IDV dimension is reformulated into Autonomy/Conservatism which also indicates similarities in the rankings of nations although 'the proportion of variance shared by the ratings of nations in the two studies indicates that they are far from identical'. In terms of UAI and MAS some correlations are evident as outlined above but 'The relatively low magnitude of these dimensions suggests, however, that the conceptual content measured by these Hofstede dimensions and by the value types is quite different, and/or that the nations have changed considerably in 20 years'.

The value types show a reasonable pattern of association with Hofstede's dimensions but the conceptual differences between the two studies reveal some surprisingly different characterizations of nations. Hong Kong is included in the analysis but the UK unfortunately is not. This means that we cannot use the UK in comparison with Hong Kong as throughout the rest of the chapter but as a proxy we can compare the USA with Hong Kong.

The first surprise is that on the narrower definition of individualism represented by Autonomy, the US sample does not show to be particularly autonomous individualistic although the US score is higher than Hong Kong for Affective and Intellectual autonomy. The US does appear to be high on Mastery along with Hong Kong which reflects the entrepreneurial culture of both countries and, as expected, both countries score relatively low on Harmony. The other scores represent differences that might be expected but there is no apparent bipolar difference in scores between the USA and Hong Kong, which supports the proposition that Hong Kong is something of a cultural melange between Eastern and Western value systems.

Summary   The principal value of Schwartz's culture-level model is that, if further validated, it offers the prospect of refinement of Hofstede's work. The arrangement of value types and broad dimensions into a continuum which organizes them into an integrated structure of conflicts and compatibility's rather than discrete categories is more intellectually coherent and may prove to elevate Schwartz's model into a position of a seminal work. The model provides a more complex relationship between cultural variables and is sometimes more appropriate in terms of observable phenomena. The model also enables us to categorize two broad cultural archetypes of societies with substantively different assumptions about life and work. The first archetype centrally adopts autonomous values along with value tensions between Mastery in terms of self-enhancement and EC/Harmony in terms of self-transcendence and can be labelled *modernist/contractual cultures*. The second archetype centrally adopts conservative values and accommodates value tensions between Hierarchy and Harmony and can be labelled *traditionalist/relationship cultures*. Before discussing what these differences might mean for management theories, work and organizations, the work of one more influential contributor to our understanding of culture requires examination.

TROMPENAARS' SEVEN DIMENSIONS OF CULTURE

Hofstede's work may be seen as an empirical extension of a framework first proposed by Inkeles and Levinson in 1969.[15] Trompenaars[9] has similarly produced apparent empirical support for a combination of dimensions partly based on Parsons and Shils' 'General Theory of Action'[32] and Kluckhohn and Strodtbeck's 'Variations in value orientations'.[11] In considering the former study Hofstede implies that the theory is victim of an 'ecological fallacy' since 'they do not take into account that different variables could operate at different levels'. Nevertheless, despite the fact that the Hofstede and Trompenaars studies reflect different frameworks and the former is more academically rigorous, their conclusions are remarkably similar. This is particularly so in their attack on the universal validity of Western management theory and practice. Trompenaars' dimensions have been shown to be conceptually related principally to IDV and PDI[33] and as such can be interpreted as supportive of Hofstede's model by emphasizing some of the consequences of IDV and PDI for organizational behaviour, attitudes and beliefs.

Trompenaars is more concerned with the concept of culturally relative *meaning* at the individual level of analysis and defines seven dimensions of culture. The first five come under the broad heading of 'Relationships with people' which includes Universalism versus Particularism, Individualism versus Collectivism, Neutral versus Emotion, Specific versus Diffuse and Achievement versus Ascription. The sixth dimension concerns 'Attitudes to Time' and the final dimension 'Attitudes to the Environment'. It is useful to look at these in turn and in relation to the dimensions of Hofstede, again using the UK and Hong Kong as illustrative examples of cultural difference.

- *Universalism versus Particularism*: This concerns 'rules' in contrast to relationships as principal determinants of interpersonal behaviour. In a strongly universalist culture such as the UK and the USA[9] personal relationships should not interfere with business decisions. Nepotism is frowned upon and contractual agreements are the referees of conduct. Logical, 'rational' analytical thinking and impartial professionalism are ideal characteristics to cultivate and standards to maintain. Particularism is statistically associated with Hofstede's Individualism as Particularist cultures such as Hong Kong[9] are normally also Collectivist[15] and therefore also high PDI.[3] In such cultures institutionalized obligations to friendship and kinship are considered 'moral' requirements (the CVS equivalent of Collectivism is labelled 'Moral Discipline' and the equivalent of Power Distance is 'Integration') which are maintained through personalism, 'face', paternalism and other Confucian social network mechanisms. In such cultures cognition emphasizes 'connectedness' and holistic understanding of the *gestalt* using intuition and synthetic mental processes rather than rational and analytical techniques.

- *Individualism–Collectivism*: Trompenaars' second dimension is almost identical to Hofstede's dimension of the same name and is consequently also conceptually related to the CVS dimension of Moral Discipline. It is associated by Trompenaars and Hofstede to the concept of *Gemeinschaft* and *Gesellschaft* with, for example, Hong Kong retaining the traditional, family-based characteristics of the former and the UK adopting the 'modern' characteristics of the latter. Trompenaars warns, however, of the danger of oversimplification since the concept of 'collectivity' is heterogeneous.[9] This warning arguably also applies to the concept of individualism, also in the light of Schwartz's models.

- *Affective versus neutral cultures*: This dimension concerns the extent to which emotions or feelings may be expressed in interpersonal communication and Trompenaars puts British as more 'neutral' than Hong Kong culture although, interestingly, US culture is shown more 'affective' than both. This dimension does not seem directly related to any of those from Hofstede or Bond. Hofstede[15] does suggest that in general there is a greater need for affective relationships in individualistic societies partly because relationships are more by choice than in collective societies where they are more prescribed.

- *Specific versus diffuse relationships*: This dimension concerns the difference between 'specific' or low-context cultures like the UK where relationships are separated by the role of each party and 'diffuse' or high context cultures like Hong Kong where relationships exist in 'multiple areas of our lives and at several levels of personality at the same time'.[9] This distinction means that in a diffuse society personal, leisure and family life is not rigidly distinct from life at work and relationships transcend many or all aspects of life. There is a conceptual relationship with IDV and PDI in that relationships with superiors and with peers are interdependent and integrated in the sense that they do not end when one returns home in the evening as 'everything is connected to everything'. This, for example, concerns marketing as the relationship with customers is also diffuse and 'upfront investment in building relationships in such cultures is as important, if not more so, than the deal'. One principal concomitant within Hong Kong and other Asian societies is the prevailing importance of 'face' in all interpersonal relationships. This is often difficult for managers from 'specific' cultures to understand and deal with when dealing with people from more diffuse cultures and we will return to the issue in more detail below when discussing 'relating to nature'.

- *Achieving or ascribing status*: In some societies status is accorded on the basis of achievement whereas others ascribe status on the basis of durable characteristics such as age. For example, Hong Kong is shown as a more ascriptive culture than the UK and this dimension seems conceptually related to PDI and IDV. Achievement in ascriptive cultures is less an individual and more of a collective concern and organizations in these societies justify a high power distance and the resulting hierarchy as requisite 'power-to-get-things-done'. Power in such cultures does not require legitimizing in the same way as in achievement-oriented cultures and abuse of power is checked by the moral responsibilities inherent in patron–client type relationships.

- *Perceptions of time*: Different attitudes towards time (past, present and future) are reflected by the contrast between notions of time as linear and 'sequential' and notions of time as circular and 'synchronic'. Such differences affect how we coordinate, plan and organize. The UK is a 'sequential' culture where the focus is rational efficiency epitomized by maxims such as 'there is a time and a place for everything'. In contrast, a synchronic culture allows parallel activities and is less oriented towards punctuality and the focus in a synchronic culture is more likely to be upon effectiveness than efficiency. Trompenaars in discussing this dimension gives no comparative measure of orientation to compare the UK with Hong Kong.

As indicated above, the UK is described as 'sequential' and by inference we would expect Hong Kong to be 'synchronic' since 'Cultures which think more synchronously about time are more we-oriented (collectivist) and usually more particularist in valuing people known to be special'. There is a connection between this dimension and Hofstede and Bond's LTO/Confucian Dynamics as 'Individualist cultures with a sequential view of time, like America and Britain, are usually short-term in their business strategies. Collectivist cultures with a synchronous view of time, like Germany and Japan, are typically long-term strategically'.[9]

- *Relating to nature*: The distinction here concerns different attitudes towards the natural environment and beliefs about nature's ability to be controlled. 'Inner-directed' cultures wish to subdue nature and tend to identify with mechanical models for institutions whereas outer-directed cultures feel more dependent upon the environment and see themselves more as a part or product of the environment. The UK is shown to be more internalized than Hong Kong at the personal level but similar in attitudes to the natural environment. There is a connection between this dimension and Hofstede's Individualism as 'In the collectivistic Chinese society (and in other Asiatic societies, such as Japan, as well), the individual is not "inner-directed" at all but controlled by a need for not losing face.'[15] A link is also clear with 'human heartedness' (or '*jen*') and therefore Masculinity since 'The Chinese use the word *jen* (*jin* in Japanese) for "man" in order to describe the "human constant" which includes the person himself plus his intimate societal and cultural environment which makes his existence meaningful. The Chinese will modify their views more easily in terms of their environment'.

The seven cultures of capitalism

In collaboration with Charles Hampden-Turner, Trompenaars applies his cultural dimensions to six Western industrial countries plus Japan.[34] In this text the dimension 'neutral versus emotional' is replaced with an alternative dimension 'equality versus hierarchy' which appears to closely resemble Hofstede's Power Distance. Not surprisingly, the major dichotomy is shown between Anglo-Saxon and Japanese culture with France, Germany, Holland and Sweden adopting varying positions between them.

The message of Hampden-Turner and Trompenaars is to submit that as cultures face dilemmas in relationships with people, with time and with the environment differently it is necessary to recognize and reconcile differences and attempt to synthesize the advantages inherent in all cultures. It is a reiteration of the view that there in no 'one best way' of managing and no objective truth in how to best generate wealth. The mechanistic metaphors attributed to organizations and markets is largely a product of Anglo-Saxon culture which cultivates a tendency towards 'scientific management'. Cultures which most tenaciously hold to this mechanistic model are the poorest performers even by their own 'objective' measurements except perhaps in commodity markets where quality and value added are less important. Japan's success and Britain's lack of it has, therefore, much to do with 'national' culture according to this perspective.

CONSEQUENCES FOR MANAGEMENT THEORIES, WORK AND ORGANIZATIONS

Modernism versus traditionalism, work and the environment

It is generally agreed that changes in the sociocultural environment induce 'acculturation' in the individuals within it. Most studies in this area concentrate on the effects of modern industrialization and the consequent transition from traditionalism to modernism.[10] Acculturation takes place at the collective and individual level and modernization theories, which attempt to explain the relationship between collective cultural change (or '*zeitgeist*') and individual psychological responses, tend to treat the latter as either independent, mediating or dependent variables. These approaches obviously generate different perspectives but they have two things in common. The first is their focus upon individual behavioural variables and the second is that these variables need to be measured.

Management theories are often culture-bound. For example, McClelland's Achievement motivation can be regarded as culture-bound in modernist/individualist culture.[35] This theory, which treats personality as an independent variable in modernization, submits that a sufficiently high level of achievement motivation (N_{Ach}) along with achievement opportunity are prerequisites for modern industrial development to take place. This premise is more a reflection of the ideological concomitants of modernism/individualism as 'This prescription is a good generalization of the Protestant ethic, of the "American Dream," and the dreams of many others to acquire the material comforts that an environment that richly rewards hard work can provide'.[10]

Similar achievement motives might have been expected in Hong Kong and the UK in terms of McClelland's 'need for achievement' (and esteem) since both countries have weak UAI and strong MAS scores,[6] although how achievement is interpreted may differ between societies because of differences in long-term orientation, individualism and in the nature of masculinity. It may be that a more general paradigm incorporating achievement with these and other factors will be developed in time to form a more appropriately universal theory of motivation.

Other needs such as 'respect, harmony, face and duty' are somewhat neglected in the somewhat ethnocentric view of the world provided by McClelland and other Western management theorists and as a result these theories in their original form do not qualify as adequate foundations for cross-cultural study. This extends to more recent theory also as Hofstede explains the 'popularity in the United States of "expectancy" theories of motivation, which see people as pulled by the expectancy of outcomes, mostly consciously'[15] as explicable in terms of the assumed 'calculative involvement' of highly individualistic Americans in organizations. By implication expectancy theories are not considered to be appropriate in a traditionalist/collective society like Hong Kong.

Individual versus collective interests, work and human relationships

Triandis[36] proposes that we distinguish individualism–collectivism at the group level with 'idiocentric–allocentric' values at the individual level. Further studies identify the relationship between the two domains. In a study of Chinese and Australian subjects Forgas and Bond[37] show the individualistic Australians with idiocentric values and the collectivist Chinese with more allocentric values. Individual or collective interests are clearly also related to modernism or traditionalism with individualism associated with modernism and collectivism with traditionalism.[7]

The cultural characteristics of a country affect conceptions of human nature produced in a society will influence the managerial theories produced therein. One influence is the degree of individualism which, according to Hofstede, provides an environment where theories of motivation such as those of Maslow are inappropriate for collective societies where higher motives are unlikely to be 'self-actualization' (as in Anglo-Saxon cultures) but the interests and honour of the in-group and harmony/consensus in the society collectively. Real motivators (as opposed to 'hygiene factors' in Hertzberg's terms) are likely to be different in Hong Kong from in the UK because of power distance.

In Hong Kong, large power distance leading to dependence should be seen as a real motivator as 'the motivator should rather be labelled the *master*. He differs from the "boss" in that his power is based on tradition and charisma more than on formal position.'[6] Maslow's needs hierarchy has been shown to be structurally similar among *managers* in fourteen countries although the same study indicates relatively large differences in need satisfaction.[38] Hofstede casts doubt upon this study and accuses it of the confusion of the 'reverse ecological fallacy' of the construction of cultural (ecological) indices from variables correlated at individual level which in this case involves forcing data into classifications compatible with Maslow's theory.[15]

A corollary of the achievement motive in individualistic/modernist cultures are the consequently culture-bound attitudes to competition and performance. Modern Western industrial societies tend to encourage individual competitiveness[39] and 'each individual is out for himself'.[40] Performance, merit or 'equity' are the approved criteria for allocating reward in achievement oriented–society[41] whereas ascriptive criteria, need and 'equality' are more influential in collective cultures[42] where a greater propensity to cooperate, particularly among in-group members,[43] is more common than competitive behaviour and attitudes.

However, in examining whether individual contribution to work sharing varies between individualistic and collectivistic countries, Latane and his associates identify a near-universal practise of 'social loafing' in that people working in groups where individual outputs are not measured tend to contribute less effort than when they work individually.[44] In reporting this phenomenon Segall *et al.*[10] cite evidence in studies of collectivist non-Western societies such as India, Thailand, Malaysia, and Japan with a range of tasks and subjects examined.

A notable exception was again a study in China which showed in contrast a degree of 'social striving' among Chinese workgroups which was also evident in another study of Taiwanese schoolchildren compared with American schoolchildren.[45] In support of this, Hofstede[6] reports on a comparative study of Chinese and American management trainees, where a series of tasks were undertaken individually or collectively and anonymously or undisguised showed that the Chinese participants (in stark contrast to the Americans) performed best with a group goal and anonymously. In the same way another study involving Chinese compared to American subjects showed a greater propensity to share responsibility among the Chinese subjects.[46]

Culture and organizational structure

Hofstede maintains that (culturally derived) implicit models of organizations cannot solely explain why Hong Kong and Singapore 'have been doing very well in modernising themselves'[6] but restates that structure of organizations has cultural antecedents. Combining Mintzberg's five typical configurations of organizations with his four cultural dimensions leads Hofstede to propose that the implicit model for Hong Kong organizations is the 'simple structure' which corresponds to the 'family' model whereas in the UK it is the implicit structure in the 'adhocracy' which corresponds to the 'village market'. Characteristics of each implicit structure are quite different particularly concerning preferred control/coordination and key parts of the organization. Essentially the focus, according to this model, within Hong Kong organizations is the 'owner' whereas in UK organizations it is the 'support staff', reflecting a fundamental difference in power distance. If one accepts this then it seems clear that Hofstede is providing a theoretical basis which is empirically supported by the work of Redding, indicating that organizational structure is one vehicle through which the comparative cultural advantage inherent in Hong Kong (relative, for example, to the UK) manifests itself in economic activity. Redding's work elaborates on the detail of the simple structure/family model and describes both limitations and inherent benefits.

This is not to suggest that simple, family-owned and managed organizations working in networks are *per se* somehow more effective than adhocracies, rather it suggests that in Hong Kong 'this special form of organization is peculiarly well adapted to its socio-cultural milieu'[3] enhancing the possibilities for culturally contingent excellence and contributing to our own understanding of the reasons for the phenomenal success of East Asian societies with an '*economic culture*' like Hong Kong.

SUMMARY AND CONCLUSIONS

In this chapter we have met three 'principal authors' in the subject area of national culture, namely Hofstede, Schwartz and Trompenaars, and we have seen the ways in which Hong Kong and the UK differ through their eyes. We have seen that Hofstede's model has been recognized as the seminal work in the field and provides a means by which cultures may be compared on the basis of four 'universal' cultural variables. We have also seen that this model may still need some improvement and that Hofstede has himself more recently added a 'fifth dimension' to the original model as a result of the work of The Chinese Culture Connection. Schwartz's models were both similar to and different from that of Hofstede. They are similar in that the values described are comparable to those of Hofstede — the differences are attributable partly to the fact that Schwartz's models are not restricted to work-related values. The principal difference was described as the assertion that individual and collective value systems are structurally equated and hence that cultural value systems are not discrete from each other but should be thought of as existing in a continuum of interrelated preferences. Trompenaars' model was shown to be conceptually related to Hofstede's dimensions of Individualism–Collectivism and Power Distance and offers some practical answers for managers involved in cross-cultural ventures.

All three of these models contribute to our understanding of the nature and importance of national culture to management and organizations. There is still, however, work to be done to unify these theories into a comprehensive and simple framework of reference for cultural analysis and management.

STUDY QUESTIONS

1. What is culture and how can it be measured?
2. What common threads can be found linking the various socio-psychological models of culture?
3. What do the models of culture tell us about the ways in which cultures interrelate?
4. In what ways can socio-psychological studies of culture provide support for managers of international businesses?

REFERENCES

1. Bond, M.H. and Hofstede, G., The cash value of Confucian values, in Clegg, S. and Redding, S.G. (eds), *Capitalism in Contrasting Cultures*, Walter de Gruyter, Berlin and New York, 1990.
2. Ouchi, W.G., *Theory Z*, Addison-Wesley, Reading, MA, 1981.
3. Redding, S.G., *The Spirit of Chinese Capitalism*, Walter de Gruyter, Berlin and New York, 1990.
4. Ralston, D. *et al.*, Differences in managerial values: a study of U.S. and PRC managers, *Journal of International Business Studies*, 2nd quarter 1993.
5. Kroeber, A.L. and Kluckhohn, C., *Culture: A Critical Review of Concepts and Definitions*, Vintage/Random House, New York, 1963.
6. Hofstede, G., *Culture and Organizations*, p. 64, McGraw-Hill, London, 1991.
7. Berry, J.W. *et al.*, *Cross-Cultural Psychology: Research and Applications*, Cambridge University Press, Cambridge, 1992.

8. Jahoda, G., The ancestry of a model, *Culture & Psychology*, **1**, 1995, 11–24.

9. Trompenaars, F., *Riding the Waves of Culture*, The Economist Books, London, 1993.

10. Segall, M.H. *et al.*, *Human Behaviour in Global Perspective: An Introduction to Cross-Cultural Psychology*, Pergamon Press, Oxford, 1990.

11. Kluckhohn, F.R. and Strodtbeck, F.L., *Variations in Value Orientations*, Greenwood Press, Westport, CT, 1961.

12. Usunier, J.C., *International Marketing: A Cultural Approach*, Prentice Hall, Englewood Cliffs, NJ, 1993.

13. Rokeach, M., *The Nature of Human Values*, Free Press, New York, 1973.

14. Ng, S. H. *et al.*, Human values in nine countries, in Rath, R. *et al.* (eds), *Diversity and Unity in Cross-Cultural Psychology*, Swets & Zeitlinger, Lisse, 1982, pp. 196–205.

15. Hofstede, G., *Culture's Consequences*, Sage, Beverly Hills, CA, 1984.

16. Schwartz, S. H., Universals in the content and structure of values: theoretical advances and empirical tests in 20 countries, *Advances in Experimental Social Psychology*, 1992.

17. Schwartz, S.H. and Bilsky, W., Towards a universal psychological structure of human values, *Journal of Personality and Social Psychology*, **53**, 1987, 550–62.

18. Schwartz, S. H., Beyond individualism/collectivism; new cultural dimensions of values, in Kim *et al.* (eds), *Individualism and Collectivism; Theory, Method, and Applications*, Sage, Beverly Hills, CA, 1994, pp. 85–119.

19. Bond, M.H., Finding universal dimensions of individual variation in multicultural studies of values: the Rokeach and Chinese Value Surveys, *Journal of Personality and Social Psychology*, 55, 1988, No. 6, 1009–15.

20. Hofstede, G., Scoring Guide for VSM, IRIC, PO Box 143, 2600 AC Delft, The Netherlands, 1982.

21. Tönnies, F., Community and Society, Harper & Row, New York [1887] (1963).

22. Bond, M.H., Chinese values and the search for culture-free dimensions of culture: the Chinese Culture Connection, *Journal of Cross-Cultural Psychology*, **18**, No. 2, June 1987, 143–64.

23. Adler, N.J., *International Dimensions of Organisational Behaviour*, PWS-Kent Publishing Co., Belmont, CA, 1986.

24. Triandis, H. C., Review of culture's consequences: international differences in work-related values, *Human Organisation*, **41**, Spring 1982, No. 1.

25. Goodstein, L. D., American business values and cultural imperialism, *Organisational Dynamics*, Summer 1981, 49–54.

26. Hunt, J. W., Applying American behavioural science: Some cross-cultural problems, *Organisational Dynamics*, Summer 1981, 55–62.

27. Schwartz, S.H. and Bilsky, W., Towards a theory of the universal content and structure of values: extensions and cross-cultural replications, *Journal of Personality and Social Psychology*, **58**, 1990, 878–91.

28. Schneider, S. C., Strategy formulation: the impact of national culture, *Organisation Studies*, 10/2, 1989, 149–68.

29. Clark, L.A. Mutual relevance of mainstream and cross-cultural psychology, *Journal of Consulting and Clinical Psychology*, **55**, 1987, 461–70.

30. Triandis, H.C. *et al.*, Allocentric versus idiocentric tendencies: convergent and discriminant validation, *Journal of Research in Personality*, **19**, 1985, 395–415.

31. Hui, C. H. and Triandis, H.C., Individualism–collectivism: a study of cross-cultural researchers, *Journal of Cross-Cultural Psychology*, **17**, 1986, 225–48.

32. Parsons and Shils, *Towards a General Theory of Action*, Harvard University Press, Cambridge, MA, 1951.

33. Lowe, S., Hermes revisited, 1994 International Symposium on Pacific Asian Business, 7th Annual Proceedings: The Dynamics of Global Co-operation and Competition, PAMI Honolulu, Hawaii, U.S.A.

34. Hampden-Turner, C. and Trompenaars, F., *The Seven Cultures of Capitalism*, Piatkus Books, London, 1994.

35. McClelland, D.C., *The Achieving Society*, Van Nostrand, Princeton, NJ, 1961.
36. Triandis, H.C., Collectivism vs. individualism: a reconceptualization of a basic concept in cross-cultural psychology, in Bagley, C. and Verma, G.K. (eds), *Personality, Cognition and Values: Cross-Cultural Perspectives of Childhood and Adolescence*, Macmillan, London, 1988, pp. 60–95.
37. Forgas, J. and Bond, M.H., Cultural influences on the perception of interaction episodes, *Personality and Social Psychology Bulletin*, **11**, 1985, 75–88.
38. Haire, M. *et al.*, *Managerial Thinking: An International Study*, Wiley, New York, 1966.
39. Munroe, R.L. and Munroe, R.H., *Cross-Cultural Human Development*, Brooks/Cole, Monterey, CA, 1975.
40. Whiting, B.B. and Whiting, J.W.M., Task assignment and personality: a consideration of the effects of herding on boys, in Lambert, W.W. and Wiesbrod, R. (eds), *Comparative Perspectives on Social Psychology*, Little, Brown, Boston, MA, 1971, pp. 33–45.
41. Hui, C.H. and Triandis, H.C., Measurement in cross-cultural psychology: a review and comparison of strategies, *Journal of Cross-Cultural Psychology*, **16**, 1985, 131–52.
42. Kashima, Y. *et al.*, Conceptions of person: implications in individualism–collectivism research, in Kagitcibasi, C. (ed.), *Growth and Progress in Cross-Cultural Psychology*, Swets & Zeitlinger, Lisse, 1987.
43. Triandis, H.C. *et al.*, Individualism and collectivism : cross-cultural perspectives on self- ingroup relationships, *Journal of Personality and Social Psychology*, **54**, 1988, 323–38.
44. Latane, B. and Nida, S., Ten years of research on group size and helping, *Psychological Bulletin*, **89**, 1981, 308–24.
45. Gabrenya, *et al.*, Social loafing on an optimising task: cross-cultural differences among Chinese and Americans, *Journal of Cross-Cultural Psychology*, **16**, 1985, 223–42.
46. Hui, H., Measurement of individualism–collectivism, *Journal of Research in Personality*, **22**, 1988, 17–36.

FURTHER READING

Adler, N., A typology of management studies involving culture, *Journal of International Business Studies*, Fall 1983, 29–47.
Ajiferuke, and Boddewyn, 'Culture' and other explanatory variables in comparative management studies, *Academy of Management Journal*, **13**, 1970, 153–63.
Bhaget, R. S. and McQuaid, S.J., Role of subjective culture in organisations: a review and directions for future research, *Journal of Applied Psychology Monograph*, **67**, October 1982, No. 5.
Hofstede, G., Do American theories apply abroad? A reply to Goodstein and Hunt, *Organisational Dynamics*, Summer 1981, 63–8.
Kerr *et al.*, *Industrialism and Industrial Man*, Harvard University Press, Cambridge, MA, 1960.
Laurent, The cultural diversity of Western concepts of management, *International Studies of Management and Organisation*, **xii**, 1–2, 75–96.
Redding, S.G., Competitive advantage in the context of Hong Kong, *Journal of Far Eastern Business*, 1, 1994, No. 1, Autumn.
Redding, S.G., Cultural effects on the marketing process in Southeast Asia, *Journal of the Market Research Society*, **24**, 2, 98–122.
Ronen, S. and Shenkar, O., Clustering countries on attitudinal dimensions: a review and synthesis, *Academy of Management Review*, **10**, 1985, No. 3, 435–54.
Smircich, L., Concepts of culture and organisational analysis, *Administrative Science Quarterly*, **28**, 1983, 339–58.
Tse, D. *et al.*, Does culture matter? A cross-cultural study of executives' choice, decisiveness, and risk adjustment in international marketing, *Journal of Marketing*, **52**, October 1988, 81–95.

CHAPTER

SEVEN
AN ANTHROPOLOGICAL JOURNEY

INTRODUCTION

Here our journey leads us to the roots and origins of culture. Our guides will be drawn from the ranks of the social anthropologists — those whose job it is to link us to our history and to the world around us.

The trouble with anthropology

A survey of the literature will suggest — in what amounts to a paradox — that anthropology, of all the core disciplines driving contemporary cross-cultural models of management and organization, is the least relevant of them all. We say paradoxically, because the term *culture* is generic to anthropology and detailed accounts of the workings of key societal institutions are its bread and butter. A similar issue is with the term and domain of *organizational culture* which spectacular growth since the early 1980s owes little to anthropology as a core discipline. Only recently two modest collections have attempted to change that by providing an anthropological perspective to the subject.[1,2]

A discussion of this so far weakened position of anthropology is relevant to our journey because, apart from adding an understanding of where most of the scholarly effort is currently invested (and where it is not), it also illuminates a classification problem we have to face: what should be considered an 'anthropological' model? Is Hofstede's theory an anthropological model? Surely not: he employs a classical social-psychological methodology, if there ever was one. But until his recent retirement, Professor Hofstede titled the position he held at the university of Limburg as 'chair in organizational anthropology'. In his key texts[3,4] he calls upon anthropological evidence for support in interpreting his findings. Or take the case of Fiske[5,6] who derived his theory from anthropological fieldwork (including his own), but has been developing (and publishing) it in the psychological domain.

To an extent, this is a healthy state of affairs: the disciplinary dichotomy in the social sciences is somewhat artificial in any case and its usefulness questionable. However, the concentration of models in the psychological, economic and even philosophical quarters of the social sciences suggests a well-known weakness in the discipline that underlines the relatively underdeveloped state of anthropological models in organization and management in general and of its cross-cultural aspects in particular. This is a lack in explicitly drawing on anthropological concepts and methodology, an absence of 'a certain readiness of mind and heart' to acknowledge an anthropological perspective.[7]

Not only has the discipline suffered the loss of patronage with the demise of colonialism (notably in the UK and France) and an identity crisis (e.g. about the position of indigenous ethnographers; the political relevance of anthropology) but anthropology has also been reluctant to play an active role in the industrialized world, in informing organizations and their incumbents on the merits of an ethnographer's gaze. Claude Lévi-Strauss, the eminent French anthropologist noted that 'many anthropologists including myself may have chosen their profession as an escape from a civilization and from a century in which they did not feel at ease' (Lévy-Strauss and Eribon, 1988, quoted in Hofstede[4]).

The drift towards psychology

A structural hurdle for any cross-cultural model stressing an anthropological approach is our inbuilt tendency to look for psychological explanations. Goffman called it an assumption about our assumptions — *the requirement to demonstrate the sanity behind our actions*, which he considered to be the most basic rule of social action, underpinning all others.[8]

The following account, from Stewart and Bennett[9] — possibly the best study of cross-cultural differences pertinent to organizations in the anthropological genre — demonstrates this tendency well:

'Twenty executives were brought together to participate in a training program. The executives were members of a large American corporation; they had been drawn from the north-eastern part of the United States. One or two had been hired from other companies, and one was an Englishman recently arrived from abroad.

The training program was designed so they could become acquainted with each other before beginning the process of setting policy for a new plant built by the corporation in the southern part of the United States. As preparation for one of their training sessions, they had read a recent book on management techniques. During the session they discussed its content so as to clarify their own policies on management.

The group quickly became polarised. The majority of the American managers occupied one position (a few remained silent) while the British engineer — highly trained and experienced — took an opposite position in the discussion. As the managers talked, their language became more heated and the comments more personal...The Americans were exhibiting a characteristic pattern of thinking which is inductive and operational. Heavy emphasis is placed on efficiency but little attention is paid to the overall framework in which one's actions take place...

In contrast, the British engineer was specific in his search for guidance from his own ideas and past experience. He wanted to consider concrete instances to which to apply his theories and to avoid adopting the general principles of the Americans which he considered vague anticipations of the future. He judged that the Americans were concerned with uncertain generalities which might not come about, that their thinking was unclear, and their use of language was confusing. For their part, the Americans judged the Englishman to be obnoxious, antagonistic, and disruptive to the harmonious working of the group.

Neither the Englishman nor his American colleagues recognised the source of their difficulty. The cultural differences in patterns of thinking were readily projected to personal and unfavourable characteristics of individuals, who were then assigned disruptive social motives.' (Emphasis added)

The 'Bongo-Bongo' propensity

Anthropology has another in-built structural hurdle when it comes to theory building. Its methodological emphasis on small-scale, person-to-person (ethnographer–subjects) interaction within a confined community; and its accent on the specificity of cultures (as against the other disciplines: psychology, sociology, economics — that emphasize universality) have resulted in the all too familiar ethnographic aversion from classification, which Mary Douglas[10] who we shall meet in a moment, calls 'this is all very well but it doesn't apply to the Bongo-Bongo' attitude. Generalizing does not come easily to ethnographers.

What counts as anthropological?

What then would qualify incorporation in a chapter on anthropological models of cross-cultural organization and management? Given the dire state of affairs described above, a pragmatic stand is called for: anyone who insists to be working in the anthropological cannon, employing the concepts, methods and conventions of the discipline should be included; and/or if one's work clearly points towards an anthropological bias.

Altman[11] has stated that it is important to differentiate between two key aspects of any model as a means of classification: first, the level of analysis being carried out and second, the methodology in use. Level of analysis refers to the frame of reference: society, group or individual. Methodology refers to the tools employed to support such an analysis. Some congruence is assumed between these two dimensions: a larger unit of analysis (society, organization), for example, is better served by sociological/anthropological methodology; a smaller unit of analysis (individuals) may benefit from a psychological approach.

By that logic, Hofstede's model and methodology clearly pursue an individual frame of reference (subjective self-report questionnaires, carefully matched samples). His is a sort of projection from inside towards the outside — an inside-out or cultural inductive approach. The internal validity of his findings is high (and over the years they have been replicated with success); but generalization becomes an art of informed guesswork: why should country *a* cluster with country *b* and not *c* will always remain somewhat of a mystery — recall that by Hofstede's own admission, his factor analysed data accounts for only 49 per cent of the total explained variance and his commentary on that is illuminating: 'Whether explaining half of the differences is a lot or not depends on one's degree of optimism. An optimist will call a bottle half full while a pessimist will call it half empty'.[4]

Mary Douglas's model, which we shall see in a moment, aims at a different frame of reference. Its level of analysis is the society (*Gesellschaft*) or the group (*Gemeinschaft*). Hers can therefore be thought of as a *projection from outside in:* inferring the characteristics of a given culture from an externalized perspective. While conceptually her model is well construed and elegantly argued, its ability to predict and explain individual differences in specific events (its internal consistency) is limited.

The two models are therefore diametrically positioned against each other on these two dimensions and since we have already spent a good deal of time with Hofstede and his fellow inside-outers, we will now spend time with Mary Douglas and her followers (Altman in particular) and will consider the merits of the outside in perspective.

Also dwelling in the anthropological quarters is Philippe d'Iribarne. His model is a meticulous reconstruction of cultures from a uniquely singular projection of three specific work environments. Although he does not propose an overall frame of analysis, his methodology stands out as a rich source for future development. Also from France is Emmanuel Todd, whose insightful study on family structures fits well with this group. All share a common approach, which may indeed be treated as a classificatory description for an anthropological approach to theory building — a typological (ideal model) approach.

Before we depart on our outside-in expedition, it is worth noting that there are a number of important studies which should not be described as typological, notably those of the veteran of the cross-cultural trade: Edward T. Hall, the studies of Stewart and Bennett (*American Cultural Patterns,* 1991) and Bellah *et al.* (*Habits of the Heart*), and, of course, the scholarship of Florence and Clyde Kluckhohn whose seminal work spanning three decades (from the 1940s to the 1960s) has had a formative impact on many, inside and outside the anthropological sphere. If a definition is warranted, perhaps the terms *value orientations* or *cultural patterns* may best describe this approach.

Another difference between the *typological* and *pattern* approaches comes to mind: the first is primarily European (counting its principal proponents), the second is clearly American: not only are the scholars Americans, but the studies take the USA as their standard comparative benchmark.

Section structure

Before we set out, a final word of caution is in order. While the other parts of our journey have led us to look at well-developed and, in some instances, rigorously tested models, the anthropological section can only highlight a selected number of contributions in the domains of work organization and management. More often than not, application of more general contributions has to be made to these domains. This state of the art, we feel, gives us licence to introduce in some detail an anthropological model (Altman's) which specifically aims to address the realms of work organization and management — though it is still at a developmental stage.

We start by a meeting with Mary Douglas where we will be introduced to a 'meta theory' under which banner all other typological approaches will be discussed. Douglas's work is by far the most influential in this genre (as manifested in the number of scholarly works induced by her model) and therefore has the best potential for providing the framework required from an anthropological theory of the workplace in a cross-cultural perspective.

MARY DOUGLAS'S GRID/GROUP (CULTURAL THEORY)

Basic tenets

Cultural Theory, introduced by the eminent British anthropologist Mary Douglas,[10,12] — also known under its earlier name as Grid/Group Analysis (thereafter: G/G), is a typological method for comparing cultures and the forms of social organization that support them. The model, based on evidence derived from non-industrial societies, has led over the past twenty-five years to well over a hundred publications[13] and has by now been applied to a variety of societal institutions and thematic case studies, as far apart as religion,[10] Chinese medieval history, theatre, geology and mathematical sciences,[14] ecology,[15] occupational crime,[16] industrial safety[17] and risk behaviour,[18] to name a few.

The model proposes that an individual's behaviour, perception, attitudes, beliefs, and values are shaped, regulated and controlled by constraints that can be grouped into two domains, labelled as *group commitment* and *grid control*. Combined, these project four prototypes of social environment: four possible scenarios of social life. These types are presented in Figure 7.1. The following description of the constituted four prototypes of G/G is adopted from Gross and Rayner.[17]

Group, the horizontal coordinate, represents the extent to which people are driven by or restricted in thought and action by their commitment to a social unit larger than the person. High

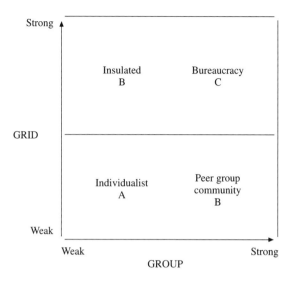

Figure 7.1   Four types of social environment (adapted from Gross and Raynor[18]).

group strength results when people devote considerable time and attach great importance to interacting with other members of their unit. In general, the more things they do together, and the longer they spend doing them, the higher the group emphasis.

Mars[16] proposes four tests for group strength: *frequency*, degree of *mutuality* and *scope* of interpersonal interactions and the group's *boundary tightness* (inclusion/exclusion). Group strength is low when people negotiate their way through life on their own behalf as individuals, neither constrained by, nor reliant upon, a single group of others.

Grid, the vertical coordinate, is the complementary bundle of constraints on social interaction — a composite index of the extent to which people's behaviour is constrained by normative role differentiation. (The term 'grid' here should not be confused with other grid models (such as 'managerial grid').[19] A strong grid environment operates whenever roles are distributed on the basis of explicit public social classifications, such as sex, colour, position in a hierarchy, office, descent (by clan or lineage), or point of progression through an age-grade system. A weak grid social environment is one in which access to roles depends upon personal abilities, skills, qualifications, etc. to compete or negotiate for them, or even of formal regulations for taking equal turns. In either case, where access to roles is not dependent on any ascribed characteristics of rank or birth, we would recognize a low-grid condition.

What is the meaning of each one of the quadrants presented in the figure?

Weak grid/weak group   Quadrant A (weak grid/weak group) is an environment which allows the maximum options for negotiating contracts or choosing allies. Consequently, it also allows for individual mobility up and down the scale of prestige and influence. The past or one's ancestry are relevant only inasmuch as they impinge on the present. Each person is responsible for oneself and for whoever else he or she chooses, not for the weak or the needy, unless one wishes it so.

Strong grid/weak group   Quadrant B (strong grid/weak group) is an environment in which the way a person may behave is strongly regulated according to one's socially assigned classifications. It is often a hierarchical environment in which most people are classified according to well-established and formalized rules. Perhaps the classifying criterion is ancestry, and all roles are based on its correlatives. Or perhaps the criterion is age, so that each person passes through a stream of age-related categories. Unlike quadrant A, the control exerted in this environment is not that of one person forcing his or her will upon another, but rather that of a whole society ready to negotiate only those deals that reinforce the pervasive social classifications.

Strong grid/strong group   Quadrant C (strong grid/strong group) is where one might find tradition-bound institutions in which everyone knows one's place, but in which that place might vary with time. Personal security is obtained at the expense of overt competition and social mobility. Examples of this type of social organization include bureaucracies that base their roles on seniority (an ascribed basis) rather than merit (an achieved basis), or a cohesive tribal society with hereditary roles. Such a bureaucratic environment might occur in the civil service or a strongly unionized industry — where promotion is based on length of service rather than competitively upon relative ability.

Weak grid/strong group   Finally, quadrant D (weak grid/strong group) is a social context in which the external group boundary is typically the dominant consideration. All other aspects of interpersonal relationships are ambiguous and open to negotiation with emphasis on egalitarianism and active participation. Leadership tends to be charismatic and lacking clear rules for succession. The suspicion of infiltration by outsiders or betrayal by group members is rampant here.

CULTURAL THEORY (G/G) OF WORK AND ORGANIZATION

Since Douglas formulated her model[12] and its further elaboration by her followers (notably Thompson et al.[20]) a number of applications have been proposed, either for the organizational or the cross-national arena. Altman[11,21] and Mutabazi et al.[22] apply the G/G model in the context of organizations, with particular emphasis on cross-cultural differences embedded in the four cosmologies of the Douglas typology.

A definition of culture

While working within the Douglasian cosmology, Altman departs from G/G in some significant ways. Altman[21] defines culture as 'a state of mind — personal, corporate, national — which construes a *Weltanschauung* (model of the world) made up of *a basic assumption about the nature of relationships between people* (at work) which is supported, sustained and changed by the advent of social-economic institutions (the major sectors of the economy), the labour market, the tradition of industrial relations, key public attitudes (e.g. the role of women in society) and pertinent legislation (e.g. the place of trade unions in the labour market)'.

On change and the perception of change

The Altman model assumes that culture is not static, as seen, for instance, in the case of national culture, which is in a constant flux of change, urged on by the force of events, be they war or fashion. Consider some key national representations of the UK: the Royal Family (in its present form), Big Ben, Ascot, Wimbledon and strawberries, fish and chips, to name a few. None of them can be easily tracked down more than 150 years or so.

Closer to our times, consider the Western economic image of Japan today (an economic superpower) and in the 1930s (producer of junk goods); the Czech Republic in the 1930s (a leader in emerging industries, like automation and aviation) and today (an assembly-line backwater for German industry). Or compare the Soviet Union, now defunct, between the early 1960s under Khrushchev — a winner in the space race, an inspiration for emerging new democracies (in Africa and Latin America), a model for social/economic development (India), a proud empire. Barely two decades later, in the latter years of the Brezhnev era, the perceived image was rather different — a superpower in retreat on the world scene (Afghanistan), a declining economy and worsening living standards (increasing food shortages, a rise in infant mortality), defeatist cynicism reigning. Only twenty years separate these images. *Change therefore is the counterbalance to the centrifugal, inward-looking tendency of the core, or basic assumption; that of the assumed nature of relationships.*

Interpersonal relationships and basic assumptions

The central postulate of the Altman model is the idea that organizational life is construed of different perceived options of interpersonal relationships (see below). In this it corresponds to Fiske's theory of sociality[5,6] which argues that up to four possible social relation types may be operational at any given time in any given context, although Altman's model suggests that a culture — whether personal, corporate or national — lends preference to one basic assumption, which acts as a core paradigm, actively organizing all related precepts — attitudes, beliefs and expectations as well as perceived actions — in tandem. This basic assumption concerns the nature of relationships (transactions) at the workplace.

In this, the model follows a similar postulate to that of d'Iribarne (who follows Bell, who follows de Tocquville) and implicitly to that of Douglas, whose theory implies that a culture may be characterized by one major configuration, which dictates an integrative social representation and mental construction, manifested in one of the four environments of the grid and group dimensions. Altman's model also builds on the groundbreaking work of Emmanuel Todd on family structures as the core paradigms of social and ideological systems. His work therefore merits a detailed mention.

Todd's typology

In his book *The Explanation of Ideology,* Todd[23] proposes that to understand the current diversity of political and ideological forms across the world (as, for instance, the seemingly haphazard adoption of the Marxist–Leninist doctrine in different parts of the world), one needs to resort to an analysis of the basic interpersonal configurations embedded in family relationships, and made manifest in ideologies covering issues like parent–children interaction, rules of inheritance (relations between siblings) and preferences for spouse choice. Clearly, with the demise of Communism in the 1990s, some doubts will be cast on the soundness of his thesis since it treated political movements as a true manifestation of the freewill of people and nations. While this judgement may have been proved to be rather naive, the basic tenets of his work still merit consideration. Todd puts forward the following hypothesis:

'The ideological system is everywhere the intellectual embodiment of family structure, a transposition into social relations of the fundamental values which govern elementary human relations: liberty or equality, and their opposites, are examples. One ideological category and only one, corresponds to each family type.' (page 17)

Todd thus embarks on an ambitious project devising a typology of family structures which

'must be both logically exhaustive, starting from first principles and setting out all the possible family structures; and empirically exhaustive, that is to say taking into account and describing all the family forms which are actually observable on the surface of the planet. Second, it must be shown that to each family form described there corresponds one and only one ideological system and that this ideological system is not to be found in areas of the world which are dominated by other family forms.' (page 18)

The principle that guides Todd (his core assumption) is that

'anthropological structure...is self-perpetuating. The family by definition reproduces people and values. Unconsciously but inevitably, each generation absorbs those parental values which define elementary human relationships: between parents and children, between siblings, between husband and wife. The power of the reproductive mechanism springs from the fact that it does not need to be conscious or expressed: it is automatic and has its own internal logic.

In practice each generation whose fundamental values are formed in the crucible of the family has the capacity to re-create in adolescence the dominant ideology of its own social world without being indoctrinated. To do so appears just and above all natural. Two brothers who have always been accustomed to receiving the same punishments and the same toys, meticulously evenly distributed, will in puberty irreversibly adopt egalitarian values.

...but it would be a mistake to restrict the idea of equality to material or economic things. Toys and punishments are simply, among a host of other feelings and emotions, a manifestation of affection...a homogenous, symmetrical emotional system in which parents display their feelings for all their children in equal measure.

For adult children equality is not simply expressed in the equitable division of goods but by the equal right of all of them to marry; conversely, inegalitarian principles allow only some of them to have a sex life, at least within marriage. Thus equality is not an economic ideal but an intuitive, mathematical concept, as applicable to the emotions as it is to the weighing of potatoes.' (pages 12–13)

A diagrammatic depiction along two dimensions: liberty/authority and equality/inequality allows for four prototypes to emerge: one sharing liberty and equality: *egalitarian family*, one sharing inequality and authority: *authoritarian family* — diametrically opposed to the first; one sharing equality with authority: *a community type family* and diametrically opposite it — *absolute nuclear family* — combining liberty and inequality (see Figure 7.2).

The 'absolute nuclear family' 'which admits the possibility of disinheritance and the right of the generations to have nothing to do with each other' is typical of England; at the opposite pole the 'community family' which is patriarchal by nature but emphasizes commonality is typical of Russia. The 'egalitarian nuclear family' stresses independence, but, nonetheless, equal inheritance is to be found in northern France as well as northern Italy, among others; and finally the 'authoritarian family' 'which is organized around strict interdependence between father and son' can be found in Germany.

Todd is not only willing to put his stake on the long-lasting implications of the differences between family structures but also proposes a global map based on this typology, drawing on historical and anthropological evidence. He is one of the few commentators on cross-cultural issues who devotes attention to Africa in his global mapping (Lessem is another one — see Chapter 4) as well as to Islam, typing in all eight different principal family structures.

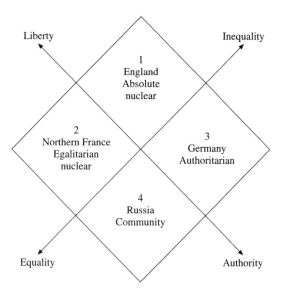

Liberty

Inequality

1
England
Absolute
nuclear

2
Northern France
Egalitarian
nuclear

3
Germany
Authoritarian

4
Russia
Community

Equality

Authority

Figure 7.2   Regions of family types within Europe (after Todd[25]).

Altman's typology of relationships

Following Todd, Altman[21] employs the metaphor of interpersonal relationships in the context of a family, transposing it unto a wider arena — the workplace. Altman considers it a key feature of the model:

> 'The single most important aspect of organizational life, differentiating between people's perception, organizational types and cultures, is the concept of relationships at the workplace. From a person's point of view, the workplace is a web of person-to-person and person-to-institution transactions and inter-actions.'

Working within the Douglas cosmology (grid and group) Altman proposes two dimensions. One emphasizes the degree of relationship intimacy — which may be seen as a variant of the 'group' axis; and the other — the degree of relationship regulation, corresponding to the 'grid' axis (Figure 7.3).

Both dimensions may also be described in terms of Tönnies'[24] well-known dichotomy between *Gemeinschaft* and *Gesellschaft* and Diaz-Guerrero's[25] further differentiation between *interpersonal reality* and *objective reality*. The more intensively regulated and intimately involved relationships will be typical of a *Gemeinschaft* organization where the principles of life are highly interpersonalized. The less regulated and less personally implicated relationships are more akin to a *Gesellschaft* answerable to an objectified reality. Put in the words of Mouer and Sugumoto:

> 'As a country develops into a modern nation, the social intensity of gemeinschaft communities, their social ties based on emotion and sentiment, loosen to become a web of impersonal social relations supported by the formal and even contractual ties characteristic of gesellschaft societies such as the United

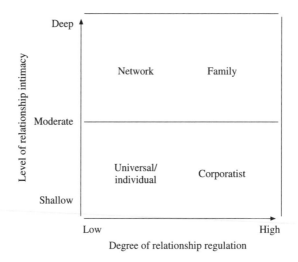

Figure 7.3 A typology of relationships *Source*: Altman[23].

States. Social ties are based on rational agreement and self-interest and are regulated by law. Groups are formed for specific purposes and accept members based on special interest or technical, educational, or professional attainments. Identity is separate from belonging; the status of the individual citizen and member of the state takes precedence over membership in groups. The status enjoyed by the individual is a product of achievement rather than a birthright as political and professional ties replace traditional social links. The changes induced in objective culture at the level of political, social and economic institutions trickle down to the subjective culture of interpersonal interaction' (Mouer and Sugimoto, 1986).[26]

While the *Gemeinschaft/Gesellschaft* dichotomy was put forward within a developmental context — the first typical of agrarian communities, the other of urban industrialized societies — this is not always the case as Stewart and Bennett point out. Japan is a current example of an industrialized country which is still operating in a *Gemeinschaft* mentality of an interpersonal reality cosmology (intimate relationships and a high degree of regulation). Thailand is an opposite case of an agrarian community that conceives of itself as highly fragmented in terms of personal relationships, operating under an objective reality code (shallow relations and a high degree of perceived independence).

Relationships at work

We now turn to the world of work and the ways in which family structures may play a role in this environment. *It is assumed that people carry with them their model of the world and that — since it is **their** model of relationships — will attempt to re-create it wherever they go, including their place of work.* But where do they get it from in the first place? Most likely from home. By home, read not the psychological familial environment created by the dynamics of an accidental group of individuals but the anthropological idea of familial structures representing longer-term and enduring societal conventions as advocated by Todd.

This is not to say that the psychological reality is not a valid base for inferences on the workplace. It clearly is, as Johnson and Indvik[27] have recently shown in the case of childhood traumas. They specifically employ the metaphor of the family and family roles at work. Attachment theory,[28–30] which has been gaining momentum over the past decade, is particularly well placed to provide the intellectual framework for such a psychological approach, as it ascertains the transferability of attachment styles (stemming from infant–mother and child–family interactions) across the life cycle.[31]

The use of metaphors as a methodological tool is not new, of course. It was central to the methods used by Goffman[32–34] to explore different facets of life, organizations included. More recently, in the context of business organizations, Morgan[35,36] has convincingly advocated the use of metaphors.

The metaphor of the family as applied to the work organization, while in itself not new (e.g. Baum[37]) may seem out of place in an Anglo-Saxon context (which indeed, as we shall see, it may be), but anyone working in the Mediterranean basin or Japan will easily recognize its validity to the workplace. In Italy, Spain, Greece, parts of France — note concepts like patron (patrone) relating in root to 'father'; note the practice of recruitment (relatives and friends of friends preferred; a local has clearly an advantage over an outsider). As to Japan, 'the Japanese company is modelled on the Japanese household. The relationships among members of the company are precisely articulated along lines of the household.'[9]

Using a family analogy, the dichotomy *Gemeinschaft/Gesellschaft* and interpersonal versus objective reality could be translated into two key questions pertinent to the world of work. These are the *question of belonging* versus the *question of independence*. Though these are not mutually exclusive, there is clearly a difference of emphasis on one or the other question, depending on one's structural position.

In a highly intimate and highly regulated environment (corresponding to Todd's authoritarian family, an extreme derivation of which would be the asymmetric family: the southern Indian cast system — corresponding to Douglas's bureaucracy type) the struggle for independence of son from father are an in-built feature of this configuration. In the classical psychoanalytic tradition, it would manifest itself in the slaying of the father figure (at least symbolically). Independence, as embedded in adolescence, can only be bought by rebellion. The fact that the death of the father does not necessarily relieve the son from his shadow attests to the depth of this intimate bond (see Figure 7.4).

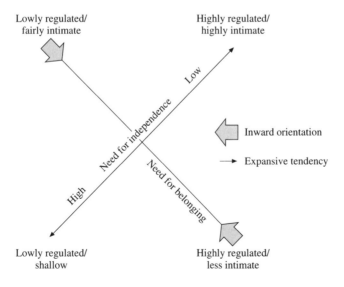

Figure 7.4   Altman typology: the two cultural axes.

The issue of independence is also central to the structurally opposite position: shallowness in relationships and lowly regulated, corresponding to the formulation of the nuclear family, particularly the absolute nuclear type (Todd) as well as to the individualist tendency (Douglas). The question of independence is central here, not because there is any need, as in the family model, to liberate oneself in order to assert one's identity (through separation) but because that is the normative expectation, that is the task at hand.

The challenge here may be defined as the *management of obligations*. Based on the principle of separation of children from parents (complete in the case of the absolute family, less so in that of the egalitarian nuclear family — Todd) from early on in life, one is encouraged to assume responsibility, stand up for oneself, become self-sufficient and resilient. The autonomous individuum is the idol. Accepting obligations (that is, reciprocity) is highly problematic in this part of the universe.

In a conceptual framework accentuated by action, an internal locus of control,[9] driven by a future time orientation[38] emphasizing movement (away from the present) and hence change (which is inherently good), stability (of relationships) which allures to a continuous present or past, is problematic. Add to that social policies, as has been the case in the UK since the Second World War, aimed at the individual rather than the family unit: child allowance paid to the mother, separate income tax, the elderly catered for by the state,[39] and the scene is set.

The question of belonging does not feature prominently in both cases. Living in the highly regulated–highly intimate pole means belonging is automatic and unconditional. One cannot disown one's father or mother ('we can't choose our parents' as the saying goes). One does not cease from being a son or daughter, even if (which is rare) disowned by one's parents. The flesh and blood bond is, by definition, irrevocable. The same would apply to a work situation. The parent–child bond will manifest itself and the expectations that follow it call for loyalty in exchange for protection.

Belonging is a non-issue also in the opposite pole, because the ideological stand is against it. In a system which encourages self-sufficiency, emotional restraint, autonomy and civil liberty, belonging to a family (and, by metaphorical implication, to a work organization) is by choice and therefore subject to review and change.

Belonging, however, is critical and therefore a key question in a highly regulated but less intimate environment (the community family on its different variants and in particular in its endogamous type (Todd) and the egalitarian type (Douglas)). A community, a brotherhood, emphasizes a tight boundary with the external world — that is, a clear differentiation between 'us' and 'them' (them practically meaning all those who are not us, namely: the rest of the world). Internally, however, it is much less differentiated: the principles that govern relationships are equality, shared responsibility, mutual guarantee.

The emphasis on high regulation of relationships (custom and laws) paradoxically impersonalizes the social control, which explains why relationships, while close and involved, are not as intimate and loaded (in the sense of a psychological complex) as in a highly regulated and highly intimate environment. Indeed they could not be since close intimacy between selected individuals would mitigate against the principle of equality.

In the endogamous community family (Todd) as exemplified by Islamic communities, relationships are focused on brothers and through them, their families. This is the basis for the extended family *(khamula)* and, by implication, the community at large *(umma)*. Belonging is critical because in this type of cosmology there is no life outside the group and the threat of expulsion, though extreme, is a real one (and necessary to maintain the social control and tighten the boundaries, which is why it is periodically employed).

Belonging is equally critical in the fourth pole (not much regulated, but pulling towards intimacy in relationships) here, precisely because there is no structural regulation. One is not driven into the protective arms of a family or a clan, yet, at the same time, there appears to be a need for a degree of intimacy in relations which does not apply to the lowly regulated but shallow pole.

This type seems to be less clear-cut than the three others, perhaps because it is less common or perhaps because we know less about it. Todd calls it the anomic type, and it is characterized by an irregular quality of relationships, inwardly oriented, but lacking the security provided by a stable, enclosed environment. The members of this typology are atomized, indeed isolates — a term used both by Todd and Douglas. They are in a perpetual state of anomie with its associated anxieties. Their only hope of overcoming this isolating tendency is by building networks — not, as the inhabitants of the lowly regulated/shallow pole do, opportunistically and *ad hoc*, but in order to fulfil their quest for a protective environment so that they can belong.

The model's assumptions are that these four meta-types with their differing origins, emphases of processes and values should account for differences in organizational structures and aligned expectations of occupational issues such as type of contract, what makes a career, organizational commitment and loyalty.

A developmental sequence

Four preferential ways of selecting a spouse   The starting point of our developmental sequence is with the family structure, which serves both as an overall conceptual framework and a latent formative force:

> The family, varied in its forms, is not itself determined by any necessity, logic or rationale. It simply exists, in its diversity, and lasts for centuries or millennia. A unit of biological and social reproduction, the family needs no sense of history or of life in order to perpetuate its structures. It reproduces itself identically from generation to generation; the unconscious imitation of parents by their children is enough to ensure the perpetuation of anthropological systems... It is a blind, irrational mechanism, but its power derives precisely from its lack of consciousness and visibility, for it cannot be questioned.[23]

Todd thus provides a starting point and at the same time puts forward the dynamics for action and change; and in doing so renders an invaluable service to the Douglas cosmology. The four essential family types presented by Todd are compared on the critical question of the principle of spouse selection. These manifest the ideology of relations formation, which is at the core of Altman's model. Four options for spouse selection emerge, based on Todd's empirical survey, three stable and one unstable:

- Spouse selection determined by parents, but within confined expectations.
- Spouse selection determined by custom — with an emphasis on marrying into the wider family.
- Decision by the persons concerned themselves, with an emphasis on exogamy.
- An unsettled model, without clear preferences, allowing for the maximum choice (including consanguinity), because little in the way of imposition exists.

Four concepts of learning and education   The evolving logic of the model leads us to examine the educational system. The differences in the concept and practice of education between adjacent countries such as Germany, France, Italy and the UK (all members of the European Union) are notable. We can identify some links between the ideology of relating, as manifested in the principle of spouse selection and the family structure; and the ideology of relating between peers and between student (subject) and teacher (authority).

A hallmark of the Anglo-Saxon model of education, so visible in North America and the UK, from the kindergarten to university, is the emphasis on learning by doing, on experimenting and learning from one's own experience as well as an emphasis on positive feedback (encouragement). Relationships with peers are open and flexible, the teacher is not as much a source of authority as a facilitator of learning. Competition is an in-built feature, a primary means for motivating (providing drive and direction) and comparing results (measuring achievements and feedback).

In the Germanic tradition, prevalent throughout the Germanic sphere of influence (which spans into Central/Eastern Europe) learning is formalized, with an emphasis on the acquisition of knowledge (theory) and know-how (practice). The resultant 'educational product' is an expert in a well-defined field. The learning method is *ex-cathedra*, an emphasis on formal exams assessing knowledge and specific applications. There are no major differences between institutions. The thrive for excellence through differentiation, so evident in the Anglo-Saxon countries (the American Ivy League and England's Oxbridge) and even more accentuated in France (the *grands écoles* system), is lacking there.

The French system emphasizes formality and knowledge acquisition (assessment by exam with an accent on deficiencies: negative feedback) and a pious adherence to the ideology of meritocracy (the equality principle — in theory at least) as laid down, some two hundred years ago, by Napoleon Bonaparte. It thus exhibits some of the key elements of the Germanic approach and some of the key elements of the Anglo-Saxon system. The ideal 'educational product' is a young pedigree, with an unrivalled command of analytical skills, but necessarily limited practical experience.

The fourth type, the community-oriented endogamic educational approach is, as anticipated by the model, inwardly looking. A fine example in this genre is present-day Algeria, which committed national suicide by abolishing instruction in the French language from its educational system, universities included. By moving to compulsory teaching in Arabic, it closed in effect the door on the outside world. Algeria, like its neighbour, Libya, thus established the hegemony of the *umma* (the community of Muslim believers). The fundamentalists' anti-foreigners terror campaign seems to have sealed the process.

The community-oriented endogamic educational system emphasizes the dual process of external negation (the outside is bad, inferior, contaminating) and internal glorification (we are the true believers, we are the best). The teacher is not just an authority on knowledge (expert) as in the authoritarian systems (Germany, France) nor a facilitator of learning (Anglo-Saxon) but, in the main, an educator: a transmitter of values. He or she is the embodiment of the wise person of antiquity. The 'educational products' may be seen in the sukhs of Teheran and Baghdad; but also in the mountains and valleys of Switzerland — the most inward-looking country-community of western Europe.

The other inward-looking educational ideology is strongly spiritual. It emphasizes an experiential approach of learning through reflection and introspection, a personal voyage of discovery and growth into oneself. The teachings of the Eastern philosophies and religions come readily to mind. Among Western thinkers, the most prominent is the Swiss (mere coincidence?) Carl Jung. The teacher in that tradition is the guru, a spiritual leader who shows the way, by means of personal induction.

The dynamics and structure of the four types   The two poles, by diverging on the same dilemmas (the quest for independence versus the quest for belonging), also share opposing dynamics. The 'independence' pole drives towards breaking out; it is expansive. The 'belonging' pole drives inwardly, towards enclosure (see Figure 7.4).

The structural features are also different. The authoritarian family (Todd), the highly regulated and highly intimate (Altman) drive towards demarcated structures, which are definitive and clearly defined. The pyramid is a common configuration for power structures.[4] The endogamous community structure — equally highly intimate and regulated — brings to mind a circle, de-emphasizing the demarcations *inside*, while emphasizing the external boundary, with a focal point (the father, the elder, the leaders) acting as sociometrical stars while emphasizing the external boundary.

With the absolute nuclear family and the egalitarian nuclear family — lowly regulated and shallow, an atomic representation suggests itself: a tendency towards maximum freedom and lack of connectedness. The isolates (the anomic family) — moderately regulated and moderately intimate — may be located at the centre of the space, whereby their confusion is manifest in, presumably, having the freedom to opt for different forms at different times. The developmental sequence is shown in Figure 7.5.

Occupational and organizational types

We now turn to consider how typological models may be used to classify occupational and organizational environments.

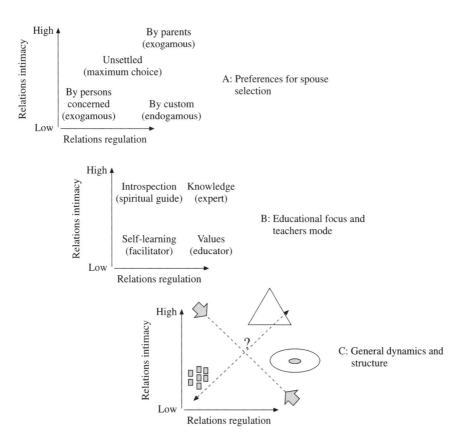

Figure 7.5   Developmental sequence (from A to C).

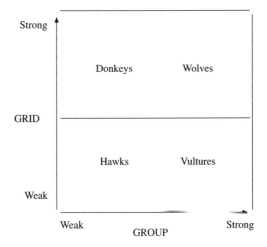

Figure 7.6   Mars's typology of work roles.

Mars' occupational typology   Mars,[16] working within the Douglas cosmology, proposes an occupational classification along the grid/group lines. He makes allusions to the animal world as a means of communicating imagery and its associated meanings (see Figure 7.6). In Mars' typology, the strong grid/ weak group (isolated subordination) is depicted as 'donkeys':

'A skivvy in a nineteenth-century one-servant family is probably the classic example here. Isolated as she was from social contact with others, unable to relate to fellow servants or the family she served, she was even excluded from contact with 'followers', that is, from male admirers. She was tightly scheduled not only over time and space, but also over work and leisure with a programme of activities which minutely controlled all aspects of her life. Her job was an extreme among "donkey" jobs.'

     Donkeys are in the paradoxical position of being either powerless or powerful. They are powerless if they passively accept the constraints they face. They can, however, be extremely powerful — in the sense of being disruptive, at least for a time — if they reject them. Resentment at the impositions caused by such jobs is common and the most typical response is to change jobs. These are, therefore, occupations where high labour turnover is common, but other forms of "withdrawal from work", such as sickness and absenteeism are also higher than normal.' (page 31)[16]

The strong grid/strong group (tight work groups) are 'wolves':

'These are occupations based on groups with interdependent and stratified roles. As well as longshore gangs and teams of miners, it includes garbage collection crews, aeroplane crews and stratified groups who both live and work in "total institutions" such as prisons, hospitals, oil rigs and some hotels.' (page 32)

The weak grid/weak group (individual entrepreneuriality) are 'hawks':

'Hawks are entrepreneurial managers, owner businessmen, successful academics and pundits, the prima donnas among salesmen, the more independent professionals and journalists... Hawkish entrepreneuriality is also inherent in occupations such as waiters, fairground buskers and owner taxi drivers. Since competition is a dominant characteristic of this type, and because the group dimension is weak, we find that alliances among hawks tend to shift with expediency and that a climate of suspicion is more common than one of trust (page 20).'

The strong group/weak grid (loose work groups) are 'vultures':

'Vultures include sales representatives, travellers and roundsmen of various kinds. The classic examples are driver deliverers, linked collectively by their common employer, common workbase and common task, but who have considerable freedom and discretion during their working day… Workers in these occupations are, therefore, members of a group of co-workers for some purposes only and they act individualistically and competitively for others. They are not as free-floating nor as free from constraint as are hawks, but neither are they as constrained as donkeys. And though individuals are members of groups, the group is not as intrusive or controlling as are wolfpacks.' (pages 32–33)

Mars, in effect, defines the occupational correlates of Todd's families. Vultures are the exogamous community family as well as the authoritarian family: bound, but expansive; wolfpacks are typical of the endogamous community family: clearly inward looking — what matters is what happens in the bounded reality of the co-workers and the designated workplace. Hawks are the entrepreneurs of the nuclear type families and donkeys are clearly the isolates, products of the anomic family.

Altman's organizational typology: high regulation–intimate relations: family type   The clearest case of a familial interpretation of workplace relationships — the family type model of the world — is where actors in the system are designated archetypal family roles: father (mother) figure, big brother, little sister… The head of the enterprise, the general director, is seen as head of a family, with the associated respect, attributed power and aligned expectations. Work colleagues are seen as siblings. Indeed there would be a propensity to recruit into the workplace *real* family members. Relations are assumed to be long term, moderate to high in intimacy and regulated: not dissimilar to a family structure.

This model is often prevalent in Latin Europe: Italy, Spain, Greece, some parts of France. But also in Ireland, for instance. These societies are characterized by a strong bondage of family and kin, distinct and disparate regional identities and recurrent tensions with central government. They tend to combine 'traditional' agricultural sectors with a developed tourist industry. The backbone of the national economy are family enterprises.

A good example in this category is Italy. Although the fifth largest industrial power in the world (the third in Europe), the majority of private Italian firms employ fewer than a hundred employees, with an average of only 7.6 employees per firm.[40] However, even the large manufacturing industrial conglomerates — the likes of Fiat, Pirelli, Olivetti, Feruzzi — are family dominated. The parent generation passing on the key positions to their heirs and the family holding a major stake in the company, in a system which Carlo De Benedetti (Olivetti) labelled 'paracapitalistic'.[4]

While a preference for the family model may be geographically bound, it is by no means exclusive. Family-type environments can be found anywhere and not only in small–medium family-owned businesses. Ford UK — the British subsidiary of the Ford Motor Company — would be an example of a major manufacturer, which in some respects resembles a family model. The Ford family (that is, the real family) is clearly perceived to be at the helm, recruitment is localized with a preference for family members of existing workers. Turnover is very low (compared to the sector), promotion is almost exclusively through the ranks (including senior jobs) and while the company is renowned for its hard-nosed, no-nonsense management style, it has always been in the forefront of welfare provisions in its sector and enjoys the reputation of a benevolent employer. Of course, there are limits to a family ideology in a large, hierarchical organization. Where it is taken too much at its face value, it is bound to founder (see Baum[37] on an attempt to create a family environment in a public bureaucracy).

The key test for survival and success in this organizational environment is loyalty. This is also a major qualification for promotion. Equally, probably the worst sin one can commit is the (perceived) betrayal of trust, as the interdependencies created by a family-type web of relations are bonded by trust. The typical organizational crises are to do with succession — the change of leadership (the real or symbolic death of the patron), the changing of the (old) guards; as well as sibling rivalries.

Low regulation–shallow relations: the universal/individual type   At the very opposite pole to the family type is the universal/ individual type. As its name implies, it is the individual, not the family or extended group, who is at centre stage; and the principles governing relationships are universal (as against the particularistic criteria of the family type). It is a 'can do' environment, where the organizational motto is 'the sky's the limit' and the bottom line is what really matters: no one argues with success. On the other hand, failure is not easily excused. Here, it does not matter *who* you are, but *what* you can do.

The entrepreneur is the economic hero in this environment. Significantly, the archetypal entrepreneur in the UK is an 'outsider' (Rupert Murdoch, James Goldsmith, Robert Maxwell, Anita Roddick, Lord Hanson, 'Tiny' Rowland, Alan Sugar, Lord King, Sir John Harvey-Jones, even Richard Branson, to name a few of the top corporate figures of the 1980s and 1990s). They are outsiders in the sense that they do not originate from the elite, or 'ruling classes' — which is one difference from the economic top brass of the family-type environment. Another difference is that these empire builders have imprinted their persona on the businesses they created and manage. This makes these enterprises vulnerable — a family succession which would be normal in a family type organizational environment is out of the ordinary here.[42]

Relationships are perceived to be between individuals, they are short term (or rather, *ad hoc*), tend to be shallow and flexible. The qualities that gel relations are mutual interests and concerns. These are subject to periodic reviews and are terminable — and 'no hard feelings'. This should not imply that friendships could not develop and flourish and long-term commitments established. It is the process of relationship involvement which is different.

In the family-type environment people come to the workplace expecting to find social relations and actively recreate a family-type framework. In the universal/individual environment people come to work in order to get the work done and be paid for it, as Homans[43] argued in his classical text. They then find that in order to do so they need to collaborate with others and eventually discover they like some of them and come to regard them as friends (as opposed to fellow-workers), engaging them in other aspects of their lives. On the other hand, they may not. That is a community of individuals.

The typical test for survival in a universal/individual environment is to deliver results. This is the ultimate (and sometimes only) requirement. It is also the key measure for career progression, as epitomized by *management by objectives*, the design–control–feedback tool which has been a hallmark of organizational life since the 1960s (and which did not fare too well in a family-type environment and was significantly altered in a corporate-type environment[44]).

Loyalty is of no consequence here. Both sides — the organization and the person concerned — review their position *vis-à-vis* the other as a matter of routine. It is seen correct for the employee to move on to another organization if the right opportunity (challenge, rewards, prospects) presents itself. It is seen correct for the organization to cut one's engagement short (downsizing, rightsizing, de-layering) if the market conditions present that to be to its advantage.

The typical organizational crises are to do with too many personal agendas and rivalries — top management pushing their pet projects and engaged in looking after their personal (division-al) interests, while neglecting the common good. Yet another typical problem is too many and too frequent reshuffles (personal and organizational). Increasingly, overwork and associated stress (results of internal and external competition) have become the hallmark of this organizational universe.

The countries that stand out in this category are the USA and, in Europe, the UK. Both have been hailed as the paradise for entrepreneurs — where innovation, risk taking and empire building are prized ('the American dream'). Of course, one finds organizational cultures of this type anywhere, but their natural habitat is where the reigning environment values maximum freedom for the individual and where enterprise is rewarded — whether it be remuneration (the UK is reputed to have the highest pay differentials of top managers compared to employees in Europe) or social recognition.

High regulation — less intimate relationships: the corporate type   Here we evidence a different form of regulation — based on social conventions — either the common law or customs (tradition, religion). One finds an emphasis on structural regulation, for instance, working hours, which are strictly adhered to and so are rest periods (lunch breaks, vacation) as is the case in Germany (where vacation times are matched with personal circumstances: families with school-age children have priority during school holidays).

Of course, there is the renowned German model of the post-Second World War regulated industrial relations (the co-determination policy). Sweden, another prime example of a socially controlled (regulated) environment, has a long-standing tradition of equal job = equal pay, irrespective of industrial sector, company size or location. While in the Islamic countries, fasting throughout the month of Ramadan is expected of all citizens and monitored at the workplace as well.

Relationships, in their own way, are also regulated by custom as defined in terms of the largest social unit, the community (*Gemeinschaft*). Not surprisingly, the key attribute for organizational success is fitting (or mucking) in and not sticking out — a regular complaint among high achievers in the Scandinavian countries. This is not just in adhering to the prescribed norms of the workplace, but it also extends to demonstrating the correct citizen virtues (choice of car, clothes, tax declaration): the Swedish concept of *lagom* (appropriateness) which dictates that the average is right and standing out is wrong — a norm seeping through all walks of life. (The term may have originated from the Vikings, who drank their beer from a common bowl. Each man would take a *laget om* (according to the law) — not to much, not to little, just the right amount.[45]) In Switzerland this translates into 'buying Swiss' (efficiently regulated by the customs officers on its borders: note the care with which Swiss cars are searched).

In Pakistan, Iran, Saudi Arabia, the Sudan and Egypt one should be careful not to commit the sin of apostasy — which is the ultimate control the community exercises over its membership. Excommunication may be the lighter sentence; death is more likely (note the murder in 1992 of Faraj Fawda and the attempt on the life of Najib Mahfuz, the Nobel Laureate, in 1994).

Commitment is to the workplace, and through it to the community at large, rather than a position (as in the universal/individual model) and social relations are less intimate than in the family model, although these may, of course, develop, particularly since there is institutional emphasis on long-term engagement. (In Germany it is still considered quite improper to change jobs more than four or five times throughout one's working life.) However, since social (non-work) relations would be in a separate category, they should not overlap with work relations (signified by being on first-name terms outside the work context and resorting to formal address at work).

Medium regulation–medium intimacy: the anomie/ network organizational type   This last type is more complicated than the other three for it is of unstable nature. This results from a structural perception of being trapped, of no escape, no alternatives. What is left is the experience of anomie — on a social level (on a personal level that would translate into chronic depression).

Perhaps the best known case of widespread endemic anomie in recent history is the case of the former Soviet people under the former Soviet regime. Writing in the last years before the regime's demise, Shlapentokh[46] in a seminal text says:

> 'Virtually every Soviet individual is regularly engaged in the infraction of dominant moral norms and laws. Indeed, few could survive in socialist society without the regular violation of the rules and principles proclaimed by the state. This anomic behaviour takes one or two distinct forms...either hypocrisy or cynicism. A growing number of Soviet people, especially the young, only barely conceal their contemptuous attitudes towards official moral values. On the other hand, a considerable proportion of the population, seeking to avoid viewing themselves as selfish and egoistic, resort to a relatively sophisticated mental construction, wherein they find regular excuses for the violation of the norms. (page 6)'

The way to combat anomie, this prolonged sense of being lost, of meaningless, is through the institution of friendship: the creation of personal social support networks.[47,48] In the Soviet system, friendship gained a role that superseded the family — sometimes it even undermined it.[46] In Communist regimes the friendship network acted also as an alternative mechanism of wealth creation and distribution in an economy of scarcity.

In the network type, relationships are believed to be long term and involved, otherwise a network cannot develop or sustain itself, but is subject to regular and frequent confirmation of commitment. This is also manifested in the very nature of transactions; while past experience may advocate expectations, they are necessarily *ad hoc* and subject to negotiation and fluctuations, as would be expected in a barter economy.

At the workplace, relationships are a reproduction of the informal support network, aiming to extend one's potential contacts inside and outside work. A key attribute to success is whom one knows and to where one has access, as these become assets to trade. Career progression is dependent not only on past performance but also vitally on the potentials of one's current circumstances. Paradoxically, while personal relations may be emphasized, they are viewed instrumentally, as the workplace itself — a seat of transactions and opportunities of a kind.

Organizational crises are typically a result of a major shift in the power structure that collapses networks, thereby requiring a restructuring and rearrangement of positions, roles and distribution of resources. On the face of it, this is not unlike the case in family-type environments, except that networks are more volatile by nature and more prone to crises than are the former.

Related meta-organizational issues: different approaches to unemployment benefits

Unemployment has become, by the mid-1990s, a permanent feature of the industrialized developed nations and a key social–political issue. Being out of gainful work puts one at the mercy of one's society. Society's views about its ungainful members are reflected most strikingly in its unemployment legislation and unemployment provisions. These amount, in effect, to a conceptualization and methodology of *social control*, one facet of the prevalent values in a given society.

Three examples of European unemployment policies are examined, using data from a recent study by Layard, Nickell and Jackman.[49] The three countries concerned — the UK, Italy and Sweden — seem to approach the matter differently from each other.

The UK policy is exemplary of a philosophy of 'standing on one's own feet' and self-reliance. Italy's philosophy pertains that wealth (and poverty) are a family matter. Sweden represents a philosophy of containment, which is congruent with the concept of wealth as a communal shared resource and safety net (or safety insurance).

In the UK, 73 per cent of those registered and eligible for unemployment benefits in 1986 received them. The duration of the benefit is in effect indefinite (since one automatically transfers to social security benefits, once unemployment eligibility transpires, and the rate of compensation remains unchanged). In 1986 it amounted to £28.45[4] for a single person per week: a princely sum on which one may not starve but hardly make a living. (Department of Social Security (DSS) figures are £30.80 for 1986. This amount did not change substantially over the years (accounting for inflation). In 1993 the figure was roughly the same (accounting for inflation): £44.65 per week.) The underlying social expectation is that one is accountable for oneself. Society is there to provide only the bare essentials, but the rest is up to each and everyone.

In Italy, only 21 per cent of those eligible for unemployment benefit received any. The reason for this low utilization becomes self-evident when the compensation rate is noted. In 1986 it amounted to 800 lira (or 40 pence) per day for basic unemployment benefit. It was only paid for a maximum of six consecutive months. Clearly, most of those eligible would not bother to claim such a petty sum in the first place. Also, alternative provisions (for illness or disablement, for instance) were considerably more generous and some may have registered under those. However, the implicit societal expectation seems unambiguous: it is not the role of society at large to support the unemployed. Who should underwrite this burden? Presumably the key social institution of Italian society: the family (the extended family, that is).

In Sweden, it is the community at large whose responsibility it is to look after its failing members. Eighty per cent of those eligible for unemployment benefit claimed it and their compensation rate was high: equivalent to some 80 per cent of wages while in full employment. This rate of compensation lasted for a period of 14 months in 1986.

In addition, Sweden provides a generous and comprehensive assistance in finding new employment, far outstripping the modest provisions of the UK (and the almost total lack in Italy). However, there is another side to this near-idyllic world of the unemployed. If after 18 months in total the person concerned does not find an alternative source of income, he or she is out in the cold (alas, literally). There are no more provisions, of whatever kind. The societal message is clear-cut: if you don't abide by the norms (and don't find employment) society has no further responsibility for you.

A revealing statistic, offered by Layard et al., may serve as an appropriate summary. It is the expenditure on unemployment benefits per unemployed person (calculated as per cent of output per worker in the national economy). In the UK it came to 14 per cent per worker in 1987. In Italy it was a meagre 4 per cent. In Sweden it amounted to 36 per cent.

Related meta-organizational issues: the social role of money

Money has emerged as the key factor in the economic and social life of Western civilization for at least the past two hundred years. As such, it has come to occupy a role which is almost independent of its monetary function: as a key cultural signifier, charting what is — for a given society, in a given time — socially acceptable and morally right. In other words, the rich are also subject to social control, not just the poor. Reflecting on the legitimized use of wealth allows us to complement the cultural map, within which working life is set. Altman[11] identifies four cultural concepts of money, corresponding to the four types.

For some, money is the great liberator from life's (and society's) constraints — an attitude shared by many of Britain's economic elite, the *'nouveaux riches'* (72 per cent of Britain's wealthiest individuals are self-made millionaires)[50] and the 'old money' aristocracy alike. Richard Branson, the most media-visible entrepreneur among the self-made, defines it as 'what money brings me is freedom — to dress as I feel comfortable, or to make my kids well again if they are ill. Most of the things it brings I'm embarrassed about — like jewellery for the wife or Rolls-Royces'.[51] Equally parsimonious is reputed to be the Duke of Westminster, heir to one of England's noblest and wealthiest families, who at the same time is known for his charity. Public opinion supports the public morale: Britain's rich are honest, hard working and no show-offs according to a Gallup survey for the *Daily Telegraph*, in January 1992.

In the Mediterranean Basin wealth begets expectations which are diametrically opposed to the perception of freedom experienced in the individual/universal world. Rather than liberation from society, money implies obligations to society. Wealth equates with honour which equates with patronage.[52] Patronage brings with it a set of privileges and obligations, entailing the dispensation of gifts and loans and, more often than not, an extravagant display of wealth as a means for accruing prestige and honour.

In the Scandinavian countries wealth is looked upon as a communal resource to be shared, no doubt, but to which one has to contribute according to norm. Money is viewed with respect but it would be considered bad taste and greediness to flash it in public. If that happens it will be subject to public scorn. Wealth is looked upon as an insurance policy and a safety net — something to be treated with caution. Hence the philosophy of a welfare society balanced by a responsible attitude towards consumption.

In the Communist system money was always a contentious issue. In a system where prices were fixed and there was supposedly no inflation, money increasingly could not buy goods and services in short supply, since money itself had no independent value: it was not traded in the free market, it could not be hoarded in a Swiss bank account. The prevalent mode of exchange, even among state enterprises, was barter.[47] That gave rise to the personal social support network, where money and money equivalent commodities became personalized: goods and services could not be bought by money alone but through exchange in one's network, barter-like.[50]

SUMMARY AND CONCLUSION

In this chapter we have looked at the various models that have been proposed as a basis for classifying cultures according to factors which are relevant to all cultures, universally. This 'Cultural Theory' provides a framework for a cross-national perspective on organizations and management. Based on anthropological theory, it is perhaps the least developed of all core disciplines contributing to this book.

Synergies with other models presented here are apparent and one may question the utility of digging out more of the same. However, we feel that the development of models based on key paradigms of a discipline (such as kinship systems in the case of anthropology) provides a vital component of a healthy cross-disciplinary debate.

These typological approaches are necessarily limited by the fact that they look only at broad generalizations and are based on only a cross-section of the vast amount of information which could be gathered about a given culture. The major strength, however, of the typological approach is to test the assumption that there are certain attributes of culture which provide some basic 'handles' by which the cross-cultural traveller can begin to grasp this subject.

The models show, for example, the importance of the family as a mediating influence in the development and maintenance of cultural systems. Taken together, the models also show that the family, and other fundamental issues such as the need for freedom and autonomy, influence not only the social construction of a given group of people but also the ways in which companies are built and developed within them.

It being the case that three-dimensional vision requires a minimum of two points of view, it is hoped that the emphasis which this chapter has placed on the sociological and anthropological issues has provided an added perspective on culture and its 'consequences', and we hope that, in taking a look at culture 'from the outside in', we have given the reader an extra dimension over that already extensively covered by the more individualistic, psychological, inside-out approaches of American and Dutch origin.

We now turn west for the final expedition of our journey.

STUDY QUESTIONS

1. Describe the principal differences between the 'inside-out' and the 'outside-in' approaches to cultural analysis, giving examples of each and discussing their relative strengths and weaknesses.
2. What are the principal relational systems that govern group dynamics?
3. To what extent does the family provide a model for understanding the differences between international businesses?

REFERENCES

1. Wright, S. (ed.), *Anthropology of Organisations*, Sage, London, 1993.
2. Hamada, T. and Sibley, W. E. (eds.), *Anthropological Perspectives on Organizational Culture*, University Press of America, Latham, 1994.
3. Hofstede, G., *Culture's Consequences*, Sage Publications, Beverley Hills, CA, 1980.
4. Hofstede, G., *Cultures and Organizations*, McGraw-Hill, London, 1991.
5. Fiske, A.P., *Structures of Social Life: The Four Elementary Forms of Human Relations*, Free Press, New York, 1991.
6. Fiske, A.P., The Four Elementary Forms of Sociality: Framework for a Unified Theory of Social Relations, *Psychological Review*, 1992, **99**, 4, pp. 689–723.
7. Czarniawska-Joerges, B., Nice Work in Strange Worlds: On Anthropology and Organization Theory, *The 1990 Annual Meeting of the Society for Applied Anthropology*, New York, 1990.
8. Manning, P., *Erving Goffman and Modern Sociology*, Polity Press, Cambridge, 1992.
9. Stewart, E.C. and Bennett, M.J., *American Cultural Patterns — A Cross-Cultural Perspective*, Intercultural Press, Inc., Yarmouth, Maine, 1991.
10. Douglas, M., *Natural Symbols: Explorations in Cosmology*, Barrie & Rockliff, London, 1970.
11. Altman, Y., Towards a cultural typology of work values and work organisation, *Innovation – European Journal of Social Sciences*, **5**, 1, pp. 35–44, 1992.
12. Douglas, M., Cultural Bias, *Occasional Paper No. 35* Royal Anthropological Institute, London, 1978.
13. Altman, Y., An application of cultural theory to organisational behaviour — Mary Douglas' Grid/Group and the case of the Israeli armed forces, *Organisational Models — Cultural Reflections*, March 1994, London.
14. Douglas, M. (ed.), *Essays in Sociology of Perception*, Routledge & Kegan Paul, London, 1982.
15. Douglas, M. and Wildavsky, A., *Risk and Culture*, Univ. of California Press, Berkeley, 1982.
16. Mars, G., *Cheats at Work*, George Allen & Unwin, London, 1992.
17. Gross, J. and Rayner, S., *Measuring Culture*, Columbia Univ. Press, New York, 1985.
18. Douglas, M., *Risk and Blame: Essays in Cultural Theory*, Routledge, London, 1992.

19. Blake, R.R. and Mouton, J.S., Managerial facades, *Advanced Management Journal*, July 1966, p. 31.
20. Thompson, M., Ellis, R. and Wildavsky, A., *Cultural Theory*, Westview Press, Boulder, 1990.
21. Altman, Y., A typology of work relations in the context of contemporary Europe, *Journal of European Industrial Training*, **17**, 10, pp. 28–34, 1993.
22. Mutabazi, F., Altman, Y., Klesta, A. and Poirson, P., *Management des Resources Humaines a L'International*, Eyrolles, Paris, 1994.
23. Todd, E., *The Explanation of Ideology*, Basil Blackwell, Oxford, 1985, pp. 31.
24. Tönnies, F., *Community and Society*, Michigan State Univ. Press, East Lansing, 1957.
25. Diaz-Guerrero, R., *Psychology of the Mexican*, Univ. of Texas Press, Austin, 1976.
26. Mouer, R. and Sugimoto, Y., *Images of Japanese Society*, Kogan Page, London, 1986.
27. Johnson, P.R. and Indvik, J., Trauma Brought into the Workplace, *Journal of Managerial Psychology*, **10**, 2, 1995, pp. 26–32.
28. Bowlby J., *Attachment and Loss, Vol 1 Attachment*, Hogarth Press; London, 1969.
29. Bowlby, J., *Attachment and Loss, Vol 2 Separation*, Hogarth Press; London, 1973.
30. Bowlby, J., *Attachment and Loss, Vol 3 Loss*, Hogarth Press; London, 1980.
31. Parkes, C.M., Stevenson-Hinde, J. and Marris, P. (eds.), *Attachment Across the Life Cycle*, Routledge, London, 1991.
32. Goffman, E., *The Presentation of Self in Everyday Life*, Doubleday, New York, 1959.
33. Goffman, E., *Interaction Ritual: Essays on Face-to-Face Behaviour*, Anchor Books, New York, 1967.
34. Goffman, E., *Frame Analysis: An Essay on the Organization of Experience*, Harper & Row, New York, 1979.
35. Morgan, G., *Images of Organization*, Sage, Beverley Hills, 1986.
36. Morgan, G., *Imaginization*, Sage, Newbury Park, CA, 1993.
37. Baum, H.S., Creating a family in the workplace, *Human Relations*, **44** (11), 1991, pp. 1137–59.
38. Kluckhohn, F.R. and Strodtbeck, F.L., *Variations in Value Orientation*, Row & Peterson, New York, 1961.
39. Dench, G., *The Frog, the Prince & the Question of Men*, Neanderthal Books, London, 1994.
40. Brierly, W., 'The Business Culture in Italy', in Rendelpowe, C., Brierly, W., Burton, H., Gordan, C. and King, P., *Business Cultures in Europe*, Butterworth-Heinemann, Oxford, 1990.
41. de Benedetti, C., 'Decline Italian Style', *International Business Week*, 2 August 1995, 14–15.
42. Bell, E., 'Cult of the Corporate Superstar', *The Observer* (Business section), 2 July, 1995.
43. Homans, G.C., *The Human Group*, Routledge & Kegan Paul, London, 1951.
44. Hofstede, G., Motivation, Leadership and Organization: Do American Theories Apply Abroad? *Organizational Dynamics*, Summer 1990, 42–63.
45. Belt, D., 'Sweden: In Search of a New Model', *National Geographic*, August 1993.
46. Shlapentokh, V., *Love, Marriage and Friendship in the Soviet Union*, Praeger, New York, 1984.
47. Altman, Y., Second economy activity in the USSR and its social implications, *Corruption, Development and Inequality*, P. Ward (ed.), Routledge, London, 1989.
48. Altman, Y., The role of personal social support networks in Soviet type centralised command economies, *10th International Social Network Conference*, February 1990, San Diego.
49. Layard, R., Nickell, S. and Jackman, R., *Unemployment*, Oxford University Press, Oxford, 1991.
50. 'Britain's Richest 500', *The Sunday Times*, 1994.
51. *The Sunday Times Magazine*, 26 September 1993, p. 58.
52. Davis, J., *People of the Mediterranean*, Routledge & Kegan Paul, London, 1977.

FURTHER READING

Bellah, R.N., Madsen, R., Sullivan, W.M., Swidler, A. and Tipton, S. M., *Habits of the Heart*, Perennial Library, New York, 1985.
Hall, E.T. and Hall, M.R., *Hidden Differences: Doing Business with the Japanese*, Doubleday, New York, 1987.
Hall, E.T. and Hall, M.R., *Understanding Cultural Differences*, Intercultural Press, Yarmouth, 1990.
d' Iribarne, Phillipe, *La logique de l'honneur*, Editions du Seuil, Paris, 1980.

EIGHT

A MANAGER'S TALE

INTRODUCTION

In Chapters 6 and 7 our northern analyst's role has been to sift and to separate, to de-layer and to expose. Before our journey's end we must now spend time rebuilding these parts into a whole, so that from the mists emerges a synergy of cultures; the means by which our transcultural business ventures will grow and succeed through the innovative management of their cultural assets and liabilities. We now therefore turn from the northern theories and our journey takes us back for a final expedition to the pragmatic west. Here we will test the mettle of our 'northern' modellers. Our western journey will therefore focus on the world of the busy manager. Here we will see the analysts' tools put to practical use. Into the foundry of the organization we will see poured the raw northern materials which will be melted and moulded into new shapes; the tools of the transcultural management trade.

By any standards these tools are rudimentary — we are still in the Stone Age of transcultural management — but they will nonetheless have a useful cutting edge. They will provide the means to organize the layers of cultural diversity; a means by which we can begin to touch the inner cultural worlds of our organizations and those of others with which we work.

DOWN TO EARTH

We have seen in previous chapters that a wide variety of factors ranging from the degree of personal freedom which we find appropriate in our lives to the ways in which we view intervention by the state in business affairs are strongly influenced by national culture. As busy managers, we are therefore sometimes not aware that our attitudes and the processes by which we reach decisions are influenced by our subconscious as well as our conscious minds. As a result, we may inadvertently take a position on a subject which is a reflection not so much of our own thoughtful processes but more of the value systems on which we draw, which have in large measure been inherited from our parents and the people with whom we grew up.

Each individual will have his or her own view on the extent to which they feel that culture affects them personally, but the evidence suggests that it is fair to make two general assumptions about culture in the workplace:

- National cultural differences do exist and these are associated with a certain number of shared values.
- These shared value systems influence people's attitudes in their adult working lives.

We have seen that these assumptions are supported by the results of a number of studies of transcultural businesses[1]. Furthermore, they point to our tendency to attribute a 'value' to our shared beliefs as a factor which may lead to conflict between people in transcultural environments.

Our main problem is that we do not have a framework of communication for examining cross-cultural issues. We can send a team to analyse the balance sheet of a prospective 'foreign' acquisition — but what cultural assets and liabilities are we buying into? What risks are we taking that we will fall into conflict with this new member of our international family?

We can (and do) send people at short notice on international assignments. The costs of a thirty-month 'stay' have been estimated at £1 million per senior executive relocation. Many fail either partly or completely, often due to an inability to cope with the new environment. At best, this is expensive, at worst, it is a huge loss, in terms of both what could have been achieved if things had gone well and also the loss of the strategic advantage which may have been gained from a proactive approach to the identification and management of what might be called the company's transcultural assets.

Take, for example, the cultural assets of a western (US)/northern (French) alliance. In the west, the world of the individual, the pioneer prevails. The western coast of America seethes with high-technology start-ups — but they have their limits. US software teams, while leading the world in 'productizing' their technology have begun to face the barriers of high-level mathematics. The French, while lacking some of the international marketing advantage of their US

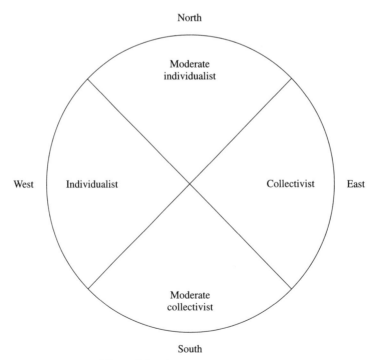

Figure 8.1   A management compass.

counterparts have a deep vein of northern rational education on which to draw. Thanks to Descartes and Napoleon they are among the world's leaders when it comes to complex mathematical modelling.

Here our businesses begin to take on new shapes — the Franco-US alliance takes on the form of a seamless interplay of transcultural assets. From the French research department of this new alliance, world-class technologies provide the raw materials of new high added-value products, to be harnessed and capitalized by their US partners.

But we must ground this somewhat eastern vision in the practical soil of the west. In order for companies to work constructively with culture it is first necessary to put in place management systems by which organizations may develop an awareness of cultural diversity and by which they may begin the process of harnessing this diversity to the competitive advantage of the business concerned.

For a cross-cultural management system to be workable it should be accessible on a number of layers. It needs to have a 'bottom-line' entry point — a basic tenet on which to build an increasing level of understanding of cultural asset management.

We have seen that the 'outside-in' models point our way in this direction. They suggest we can start with one key fundamental cultural parameter — that of relationships — the individualist collectivist divide. This would normally not be enough to provide us with a round-world view of culture but for the proposition, put forward in Chapter 6, that there exists a continuum of cultures existing between these two extremes. Our journey from the west to the east, in individual/collective terms, therefore takes us from pure western individualism, first to the north, to the moderate individualists, then to the south, to the moderate collectivists, and finally east to the profoundly collectivist cultures of the Asian world. Our basic management 'compass' is therefore shown in Figure 8.1.

Table 8.1 compares the compass model with other models described in earlier chapters and shows that there is general agreement on the characterization between cultures according the degree to which they lean in the direction of individualism or collectivism. (While all the models provide a useful basis for a comparison of Anglo-Saxon cultures, some are of limited relevance to description of the eastern world, as is evident by the lack of intuitive 'fit' with the descriptions given for this quadrant (see question marks). This may partly be a result of the fact that the researchers concerned have worked principally in the northern and western cultural worlds.)

The 'compass' model provides a simple means of framing the basic question — where am I likely to be in the individualist/collectivist continuum? Furthermore, it has the advantage that, since there exists a level of 'entry-level' commonality among geographically proximal cultures (Table 8.2), this provides a means for experienced managers to link their intuitive 'gut feel' skills to the development and use of the model in the workplace.

So far so good, but what has all this to do with managing a business? The answer to this

Table 8.1

Compass	Lessem	Douglas	Altman	Altman	Mars	Schwartz
Western	Action orientated	Individualist	Individual	Can do	Hawks	Contractual/
Northern	Thought orientated	Insulated?	Corporatist	Corporate	Donkeys	modernist
Southern	Family orientated	Bureaucracy	Family	Paternalistic	Wolves	Traditional/
Eastern	Group orientated	Peer group	Network?	Personal network?	Vultures?	relationship

Table 8.2

Culture	Geographical spread
Western	UK, USA
Northern	Northern Europe
Southern	Southern Europe/Africa
Eastern	Russia/Asia

question lies in the results of the individual level 'inside-out' studies — those of Hofstede[2,3], Trompenaars[4], Hampden-Turner[5], whose work with people in international companies has shown the existence of distinct preferences according to the culture in which they operate. In their re-analysis of previously published data, Gatley and Lessem[1] have shown that *patterns* can be found among these preferences, linking a total of twelve different preference 'variants' which are of relevance to the management of international businesses. These twelve variants together make up a profile of the culture concerned. These authors have carried out variant pattern analysis on combined data from previously published studies,[2-5] scoring relative bias on eleven of twelve variants on a country-by-country basis (numerical data are not yet available on one variant).

Brief descriptions of each of the variants used in the model are given in Table 8.3 and the compiled data for ten countries studied are shown in Table 8.4. Table 8.4 shows strong evidence of linkage between the variants, allowing national cultures to be classified into groups and sub-groups according to their variant scores. The data also show clear evidence of the polarization between what have been termed the north-eastern cultures (USA, Northern Europe) and the south-eastern cultures (southern Europe and Asia).

The importance of this study is to show that there is a certain level of *predictability* in the way cultures vary. That is, they do not vary in a random fashion — strongly individualistic cultures such as the USA tend to be also cultures which value a business's profit above its social contribution whereas the opposite is true of collectivist cultures such as Japan. By the same token, individualist cultures also tend towards a short-term view whereas collectivist cultures take a longer-term approach to business planning.

Viewed in the light of the models described in earlier chapters, a picture emerges of the fundamental importance of recognizing the level of individualism (or collectivism) which exists in a culture, it being the case that profound pattern differences exist between cultures which occupy the polar opposite positions of the continuum. From a business perspective this provides an opportunity for the development of a form of cultural shorthand for discussion and analysis of cultural issues which are relevant to the workplace. Using this information in combination with our management 'compass', we can now begin to plot a course according to the level of individualism which predominates in a given culture. From this we can develop a means to predict the ways in which value systems will change as we move from individualist cultures to those in which collectivism predominates.

THE CPAS AUDIT SYSTEM

The above observation has been used as the basis for the development of a Cultural Profiling and Analysis System (CPAS), which provides a means of generating a pattern of cultural

Table 8.3   Notes on cultural variants

Cultural variant	Brief description
Superstructural variants — orientation to:	
Time orientation	Time may be viewed as a sequence or as circular phenomenon — tends to affect the degree to which people take a long-term view on business
Emotional orientation	The way in which the expression of emotion is viewed in the workplace. In controlled/suppressed cultures emotional outburst may be considered a sign of weakness
Hierarchical orientation	Organizational structures and the interaction of the people within them
Relationship orientation	Relationships may be specific to the workplace or may extend into private lives of working people
Status orientation	Allocation of status may be based solely on performance or may include considerations of social standing as a factor in the ability of an individual to exert authority over others
Profit orientation	Business and profits may be viewed as separate from or as integrated within the social system within which it operates
Subsoil/bedrock variants	
Systems orientation	The extent to which person-centred values are viewed as central to the management of businesses. Rational/utilitarian cultures see this as less important than humanist cultures
Ambiguity orientation	The way in which people approach situations of ambiguity. 'Accepting' cultures tend towards a have-a-go approach whereas 'avoiding' cultures will go to considerable efforts to analyse associated risks/outcomes before taking action
Rule orientation	'Universalist' cultures see the letter of the law as a central pillar to social and management practice. 'Particularist' cultures interpret laws to make them meaningful at a local level
Control orientation	The extent to which people feel they can/should assert control over the world around them
Gender orientation	The degree to which people share a need for 'masculine' independency or 'feminine' interdependency
Group orientation	The extent to which people interact as individuals or as social groups

preferences using what has been termed the twelve-point model (Figure 8.2). The model allows comparison of a given pattern with corresponding profiles, either from published information or from local studies of cultural value systems. Figure 8.3 shows the CPAS twelve-point profiles of those cultures with variant extremes to left and right. The analysis shows the polar positions of the western and eastern cultures, exemplified in these figures by the USA and Japan. Figure 8.4 shows examples of northern and southern transitional cultures existing between the two.

PRACTICAL USE OF THE MODEL

The CPAS model has been used in management workshops, both to assess the cultural profiles of participants and to provide a means for evaluation of likely cultural conflicts and

Table 8.4   Separation of north-western and south-eastern cultures — the first cultural divide. Average relative data scores by country — countries ordered according to relative variant scores

Bias Cultural variant	Group Cultural bias	North-western					South-eastern				
Strategic horizon	Short term	SP (5)	UK (18)	IT (21)	USA (24)	CA (34)					
	Long term						FR (49)	NL (61)	SIN (62)	SW (72)	JAP (88)
Expression of emotion	Expressive	IT (0)	FR (9)	USA (20)	SIN (24)						
	Controlled						NL (56)	UK (78)	JAP (78)		
Hierarchical orientation	Democratic	SW (5)	CA (19)	USA (20)	NL (38)	UK (46)					
	Bureaucratic						JAP (53)	SP (60)	FR (85)	IT (87)	SI (100)
Relationship orientation	Context-specific	SW (1)	NL (7)	UK (9)	USA (10)	FR (18)					
	Broad context						IT (28)	CA (30)	SP (59)	JAP (64)	SIN (69)
Status orientation	Achievement orientated	USA (0)	CA (8)	UK (27)	SW (29)	FR (49)					
	Ascriptive						IT (64)	SIN (64)	NL (65)	JAP (90)	SP (100)
Profit orientation	Profit orientated	CA (9)	USA (11)	NL (24)	UK (31)	SW (36)					
	Socially orientated						IT (40)	SP (43)	FR (88)	SIN (91)	JAP (100)
Systems orientation	Rational Humanist	Study in progress									
Ambiguity orientation	Accepting	SIN (0)	SW (25)	UK (32)	USA (45)	CA (48)					
	Avoiding						NL (54)	IT (80)	FR (93)	SP (93)	JAP (100)
Rule orientation	Rule adherent	USA (11)	CA (17)	NL (33)	SW (35)	UK (40)					
	Rule interpreting						JAP (58)	FR (77)	IT (78)	SIN (85)	SP (93)
Control orientation	Assertive	USA (0)	CA (16)	SP (24)	FR (27)	NL (42)					
	Responsive						UK (53)	SW (71)	IT (72)	SIN (95)	JAP (100)
Gender orientation	Masculine	JAP (0)	IT (28)	UK (32)	USA (37)	CA (48)					
	Feminine						SIN (52)	FR (58)	SP (59)	NL (90)	SW (100)
Group orientation	Individualist	USA (8)	CA (12)	SW (29)	UK (29)	SP (32)					
	Collectivist						NL (36)	IT (43)	FR (58)	JAP (71)	SIN (93)

◄———— Left-hand bias | **Median score line** | Right-hand bias ————►

Cultural profile

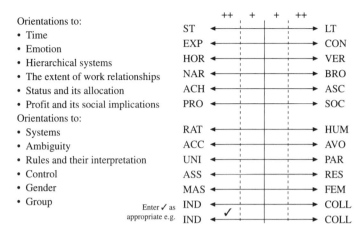

Notes on cultural orientations

Orientation	Abbr.	Description	Abbr.	Description
Time	SP	Tendency towards short-term thinking	LT	Tendency towards long-term thinking
Emotion	EXP	Feelings expressed at work	CON	Feelings not expressed at work
Hierarchies	HOR	Flat, bottom-up organization	VER	Vertical, top-down organization
Extent of work relationships	NAR	Work is work and home is home	BRO	Work extends into private affairs (position, title, responsibilities to superiors)
Status and its allocation	ACH	Status granted on basis of achievement	ASC	Status linked to age, social standing, etc.
Profit and its social implications	PRO	Profit is main goal of the business	SOC	Social contribution is main goal of the business
Systems	RAT	Task orientated	HUM	Human orientated
Ambiguity	ACC	Empirical, experimental, action focused	AVO	Circumspect, analytical, organized
Rules	UNI	Letter of the law important. Rule based	PAR	Spirit of the law important. Moral based
Control	ASS	Assertive, confident	RES	Reflective, tending to seek confirmation of opinions
Gender	MAS	Dominant, ruthless	FEM	Sensitive, supportive
Group	IND	Individualist, independent	COLL	Collectivist, interdependent

Figure 8.2   The CPAS twelve-point model (adapted from Gatley and Lessem[1]).

synergies between workshop groups and the commercial geography in which they operate. The four points of the compass are used as a means by which people can begin the process of moving cultural value systems from a 'gut feel' intuitive level to a more rational, analytical level. This can then be followed by a re-evaluation of these innate value systems in a broader, more global context.

A CPAS questionnaire is used to provide a 'broad-brush' evaluation of individual cultural preferences. The questionnaire comprises a total of sixty questions covering twelve cultural variants (five questions per variant) and provides a means of assessing individual and team profiles using the twelve-point model. An extract from the questionnaire is shown in Figure 8.5. Respondents are asked to score their responses on a scale A to E according to their preference for one of two options given.

Responses are converted to numerical values using a conversion algorithm which provides

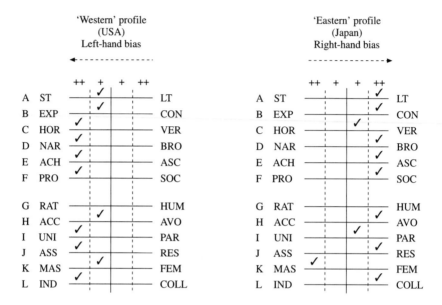

Figure 8.3 CPAS cultural analysis — cultural profiles.

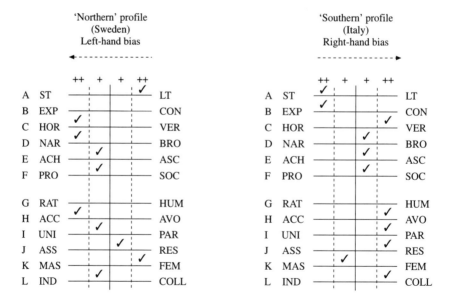

Figure 8.4 CPAS cultural analysis — cultural profiles.

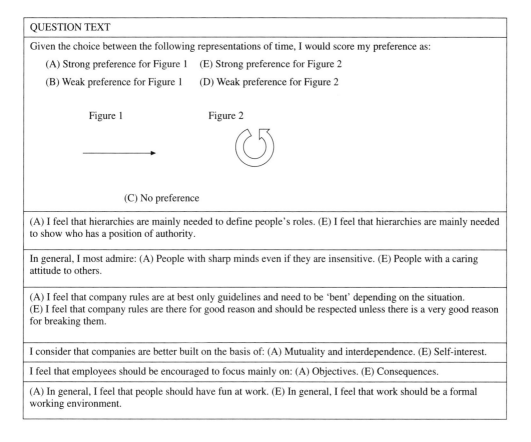

QUESTION TEXT

Given the choice between the following representations of time, I would score my preference as:
 	
(A) Strong preference for Figure 1   (E) Strong preference for Figure 2
 	
(B) Weak preference for Figure 1   (D) Weak preference for Figure 2
 	
    Figure 1   Figure 2
 	
            (C) No preference

(A) I feel that hierarchies are mainly needed to define people's roles. (E) I feel that hierarchies are mainly needed to show who has a position of authority.
In general, I most admire: (A) People with sharp minds even if they are insensitive. (E) People with a caring attitude to others.
(A) I feel that company rules are at best only guidelines and need to be 'bent' depending on the situation. (E) I feel that company rules are there for good reason and should be respected unless there is a very good reason for breaking them.
I consider that companies are better built on the basis of: (A) Mutuality and interdependence. (E) Self-interest.
I feel that employees should be encouraged to focus mainly on: (A) Objectives. (E) Consequences.
(A) In general, I feel that people should have fun at work. (E) In general, I feel that work should be a formal working environment.

Figure 8.5   Extract from audit questionnaire.

percentage bias scores on each of the twelve model variants (the encoding is not revealed to the respondent during completion of the questionnaire). A computer database is used to generate individual cultural profiles and provides a means of comparing them with the median (calculated average) group response. This median response is in turn compared with the minimum and maximum individual scores for each variant, which provides a picture of the variation which exists within the group on each of the variants analysed. Profile comparisons can then be made against stored national pattern profiles on a country-by-country basis.

The profiles are used in the workshops as the basis for discussion of individual preferences within the context of the variations which exist within the group as a whole. This not only serves to bring innate value systems to the surface but also provides a means for comparing and contrasting the different cultural preferences that exist within the workshop group.

Example study

In a study of working practices among Italian managers the CPAS questionnaire was used to provide information on individual and group preferences on a number of cultural issues relevant to business management and competencies. Shared values were analysed through the calculation of

Table 8.5

CPAS variant	Median score	Group bias	Notes
Strategic horizon	12	Short term	Focus on short term. Tight agendas for meetings and keep your eye on the ball
Expression of emotion	13	Controlled	Respect task orientation and self-control but believe in having fun at work and expressing emotions freely
Attitudes to hierarchy	14.5	Flat — open structures	Function not power, question orders *but* not more than one boss please
Context of relationships	10	Narrow context	Deal is a deal. Separate work and home. Get to the point
Systems for allocation of status	10.5	Achievement orientated	Promote the achievers. What you know, not who you know. Skills, not age
Commercio-social integration	13	Profit orientated	'Bottom-line' is the best measure of performance
Rational/humanist orientation	11.5	Rational	Precaution, not compassion. Observe people's rights rather than their feelings
Attitudes to ambiguity	18	Uncertainty avoiding	Plan, analyse, avoid ambiguity
Attitudes to rules	16.5	Rule interpreting	Contracts evolve, relationships not rules. Spirit of the law over the letter of the law
Assertiveness/tendency to control	15	No bias	
Masculinity/femininity	21	Feminine/ interdependent	Cooperative, interdependent. Family quality of life important
Individualism/ collectivism	17.5	Collectivist	Like to work in groups/prefer group reward systems. Use consensus in preference to majority voting

median scores for each variant. Table 8.5 shows the results from the CPAS analysis and Figure 8.6 shows the group median data converted into a CPAS profile.

INTERPRETATION OF RESULTS AS PER EXAMPLE STUDY

Care should obviously be taken in drawing conclusions from limited amounts of data and the following interpretation would normally be the point of departure for a series of discussions designed to evaluate the validity of the analysis. The following is therefore put forward for the purposes of illustration of the type of considerations which may be encountered during workshop discussions.

This particular profile would suggest that, in general, the group leans towards a preference for a collectivist, interdependent working environment and shows a tendency towards an interpretative approach to rules. The profile indicates that the group would tend to approach situations of

Italian management profile

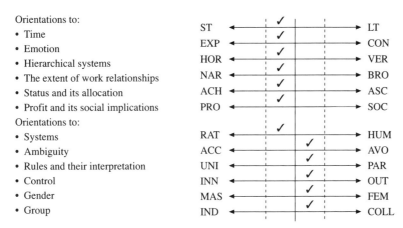

Figure 8.6 CPAS profile.

uncertainty in an analytical and pre-emptive manner and would be inclined towards a rational rather than humanist approach to business. This would lead them to take a relatively functional and task-orientated view on the workplace rather than a more interpersonal people-orientated view.

In terms of their attitude to business, the profile suggests that the group would tend towards the view that a company should focus on its profit rather than its social responsibilities, and they would consider that rewards should be given primarily on the basis of achievement. The data suggest that the group would have a tendency towards the view that home and work relationships should be kept separate and would be more comfortable with an open, flat management system than a more formal and hierarchical structure. In terms of their attitudes to the expression of emotion, the profile suggests a positive attitude towards emotional self-control.

In cultural terms, this group therefore exhibits a strongly northern (rational/analytical) influence, which is tempered by a southern (moderately collectivist) orientation. There is a noticeable absence of polar western influence, as there is also a lack of polar eastern orientation.

CULTURAL ASSETS AND CULTURAL LIABILITIES

In combination with the 'four worlds' model of culture presented in Chapters 1 to 5, the questionnaire results provide the beginnings of a means of assessing the cultural 'assets and liabilities' of the workshop participants. This involves the analysis of cultural resources in each of four quadrants, a brief overview of which is shown in Figure 8.7.

Cultural Assets

Taking the median data for the purposes of illustration (a complete analysis would need to look at the variation within the group), Table 8.6 shows the cultural asset profile which would be at the disposal of this particular workshop team.

Cultural liabilities

Looking in turn at the downside of the profile, in other words the cultural liabilities, the analysis would suggest that, if this team was involved in the management of high-risk ventures (e.g.

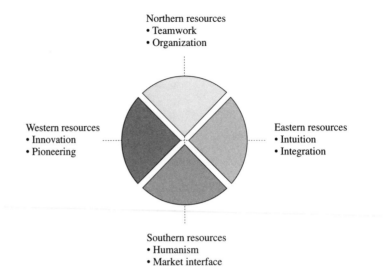

Figure 8.7   Analysis of cultural resources.

high-technology R&D), some attention would need to be given to building the pioneering, uncertainty-accepting aspects of their profile. A synergy between the strong northern (rational) and this innovative risk-taking influence would have benefits in a number of areas, notably product innovation and development. The group profile indicates a culture in which objectives rather than consequences are the major focus of attention. Attention may therefore need to be given to assessing its abilities in the strategic, mid- to long-term arena.

SUMMARY

Analysis of the data from studies of international companies supports the view that there are significant differences between managers' preferences according to the geographical/cultural location of the companies concerned. The data also support the premise that the level of individualism which predominates in a culture is a major determinant factor in the pattern of preferences which pertains to the group under study. The CPAS cultural audit system provides a means of assessment of these cul-

Table 8.6

Cultural typology	Natural resource/cultural focus	Business leverage	Group analysis ✓ = predominant influences
W = western	Action	Technical — pioneer — product	
N = northern	Organization	Systems focus/organizational management	✓
S = southern	People	HR management/people/customer focus	✓
E = eastern	Harmony	Integrator — holistic focus	

tural preferences, both within the context of the group and also within the context of their organization and the national culture(s) within which they operate.

As was stressed at the beginning of this chapter, these tools of cultural analysis are, at best, rudimentary, and care should be taken at this stage of their development, especially where they may be considered as adjuncts to other, more established systems of 'human resource' management. If, however, we are to treat human beings as a form of capital, then we should at least attempt to do so against the background of an understanding of their cultural values and preferences. At worst, this will add a further dimension to our skills; at best, it may also provide the basis for a substantial improvement in the returns we achieve from accessing the synergies which exist within our international cultural asset base.

STUDY QUESTIONS

1. How is the level of individualism which exists within a culture related to the type of commercial environments which operate therein?
2. Describe the patterns which exist within cultural variants and relate these to one of the key business functions (R&D, marketing, production, finance, etc.).
3. Discuss the potential uses of cultural analysis as an adjunct to established systems of human resource management, including the implications which this may have for strategic planning within international businesses.

REFERENCES

1. Gatley, S. and Lessem, R., Enhancing the competitive advantage of trans-cultural businesses, *European Journal of Industrial Training*, **19**, 1995, p. 9.
2. Hofstede, G., *Culture's Consequences*, Sage Publications, Beverly Hills, CA, 1980.
3. Hofstede, G., *Cultures and Organisations*, McGraw-Hill, London, 1991.
4. Trompenaars, F., *Riding the Waves of Culture*, Economist Books, London, 1993.
5. Hampden-Turner, C. and Trompenaars, F., *Seven Cultures of Capitalism*, Doubleday, New York, 1993.

THREE

GLOBAL SYNERGIES

JOURNEY'S END

As we come to the end of our journey, we look back to see that the northern and southern routes have now taken their rightful place in our global businessphere. These 'new worlds' offer us a treasure chest of cultural assets and, with their eastern and western partners, they take us to the threshold of a new era of transcultural business venturing.

But this world of multicultural assets is surely only for dreamers. We pragmatic western business executives have tasks to fulfil, profits to make. Leaders are born, not made, the world is full of individuals, not culturally predestined robots. We southern managers know that business is done through people near to you, whose families you know and love, not people in far-flung places who know little and understand even less; we directors of northern corporations need no advice from philosophers about how to run our international companies; and finally, from the east, I hear the elders saying 'who are you in Anglo-Saxon garb to teach us of the world of vision and of harmony?'

And yet we seem to have so much still to learn. Somewhere along our journey together we became aware of something we had sensed but never touched. We had always wondered what lay beyond the clouds of human misunderstanding, and we had seen, but only through the eyes of our children, a world where diversity was a source of wonder and not of war. As it peers into the mists of synergy, Africa is teaching us that there can be hope where none seemed to be. It seems that country may yet re-awaken in us a yearning to learn and grow.

As business executives we need to play our role in building new ways to embrace and harness the rich diversity of our global assets. If we can do so in ways which will serve not only to build new and vibrant businesses but also to build bridges across which we can reach a new understanding of ourselves and the colourful world in which we live, then our journey together will have been the better for it.

So what have we learned from our transcultural odyssey? It seems to us now that our multicultural world extends as a long continuum of interrelationships, stretching far out to the west, to the worlds of our puritan individualists, where profit and achievement are the driving forces of industry. As we move towards the east, passing as we go through the northern corporate and southern family worlds, we see the scenery of our cultural paradigms slowly changing until we reach the 'yang' of our cultural dialectic — the collective eastern worlds of harmony and integration.

As we begin to understand this continuum of human values, we sense a growing awareness that this family of cultures has much to offer us as international managers. As we watch the economic pendulum swinging away from its long-established western pole towards a new position in the east, new opportunities emerge for global trade. But we sense that the new economic dynamic will likely dance to a different tune from that we are used to in the west.

To be successful in this new corporate world we will need to become skilled in the use of our management compass. We will need to become sensitive to the ways in which our paradigms both support and limit us, and we will need to learn from the paradigms of others with whom we interact. Taken apart, our paradigms divide and separate us, and they do so as much for our eastern elders as they do for their corporate raider cousins in the west. True, the values of the eastern elders may be more akin to the new Asian marketplace, but their eastern ways have limitations of their own. Japan is learning to cope with the results of its disastrous property investments, China is borrowing not only western financial but also western management skills as it emerges into a new era of economic activity. Taken together the total value of the world's cultural paradigms now appears greater than the sum of its parts. This synergy of human values seems to offer the international company a new and dynamic form of asset base from which it can grow and develop — but harnessing these assets will not be easy. As with all strategic plans, success will require time, investment, commitment and, above all, human enterprise.

First, we will need to take a fresh look at the world in which we live and work. We need to overcome our individual and corporate mind sets and view the world with truly three-dimensional vision. Once we do this some assets will be quickly harnessed. Better use of our European paradigms will put long-term German investment at the disposal of hardened pragmatic entrepreneurs. In a wider frame, Cartesian French education will provide (and already is providing) cutting-edge algorithms for the program makers of US software giants.

Other more subtle assets will come into play, but at a later stage. The southern humanists of Europe and of Africa have much to learn and, in turn, much to teach us about the ways in which their nations can play a role in our understanding of their role in building wealth into the bedrock of our international economies. Only recently Professor dasGupta, in Cambridge University's Department of Economics, has written that the rules for wealth creation differ between poor and rich nations. New models are needed for economies in which there are simply not enough basic resources to make possible the much-vaunted 'trickle-down' effect of classical market economics. For these nations a new economic paradigm is needed if they are to join the rest of the world as partners in the wealth-creation process. Here may yet, for example, lie a new and important socio-economic role for the western world's much-criticized privatized water and power utilities.

We therefore stand at the gateway to an exciting but uncertain economic era. We can approach this with our tried and trusted ways, but if we do so we must be aware that there is a chance that we may be relying on a paradigm which limits us in our scope and flexibility of response. We may, in short, be driving on the wrong side of the corporate road and not be aware of it.

The alternative is to stretch our imagination beyond the known and into the unknown. Our journey has taught us that as eastern managers, this will take us into the pioneering world of the west; we can go alone or we can seek an experienced guide to help us on our way. As western managers, this territory should be familiar to us — indeed it may be here that we seek to build our competitive advantage in the years to come.

INDEX

Index compiled by *Indexing Specialist*, 202 Church Road, Hove, East Sussex BN3 2DJ. Tel/Fax: (01273) 323309